Live in Joy!

Bhante sujatha

My Wish

The Story of a Man who Brought Happiness to America

The authorized biography of

Bhante Sujatha,

Chief Sanganayaka of North America

Sujatha @ bluelotustemple·org
bluelotustemple·org

Written by:

Mary A Gustafson

Blue Lotus Temple
221 Dean St.
Woodstock IL 60098

815-337-7378

ISBN-10:069222064X

ISBN-13:978-0-692-22064-1

DEDICATION

To the Buddha

Thank you for sharing the dhamma with the world.

- Bhante Sujatha

~

To Peg Marino, 1963-2012,

The happiest person I have ever known.

Thank you for your love, support and friendship.

Mary G

-

Contents

Acknowledgements

I want to express my heartfelt appreciation for the cooperation, comments and shared experiences of the Blue Lotus Temple Sangha (Community) in Woodstock, Illinois. Their generous sharing allowed me to craft this biography in great detail. Many people told me that Bhante Sujatha had changed their life, and the gratitude for his consistent generosity and loving kindness was universal.

Bhante Dhammawasa and Bhante Muditha, Bhante Sujatha's esteemed teachers in Sri Lanka, put me at ease with their friendly, humble ways and offered unconditional support for Bhante Sujatha's mission to bring happiness to Americans.

Bhante Muditha translated the manuscript into the language of Sri Lanka and offered me the invaluable perspective of a monk who understands the Sri Lankan culture.

Bhante San introduced me to Bhante Sujatha.

Bhante San and Bhante Sumana spent hours with me, telling me fascinating stories about their lives as young monks. They were so detailed in their descriptions (with English as their second language no less!) that I was able to write *My Wish* feeling as if I had been to all the places they so richly described.

Bikkhuni Vimala provided unconditional support, taking my calls at all hours of the day and night and sitting with me for hours, patiently answering my questions.

Thank you to Tyler Lewke, my noble friend and writing partner, who introduced me to the Blue Lotus Temple

Michael Fronzcak, Bhante Sujatha's friend for more than a decade, helped me see a famous monk through the intimate eyes of a long

7

friendship. He was a kind, humble and generous guide as we traveled together through the story of Bhante Sujatha's life, and later, as we physically traveled through Sri Lanka.

Dr. John Bardi, a noble friend to Bhante and a professor of philosophy at Penn State University, provided expert encouragement and support throughout the project. His forward is a testament to the remarkable people that populate the life of Bhante Sujatha. Dr. Bardi is a kind, brilliant and noble teacher, and I am forever grateful for his beautiful observations about the book and Bhante Sujatha.

Ann and Tom Van Slyck, Bhante's noble friends in Arizona, provide a refuge for Bhante Sujatha that is described by many as heaven on earth.

Bhante Sujatha would not be able to travel the world and spread his message of loving kindness and the dhamma without the constant friendship and support of Bhante Sankicha, the abbot of the Great Lakes Vihara in Michigan. Bhante Sankicha provides generous and constant support for the monks at the Blue Lotus Temple and elsewhere.

All of the monks who generously allowed me to interview them, including Bhante(s) Chan, Samita, and Rahula, have my unending gratitude and respect.

Bhante Dhamawansa, Bhante Sujatha's Sunday school teacher, was extremely generous in sharing his razor sharp memories of Bhante Sujatha as a young Sunday school student.

Gary Devar recorded the original manuscript while I read, patiently handling all the technology, steadily encouraging me to keep moving forward and get this story out into the world.

Christopher Trent supported me throughout the writing process and offered invaluable editing services and a rich education in Buddhist concepts.

Kirk Osterman helped immensely with the crowd-funding project along with this considerable technical skills and cheerful attitude .

Tiffany Colter provided editing, publishing, writing, and coaching skills to get this book out into the world. Her Christian spiritual perspective and her solid work ethic have been inspirational.

Kristen Costello was the brilliant designer behind the original book cover concept and stayed up 24 hours at a time to meet deadlines when we were preparing the smaller book for the ceremony in Sri Lanka. Her expertise in design is unmatched in my experience.

Mark Babick managed to print the ceremonial books in a flash, as we hurried at the last minute to finish that project before we left for Sri Lanka.

My dear sister, Elizabeth Fitch and my sister in law, Erin Gustafson, have offered consistent, unconditional love, support, and guidance. They were instrumental in helping me get to Sri Lanka, and have always been sisters to me, in all the best ways.

Chris Atwater helped me immensely with the interview process, handling all the technical aspects of transferring the interviews into an accessible database.

Dawn Gerth and her staff provided me with rich food and great company at Le Petit Marche while I worked on this book.

Karen Widdowson and Erin Gustafson practically pushed me out the door for the trip to Sri Lanka, reassuring me that they would make sure my son, my dog, and my home were ok. Their support has been invaluable.

Thank you Keith, Drew, Brent, and Brandon Bryant, Alan and Matt Gustafson, and Chris Atwater. All of you must know that you have literally saved my life. Thank you.

I am grateful for the serendipitous meeting with Ryan Thompson at the writers group run by Kim Bookless in Chicago. (yes, that is her real name!). Ryan was enthusiastic and generous in his acceptance of the job of the rush eBook formatting and he was kind enough to put me in touch with Madeline Baum, who put the final touches on the cover design for this edition.

Thank you Ray Suchy for helping with Lou Lou and so much more. You are a true noble friend.

Chris and Ed Gerulat have helped immensely with support for me and for my son at college in New York during this project. Thank you both for the limo ride!

I cannot begin to express my gratitude for the influence of Bhante's hard working, humble parents, Heenbanda and Lalitha, and his loving sister, Manel. Manel's son, Krishan, translated the interviews with his grandparents, making their deep wisdom accessible to all of us.

Leo Zimmerman, you are a gift. Thank you for engaging in your own dreams while your mom went for her own. I know it wasn't easy, and I am grateful for your obvious, inherent goodness and grace.

Finally, of course, I am saying an impossible to convey thank you to Bhante Sujatha, who let me into the magical story of his life, and inspired me with his tale of a humble and holy path to a dream come true. He is a living example of a Bodhisattva to many grateful people.

Thank you.

-Mary

Acknowledgement from Blue Lotus Sangha

Within the western society we live in, many of us tend to look externally for ways to achieve peace and balance in our lives. Bhante Sujatha has worked tirelessly to demonstrate that the deepest love and peace can be found within. The idea that we already possess the qualities of equanimity, peace, and compassion is a challenging concept at times, but Bhante reminds us through the love he shares in his heart that peace is not bound to circumstance, but rather is actively cultivated through practicing bhavana (meditation).

He has led and inspired many communities (through his example) to understand that we all have the ability to see love in every situation. He has empowered countless individuals to seek out truth in their lives. He has smiled in the face of profound adversity, and in doing so has shown us that we may always take refuge in the Buddha, the Dhamma, and the Sangha. We are forever grateful for his loving presence in our lives, and deeply look forward to being a part of his loving relationship with the world.

-John LaDeur and Jennifer Wong –on behalf of the Blue Lotus
Temple Sangha

Tributes

Bhante, you being you, has helped me to change my heart, my mind, and my soul.

Thank You.

Namaste,

Ann Van Slyck

Tributes

For more than 20 years, I've had the distinct privilege of having Mary Gustafson as my best friend. We've traveled the inner and outer roads of life together. Traveling thru this life with Mary as my constant friend and inspiration is something I cherish as I get to see what's possible when people show up, tell the truth and become willing to go to any lengths to bow with dignity and live with nobility. Bhante Sujatha is my brother... If you could see our insides you'd see the undeniable family resemblance and my love for him isn't measurable. I don't use words to describe it. I use action, which is all he wants from any of us. His profound impact has changed everything. The story of his relentless desire to add more love in the world could not be told by anyone better than Mary as she has X-ray vision into the soul of this man and with total perfection found the best of him and his wisdom to share with all of us in this sacred text. I am humbled, elated, and deeply moved to be part of this journey with them and consider this moment sacred. The ripple of love that will forever touch people is so beautiful it almost blinds me.

To you both, I'm bowing as low as my body can possibly go.- Tyler Lewke

FOREWORD

BY DR. JOHN BARDI

This is a remarkable book. It will entertain you, inform you, and almost certainly illuminate your spiritual life. It might even be the type of book that marks a "before and after" moment in your life.

But don't be fooled. This book may present itself as being about Bhante Sujatha, but actually the book is *like* Bhante Sujatha. Both Bhante and the book come to us softly, with a light and gentle touch, but if we stick with them, we are likely to find our highly conditioned understanding walloped along with the settled routines of our moment-to-moment state of being. This helps us to change and grow spiritually.

I teach Asian philosophy at the Mont Alto campus of Penn State University, and Bhante Sujatha has visited my campus several times. On each visit I have seen him interact with students I know well, giving me the opportunity to note the incredible impact he has on them.

Two things stand out to me regarding his impact:

The first is that his appeal somehow cuts across the lines that normally divide students and their interests. Hard-core atheists as well as devoted Biblical fundamentalists; student athletes as well as math nerds; social butterflies no less than ponderous thinkers—all of them find something gripping in Bhante's presence.

I think this is because beneath the sociological and stylish differences that divide and categorize these students, they are all equally human. Bhante touches into this universal human foundation with them.

And the second thing that stands out about his visits is how long lasting his impact on these students turns out to be. While many of them immediately began a meditation practice after interacting with Bhante, I am struck by how many of them were still continuing more than a year later.

But even those students who do not immediately take up a meditation practice often feel an impact. Bhante rocks their world when he reveals that functioning internally as a sort of "bleeding heart on steroids" is actually a path to happiness and personal fulfillment. They are intrigued to consider that caring for others rather than thinking only about oneself actually leads to that sense of happiness and feeling of personal fulfillment they all so desperately want. For many, this awakens in them a more spiritual focus in life. They begin to sense the deep spiritual significance of how they conduct their otherwise seemingly mundane, everyday lives.

What I saw Bhante do with my students—opening a new and great possibility for them—is what this book can do for you. The author does a brilliant job of letting us into Bhante's inner experience, both as child monk learning mindfulness and loving kindness and also as a wise monk in America, not only teaching people the practices of mindfulness and loving-kindness, but showing them by living example how to apply them in the turbulence and chaos of ordinary daily life.

It really is all very simple when you come right down to it. As Bhante says, it is just a matter of *practice*.

One would be tempted to assume that Bhante must be a uniquely gifted speaker with personal command of all sorts of rhetorical tricks by which he is able to summon and hold the attention of these members of a jaded generation. His striking success with them would lead one to picture him as a sort of pied piper of disaffected college youth.

But Bhante is not like this at all. He has no tricks or unusual oratory skill. To the contrary, he is completely unassuming and absolutely ordinary. What so profoundly strikes my students is not his delivery or technique or even his words (as wonderful and entertaining as his words are). Rather, it is his *presence* that strikes them, riveting their attention in place. *Bhante is less of a behavior and more of a condition.* He stands before them in the **condition** *of being completely "present."*

I think the reason why Bhante's well-established condition of mindful presence has such a resonating impact with my students is because it directly addresses and impacts their actual (if mostly hidden) state of being, which is one of fear, worry, and deep trepidation about the future. Bhante's presence and loving-kindness resonates with particular potency.

Although it is not always admitted, there is great dissatisfaction and unhappiness in our consumer culture. We are wealthy and privileged...and suffering. This suffering is especially pronounced among those in our society who are not experiencing the hunger and material deprivation we associate with poverty. Such people are often experiencing an even greater poverty, a poverty of spirit.

This spiritual poverty is not random. In our highly individualized culture, we constantly elevate the individual, turning individualism into the coin of the realm without ever acknowledging that the 'tail' side of the coin is selfishness. Individualism and selfishness are the two sides of the same coin. Selfishness could be called unhappiness in practice.

Now the inherent unhappiness of selfishness is not the result of ideas, judgments, or even of moral values. It is a function of the nature of things. We *are* connected, and there *is* great joy, meaning, and happiness to be found in our awareness of this connection. When we block out or attempt to deny our essential oneness with others, we suffer—not from blame or moral judgment necessarily, but from *absence.*

Watching Bhante, it is clear he does not offer judgments. He **connects directly with this poverty of spirit, accepting it without judgment, and offers a living example of a different way of being, one that is happier, more at ease, and decidedly more loving and kind.** In other words, Bhante, for all of his humor and funny stories, is a deeply serious friend, functioning to help us *change* the very foundation of our way of being in the world. (This is the "wallop" I mentioned earlier.) And he doesn't just talk about it. He is the change. He models it. By his very presence, he opens the possibility for people of a different way of being in the world.

That changes everything.

We live in an "outside/in" mode, which is the foundation of our market society. This conditions us to believe that our feelings, especially our feelings of happiness, are caused by what is happening in the outer world; if we feel bad or sad, we need to change something in the outer world, usually either by buying something or by acquiring a new relationship. Conversely, on those times we experience well-being and joy in the moment, we automatically assume it is because things are "going our way," that we have in our possession the right product or the right relationship. Of course, all of these things on the outside can be lost, thereby (we think) ending our happiness, so there is hidden in this outside/in materialism a constant, throbbing fear of loss.

Therefore, we live, act, and function as if the most important factor in our life is what is outside and coming in, not what is inside and going out. Indeed, this connection between external event and inner response seems so natural and necessary that, without even realizing it, we abandon our capacity to respond mindfully, lovingly, and kindly to events. Instead, we become emotional slaves to those events, letting the events determine the quality of our inner presence.

This outside/in connection is so well established in our culture that if we want to communicate to others that we care deeply about something unfortunate that has happened, we show how incredibly upset and "out of our minds" we are. Conversely, if we manifest a balanced internal peacefulness in the face of troubling external difficulty, others will often 'read' us as simply not caring. We say things like, "If you are not outraged, you are not noticing."

It is in this context that Bhante offers an alternative way of being in the world, an inside/out way. As Bhante both explains **and models**, without your *peace* (or *presence* or *mindfulness*), you cannot function as a truly sensitive, empowered human being, knowing instinctively what to do to heal, pacify, or transform whatever difficult situation we find ourselves in. *By losing our presence of mind, we lose our capacity to be a transformational presence and instead become a mere extension of the difficult situation.* Alternatively, by maintaining our presence of mind, we can become a calming, healing, transformational influence within it. No longer a mere extension of the difficulty, the power of our presence allows us to be a healing influence within it.

Interestingly, I have found that many people today *want* this. They just do not know *how* to be present in all circumstances. Even worse, because they have been conditioned with this profound outside/in error, they often think that being a sensitive, caring person means totally losing their cool in dramatic situations.

Bhante is incredibly clear on this point, cutting right through the suffering (and all of its justifications) to the simple truth. Having collected our minds, we can be in the situation in a different way, one that helps others to feel the presence of light and love—even while they are experiencing temporary feelings of loss, trauma, and fear.

Again, the presence or peace I am talking about here is a *condition*, not a *behavior*. It isn't the sort of thing we aspire to learn to fake. It is, rather, the sort of thing we aspire to become.

So how can I get into this condition?

Well, this is the question of questions, the very essence of the spiritual life. I have often heard Buddhists draw a distinction between those who *seek* and those who *practice*. The idea is that seeking is a preliminary stage, one that leads to *practice*. At some point, however, one has to stop seeking and begin to practice.

Romantic relationships provide a clarifying parallel here. Sometimes those who claim earnestly to desire a relationship but who actually turn down every promising opportunity for one on the grounds that they are seeking the "right" person—often such a person is actually in the process of actively *avoiding* a relationship.

And here, is where Bhante's spiritual genius shines the brightest. Having taught philosophy for more than thirty years, I have learned the supreme importance of identifying the automatic operating assumptions that shape our lives beneath the threshold of our ordinary awareness. We rarely consciously choose the most basic assumptions that shape our lives. Rather, they are culturally conditioned into us as well as being psychologically generated from earlier traumas. In this way they become unconscious mental constructs that function automatically *beneath* the level of our ordinary awareness to shape our experience. For example, we tend automatically to assume that getting a new car, better sex, or hard-to-get concert tickets are good things. The point here is not that these are not good things, but that we are functioning *automatically*. We are not able to discern.

To clarify this point, imagine that we intend to drive west but are actually driving east and that, suddenly, we realize we are on the wrong road. Now imagine, further, that hidden beneath the level of our ordinary awareness is an operating assumption that, when lost, our only option is to turn either north or south. (Not a lifelike example, but it clarifies the point.) In this instance, even when we discover we are heading the wrong way, we still will not be able to get on the right road because this automatic unconscious assumption will limit the corrective power of whatever changes we might make. In other words, regardless of whether we turn north or south, we will still be heading in the wrong direction.

19

How utterly horrible to consider that unconscious conditioned constructs in our minds limit us so profoundly! In **Buddhism it is often said that there are so many dhammas (teachings) because there are so many more mistakes, with the mistakes always outnumbering the dhammas by a huge margin.** In other words, there are many more ways of going wrong than there are ways of going right. So what is a person to do? Again, this is where the genius of Bhante comes in.

Speaking personally, I have explored global Buddhism in some depth as well as the spiritual practices of other world religions. There are many wonderful 'correctives' available throughout the different spiritual traditions. Indeed, there are so many that the situation soon gets confusing. **The one practice I have found that cuts right through the confusion, offering the suitable corrective no matter what the presenting problem is, thus rendering depth analysis unnecessary, is the practice of loving-kindness. You could say that no matter what one's problem is, the practice of loving-kindness addresses it**, leading a person naturally to take the steps and make the corrections that are necessary to heal and lead to happiness.

That is why Bhante's teaching—so deceptively simple—is so amazingly effective and powerful. **Meditate (to practice being 'present' in all circumstances) and constantly practice loving-kindness (which is a natural expression of 'presence').** That is it!

Of course, this is much more easily said than done. This, once again, is where Bhante *the monk* is relevant.

I recently had some work done by a master mason. I was deeply impressed with his skill at placing brick and shaping stone. When I commented on his amazing skills, He told me his father was a mason as well as his grandfather. He said that even though the tradition of masonry goes back to the beginning of time, this tradition is being lost today. People who call themselves "masons" no longer have the depth of experience and skill with stone and brick than

20

masons of the past used to have.

The same is true of monasticism. This book wonderfully captures Bhante's early life as a poor person in a traditionally Buddhist culture. Of course, that life, even in Sri Lanka, is changing, as is monasticism generally. Like the mason I talked with, Bhante is a throwback to a way of life that is altering rapidly and changing from what it was. A person today can still become a monk, of course, but very few people have the opportunity to develop in a cultural context like Bhante did, working on mindfulness and loving-kindness from early childhood and with full cultural support. In this, Bhante is a sort of living cultural treasure. And as a living cultural treasure, he is making a gift of spiritual treasure to the world—and especially to Americans. He is teaching them how to be happy.

This book brilliantly captures his teaching, bringing it to you in the context of his remarkable life. Of course, from a more cynical, western point of view, some of his childhood recollections might seem a little idealistic and a mite "too fondly" remembered. For example, were his teachers as pure and consistently noble as he remembers them? Was his strict, grumpy teacher wisely giving him an important lesson…or just having a bad day?

In the end it doesn't matter. This book is about Bhante, not his teachers. What matters is how Bhante thought, loved, lived, and responded. And what matters is how we—each of us—thinks, loves, lives, and responds. And in that, Bhante blesses us with his life and how he lives it. He is, if you will, an experiment in living. And that—to come full circle—is what impressed my students. He opened to them the *possibility* of a different way of being, one that is peaceful rather than anxious, loving rather than selfish, and consistently happy rather than mostly sad. In their world of limited psychological and emotional options, Bhante opened before them a door to another entire world, another complete way of being.

Moreover, because of his great humility and refreshing, self-revealing honesty, **they had the sense that if he could do it, then so could they. It may not be easy (though the difficulty comes**

more from inner resistance than from the inherent difficulty of the task) and it may not be quick (though the time it takes comes more from the stubbornness of our inner resistance than from any objective requirement), but it is definitely possible.

At the bottom line, this is about *changing* — about being in the world in a new way, where your behavior is not what it used to be. To have changed thoughts with no changed behavior means you're not in a position to make any contribution, whatsoever, to the world.

Imagine there was someone who was recognized as a master Bluesman, someone who had been born into and grown up in a family of authentic Blues musicians. But imagine, further, that this master Bluesman was actually a master musician. He had been born into the Blues and mastered its forms, but now he had grown beyond cultural identification and prescribed forms and was now playing pure, formless music. At the same time the Blues permeated him and provided form to him, he had "let the Blues go."

This is Bhante. He grew up in a Buddhist culture and became a monk at an early age. But now there is a global jam session occurring, and Bhante, born into the Blues, is now making beautiful global music in the world band. Bhante is a *master world musician,* and his music, while rooted in the blues, actually fits in seamlessly with every music style in the world. Everyone, from country fanatics to punk rockers, from Eastern gong players to African drummers, hears his contribution as a part of their musical genre.

In other words, Bhante Sujatha is a Sri Lankan Monk, but his message (and the lessons of this book) is not culturally Sri Lankan or even dogmatically Buddhist. It is universal, global, and human and oriented entirely to helping people find happiness.

INTRODUCTION

BY BHIKKHUNI VIMALA

Bhante Sujatha met Mary Gustafson for the first time in July 2012. In only a month or two, he asked her to write the story of his life. I know Bhante had been looking for someone to do this for a few years, but he made his decision soon after he met Mary. And his choice was impeccable.

Somehow he knew Mary was the right person for such a daunting task. The project entailed writing a biography spanning two different cultures and languages; interviewing hundreds of people all over the world who spoke several languages; and getting not just the facts but the very essence of this dynamic yet simple man—a Sri Lankan monk destined to be an ambassador for peace and happiness in America.

It is clear to me and it will be clear to the reader that Mary is the right person to capture the beauty and poignancy of Bhante Sujatha's childhood, even though she is writing about a culture she did not know. Her descriptions capture the lush paradise of Sri Lanka and the poverty of so many, including Bhante's family, at that time in the country's history. The experiences of the little monks and their teachers, very young men themselves, come alive in her storytelling and her attention to details of everyday life.

Mary is also the right choice as the writer who could capture the monk's vision and his mission in the world at this time. She does it very succinctly and with a crisp, fresh voice. She doesn't use overworked clichés, and she doesn't whitewash Bhante's personality or his experiences. I have known and been Bhante's student for over six years, but it was Mary's story that really opened my eyes to his broader mission in the world and made it suddenly seem so obvious. I see Bhante differently and more deeply after reading Mary's book, and I will always be grateful to her for giving me a new appreciation of someone I thought I knew rather well.

With only sketchy details given to her about the dimensions of her book, Mary jumped into her project with gusto, continuing to raise her teenaged son while working as a mortgage banker. She has spent hundreds of hours in personal interviews, and written hundreds of letters with hundreds of questions, often needing a translator at every step of the way. And with Bhante's busy schedule, making appointments to talk to him often meant driving him to the airport in early morning hours or late at night, or driving him to speaking engagements or meditation classes all over the sprawling Chicago area. She made opportunities to find every precious minute she could squeeze from him to help put the puzzle of his life together from all the interview pieces she had.

This book is a clear tune, like the sweet pure sound of a perfectly pitched flute playing the melody of a much more complex composition. For all of the stories and all of the people who are a part of Bhante Sujatha's life to this point, you must read the entire book.

Mary's energy and optimism in the face of reality is a perfect match for Bhante Sujatha's personality. Her vision of him is as clear and intuitive as his vision of his own mission. Her stories will come alive for you and you will see the little monk being stubborn and determined; feel the love his parents and sister always have for the indomitable little monk; and admire the discipline and courage of the young teachers who guided his way in.

MY WISH

"NO MATTER HOW HARD THE PAST, YOU CAN BEGIN AGAIN."

LORD BUDDHA

PROLOGUE

It is dusk in the mountains. A small mud house is outlined in the orange haze of the fading sun on a hilltop in Peradiniya, Sri Lanka.

Inside the house, 2-year old Neil Bandara is laying in the crook of his father's arm, enjoying the warmth of a small fire on the dirt floor. Fragrant vegetable curry simmers in a large black pot suspended on twin iron bars over the mossy fire. The smell makes Neil's father dizzy with hunger.

His 5-year old daughter Manel sits near him humming, while she stirs the stew with a large wooden spoon. A monkey caws in the distance, and the crackle of the fire soothes Neil, who smiles as he rests with his family.

The house is lit by candlelight.

A small statue of the Buddha sits on a plywood shelf attached to the wall near Neil's narrow bed, the only furniture in the house. The rest of the family's sleeping mats are rolled up and stored neatly underneath the bed.

Manel sighs. She is tired of stirring. She takes the heavy spoon out of the pot and rests it on her eating mat.

"Poppa, will Momma be back soon?"

Heenbanda hopes that his wife is walking up the hill now, almost home. Lalitha is doing road labor again, for 5 cents a day. Heenbanda is planning on telling her to quit immediately. He must find a way to support his family properly.

27

"Yes," Heenbanda says to his daughter. "Yes, your momma will be back really soon, and she'll have lots of rice for the stew."

Manel frowns. Heenbanda winces as he hears her stomach growl. He leans back and picks up a machine part from a repair pile on the floor, studying it to distract himself from his family's hunger.

"I think your little son is trying to see the stew, Papa," says Manel, watching Neil squirm as he reaches towards the pot.

Heenbanda looks up from the machine part. "What? Oh! Chuti Putha (little son), do you want to see the stew?"

Neil looks up at his father and points at the pot, smiling. Heenbanda leans over so that Neil can see the stew.

Suddenly, Neil shoves his tiny hand into the boiling mixture. Manel screams. Heenbanda jumps up and drops the machine part, yanking his little son's hand out of the stew as he backs away from the fire.

"Chuti Putha! Chuti Putha! (Precious son, precious son.) What are you doing? Why would you do that?"

Neil is sobbing, screaming with pain as he sucks on his blistered hand.

"Apache (Daddy), Apache! Help me!"

Bhante Sujatha, now a 90 pound, 45-year old Buddhist monk, smiles at me as he tells this story. He has just shared his childhood name with me for the first time: Neil Bandara.

We are sitting on battered chairs in the dingy basement of the Blue Lotus Temple in Woodstock, Illinois with a tape recorder set up between us. The cold basement, where the Blue Lotus Temple started ten years earlier with a small weekly meditation class, seemed like a good place to interview Bhante Sujatha (pronounced

28

"Bantay Soojatha") for this biography.

"I don't know if this is important for the book, but I still have scars. See?"

I do. His hand was obviously burned, and I wonder how I never noticed it before.

"I think they used oil to stop the pain. I don't remember. I was okay. I was just trying to stir the pot, you know? Just using my hand instead of a ladle."

I smile.

His hand is scarred, he suffers from chronic pain, he has no money, he is the head of a Buddhist temple in a former Christian church in a Bible-thumping, overwhelmingly white Midwestern town, and he is the happiest man I know.

"Bhante," I ask, "aren't you always stirring the pot somewhere?"

He laughs. "I guess so. I do like stirring things up, don't I?"

I smile at him. I think of the protesters marching outside the Christian church when he first arrived, carrying large posters with the word PAGAN in bright orange marker.

"Yes you do, Bhante, yes you do."

Chapter One

The Cobra

"Stop it, dog! You'll trip me!"

Lalitha is squinting in the bright morning sun, kicking at a half crazed dog who will not stop bothering her. She carries a basket of wet laundry on her head as she hikes up the hill from the Mahaweli River to her small mud home in Peradiniya, Sri Lanka. Her white cotton skirt is damp, and her hands are slippery with sweat.

Halfway up the hill, she drops the heavy basket on the ground as she leans against a mango tree, rubbing her long brown hair up and off her wet neck. The dog, a wild pack animal that adopted the Bandara family when Manel started to feed him food scraps, runs up and jumps on Lalitha, knocking her back against the tree.

"What in the world is wrong with you?" Lalitha scolds. The dog barks in her face and runs a few steps up the hill, turning to see Lalitha still resting against the tree. He runs back, jumps up, and barks in her face again.

"Is something in the house?" Lalitha asks. "Is there an animal?"

The dog wags his tail and barks loudly, twice, pushing his muddy paws hard into Lalitha's small shoulders.

Lalitha frowns. Her 5-year old son, Neil and her 7-year old daughter, Manel are alone in the mud house. The dog drops to all fours, barks again, and bites on Lalitha's skirt, pulling her towards the path.

Lalitha kicks again at the dog. "OK! OK! Now let go!"

Heaving the laundry basket up to her shoulder, Lalitha starts to run. She forgets to grab her skirt and trips, scraping her shin painfully on a loose rock as she makes her way up the 187-step staircase from the vast Mahaweli River to the tiny mud home that she and her husband, Heenbanda, built by hand.

The dog beats her to the door, wagging his tail while he emits a growly whine. He shrugs his shoulders up near his snout and slinks down to his front paws, pressing his ears back while he stares at the single bed near the Buddha statue. Neil is softly snoring in that bed, and Manel is sitting by the fire, facing the door.

"Doggy, what are you doing?" shouts Manel. "Come over here!"

The dog ignores Manel, preferring to guard his adopted mistress. The noise wakes Neil, who stirs and yawns, stretching his arms behind his head. Lalitha stands behind the dog, carefully following its gaze.

Neil sits up and kicks off his light cover, letting it fall to the floor. Lalitha sees the cobra under the bed just in time to stop her young son from putting his feet down right next to its angry, expanded head. She whispers loudly. "Stop! Stay on the bed!!"

The cobra is frightened. He hisses loudly to scare off these people, who seem intent on invading his cozy sleeping space. He had slithered into the house while the family slept, trying to find a hiding place from a relentless mongoose. Lacking the receptors that cause cobra bites to kill, mongoose is the cobra's only natural predator.

"Momma, what was that noise?"

Neil's brown eyes, framed with enviably thick eyelashes, look enormous in his tiny face. He uses the heel of his hand to rub the sleep out his eyes while he yawns and asks again, "What was that?"

Lalitha watches her little son shudder with a morning chill in the heat.

"Mama? Is there a snake?"

"Yes. Stay on the bed."

Lalitha knows better than to show her fear to the cobra or her son. Smiling to reassure Neil, she takes a step forward, triggering the snake to rear up and hiss again.

A cobra can bring down an elephant with a single bite. While the snake could easily kill her, Lalitha will not kill this snake or harm any living being. She is a Buddhist and is living according to the precept (a Buddhist rule) that tells her to cause no harm to another being.

The smell of milk scalding on the cook fire reminds Lalitha that her children are hungry. She is terrified that the milk will burn. Her family cannot afford to lose a meal.

"Manel, please, stir the milk!" Lalitha says, trying not to alarm her daughter.

Manel obediently picks up the ladle from its resting place near the fire and scoots around to the other side of the pot, where there is a convenient log set down. She sits up on the log and leans over to stir the milk. As she is lowering the ladle into the pot, she sees the cobra. Manel freezes with fear and drops the ladle.

Lalitha hears the ladle fall. She does not turn to see Manel. She knows she cannot take her eyes off the snake.

"Momma!" says Manel, "Momma, there is a cobra!"

Neil looks from his sister to his mother. His dark face turns pale with fear as he realizes that this is not some harmless garden snake under his bed. It is a deadly cobra.

Keeping her breath slow and steady, Lalitha resists the urge to blink and wipe away the sweat dripping from her forehead onto the bridge of her nose. She maintains steady eye contact with Neil as she swallows and takes a long, deep breath.

"Manel, go outside and get a stick. Dip it in the kerosene and hand it to me. Then go back outside and wait. Neil, I am going to make the cobra back up, and then you must get off the bed."

"But momma," Neil cries, "I am so scared!"

 Manel jumps up and runs outside, immediately forgetting her mother's instructions. The smell of kerosene is usually enough to chase off a cobra, and Lalitha was planning to brandish the offending scent as she approached her son. Breathing a little easier in the bright morning sunshine, Manel stays to the side of the door, ready to run down the stone steps to the river if the cobra comes after her.

Inside the one-room mud house, Lalitha squares her shoulders and lifts her chin, staring the cobra down. She realizes that Manel is not coming back. Neil has backed up into the corner of his bed. Fear grips his body like a vise.

Neil watches his mother's eyes narrow as she takes another deep breath. Gaining courage from an imperceptible glance at the Buddha statue, Lalitha moves forward quickly, shortening the distance between herself and her son.

She stops and stares meanly at the cobra, commanding respect. "Get back! Get back now, Cobra!"

The cobra turns his head a little to the right, measuring Lalitha's resolve.

"I said get back! Get away from my child!"

Lalitha does her best to ignore the smell of burning milk and keeps her gaze steady. After a few minutes that seem like hours, the cobra finally bows his head and retreats, back to his hiding place in a dark corner under the bed.

Lalitha rushes to her little son, grabbing him with both arms.

"Chuti Putha! You must come now! Come!"

Neil softens under his mother's gaze and quickly slides to the edge of the bed. Lalitha hugs her son close to her, cradling his lower back with her arms as he wraps his legs around her waist. They run out the door, glued together with relief.

In the mountains of Peradiniya, Sri Lanka, where Neil Bandara lives with his family, cobras were a common sight. Young Buddhist children, schooled in rebirth and kamma, were taught to speak with them when they came too close. It was normal to see a child holding his hand out, palm down, making a motion that looked like they were pushing the cobra's head down while they said, "No! You must not come so close to children! Go away!"

I apologize for answering the phone while Bhante San, a young monk from the Blue Lotus Temple, tells me about his favorite childhood game. They called it Capture the Cobra. Bhante San would hold the snake's head down while his friend grabbed the cobra's body and stuffed it in a sack. They loved to hear the hissing sound from the jostled cobra as they ran barefoot down the dry, dirt road yelling, "Snake in the sack!"

San and his friend would stop at the entrance to the thick jungle canopy, daring each other to open the sack and release the snake

The phone call that interrupts this story is about locking in an interest rate on a mortgage. It is a challenge to be steady as I go between the lush jungles of Sri Lanka and the reality of my life as a mortgage banker in McHenry County, Illinois. This book project is bigger than I thought.

Lalitha holds her hand up to her forehead for shade and watches the doorway, smelling the burning milk and wishing the cobra would just leave. Manel and Neil are starting to get bored. As usual, Neil is the first to complain.

"Momma, I'm hungry! Can't we get our food? Can't we see the cobra again?"

"Of course not! You can play in your tree until the cobra leaves. Now go!"

Neil's mother has a compassionate nature. She feels bad that her children are hungry, and her firm response is delivered for their benefit. They must practice disciplined patience together. If the milk burns, her family will have to wait until nighttime to eat.

Lalitha half closes her eyes and silently prays that the snake is not a fool that will wait too long to leave. She wants to feed her children soon.

While Neil and Manel run off to play, Lalitha thinks about her favorite cobra story from the Buddha.

In this classic Buddhist tale, an old woman with poor eyesight thinks she sees a rope and grabs a silent cobra out of the woodpile where she is gathering wood for her home fire. She uses the silent cobra as a rope to tie up the wood and carry it home. The cobra is hurt as the woman twists his body this way and that, and then drags the pile behind her on the ground, scratching the cobra's delicate skin. This goes on for weeks, as the woman uses the cobra over and over again as a rope to carry wood and belongings back and forth. Finally, when the woman drops the snake roughly on the ground for the 100th time, the cobra escapes, slithering away as fast as he can with his now crippled body to the refuge of the temple where he meets his friend, the Buddha.

Siddhartha (the Buddha) gasps when he sees his cobra friend. "What in the world happened to you?"

The cobra can hardly hiss, but he answers slowly, "My lord, I did not want to harm a living being. I knew that if I hissed, I would scare the woman who was using me for rope. I did not want to kill her with my bite, so I remained quiet, but then I was hurt so badly I had to escape. I am sorry, my Lord. I have failed in my commitment to service."

The Buddha smiles.

"Oh, my friend, please remember that you were gifted with the ability to hiss, which surely would have let the old woman know that you were a snake and not a rope. You might have scared her, but there is never a need to harm yourself like this. Her momentary fear cannot compare to the damage done to you. Do you see that you harmed her by allowing her to harm you?"

Lalitha's musings are interrupted by the cobra, who shows its head outside the door, looking to the right and the left. The snake rears up, gives one final hiss to ward off any attackers, and slithers off into the jungle, disappearing under a pile of leaves.

Hoping to save the milk, Lalitha enters the house and dons a pair of thick gloves. She grunts as she grabs the heavy pot and roughly drops it on the floor, away from the fire. The milk is badly scalded but still usable. Lalitha removes the gloves and grabs the bowl of rice from last night's meal. She pours it into the scalded milk and stirs it quickly with the ladle, pleased to see that the rice milk will be edible.

After five minutes of vigorous stirring, Lalitha is finally able to wipe the sweat off her forehead and relax. Her children will eat and the cobra is gone. She takes a breath, and smiles.

Chapter Two

Swinging

Outside, Neil laughs as he jumps up and grabs the lowest branch of his favorite tree. He and Manel use this branch so frequently that the bark is worn thin from their palms, making it easier to slide their hands back and forth as they swing. Holding on just tight enough not to fall, Neil swings, laughing as his little body makes a bigger and bigger arc in the air.

Manel uses a stick to draw in the dirt. She has just learned how to draw tall houses with sidewalks. She saw them in a picture book at the temple last week. The ground underneath the tree is covered with stick scratched drawings of tall houses surrounded by straight sidewalks, a child's city filled with clean luxury and straight lines in the middle of crooked, muddy poverty.

As she wipes the sweat off her cheeks with her dirty palms, she feels the soft breeze of Neil's body passing over her head. She knows how good it feels to swing on that branch, feeling the cool wind on her face. She wants her turn, but she knows her stubborn little brother won't give up his perch without a fight.

Near the Kandy-Colombo road at the bottom of the mountain, Heenbanda is starting the hike up the path to his home. He thinks about the growing economic crisis in Sri Lanka and his conversation with a friend about the JVP (Janatha Vimukthi Peramuna movement) as he hikes.

The JVP started as a political movement in 1965. Heenbanda's precious son, Neil Bandara was born in 1967. The JVP appealed to Heenbanda as a way to ensure the economic survival of his family.

Heenbanda grew up on a family farm where education past the second grade was not provided. As a young man he took the advice of a trusted friend and moved to Peradiniya, where an intellectual helped Heenbanda educate himself to the 8th grade level.

Peradiniya is near Kandy, a thriving metropolis in the small country of Sri Lanka, a tiny island off the tip of India. Kandy has the world's most beautiful Botanic Gardens and many famous historical sights. In 1972, Kandy was already considered a big city, attracting many men from the surrounding villages, seeking work on construction projects or jungle clearing for pennies a day.

Heenbanda took a keen interest in the political process and became involved with the JVP, committed to changing the circumstances into which his young family was born. Rohana Wijeweera, a brilliant student and the son of a businessman, started the JVP after his own poverty became a barrier to his further education. Wijeweera's commitment to economic inequality was inspiring to a poor man like Heenbanda. He was sad to see the JVP take an unfortunate turn into extremism fifteen years later, murdering thousands of people in the insurrections of 1987 through 1989, long after Heenbanda had broken his connections with the movement.

Heenbanda had been shouting as he rode over rough dirt roads in the bed of an old pick up truck that carried the day laborers from their job site to the bus stop in Kandy.

"We cannot get ahead this way! I only made four rupees (three cents American) cutting down ten trees! I can't work enough to feed my family!"

Shouting louder as the diesel engine pushed the truck up a hill, Heenbanda continued, "I mean, now I have a family to support! I cannot associate with the JVP or any political movement! How can I feed my children, much less educate them with no money?"

Heenbanda thinks about his desperate questions as he wipes sweat off of his brow with the side of his wrist as he walks up the hill to his home, sighing, wishing he could support his family and do something to help the people of Sri Lanka.

As he reaches the middle of his journey, he stops for a moment, resting in the shade of Lalitha's favorite mango tree near the stone steps. Leaning against the small trunk, he smiles, remembering that he does have some good news for his small family. A wealthy man in Kandy took pity on him as he waited for the truck. "Feed your family, my friend," said the kind-hearted man as he handed some bananas to Heenbanda, who looked desperately poor waiting for the bus in his threadbare shirt and bare feet.

Pushing his foot against the base of the tree, Heenbanda propels his tired body up the hill, anxious to see his family and make sure that they have enough food. It has been a short day, and he is hoping for more work tomorrow. He worries about his poverty, but he is determined to keep his concern away from his children and his wife. As a man in the patriarchal Sri Lankan culture, Heenbanda accepts great responsibility as a husband and a father. His family depends on him completely for their survival. Heenbanda will never let himself let them down.

As Heenbanda gets nearer to his mud home, Heenbanda sees his young son Neil swinging dangerously high on a tree branch, while Manel crouches on the ground underneath the tree, drawing with a stick.

Heenbanda's stomach growls and he exhales loudly, using his breath to push out the pain of hunger as he readies himself to greet his family.

Manel hears Heenbanda's sigh and looks up from the dirt. She smiles as she sees the top of her father's head bobbing up the steps.

"Daddy!" she yells as she jumps up, dusting off her thighs before she races to greet her father. Heenbanda steadies himself for her hug and smiles as he watches Neil throw himself forward off the swing and land on the dusty ground, in a crouch like a cat.

"Oh, my little son! You are like a monkey in that tree!"

Neil runs after Manel who is already hugging her father's legs. He pushes his way in between Manel's arm and his father's knee, hugging Heenbanda's leg with one arm. This closeness is short lived. Heenbanda is a tough father, hardened by poverty and stress. He pushes his children away, eager to see his wife.

"Okay, okay, I must go in and speak with your mother! Let me go now. Go!"

Lalitha comes to the door and watches as Manel lowers her head, sighing as she walks back to the tree where Neil is already swinging as high as he can. Neil is laughing as he throws his small body back for another exciting flight through the air.

Lalitha shakes her head, sensing her children will soon be fighting. Reminding herself not to interfere with their relationship, she walks outside to welcome her husband, bowing to the ground as he approaches.

Heenbanda is holding a machine part in one hand as always. He stares at it while he walks, thinking about the conversation with his friend while his mind is working out the ways to fix the part he is holding. Heenbanda is a good Buddhist man, but during meditation he allows too many worries about his family to fill his head. He prefers to contemplate the problem of a machine part that needs fixing, rather than the all too real possibility of starvation for himself and his family.

As Heenbanda comes closer, Lalitha stands up and follows her distracted husband inside. She breathes steadily, readying herself to sit and listen with full attention to her husband. As a Sri Lankan woman, Lalitha cannot drive or wear pants. She is expected to practice subservience, respect and dependence on men.

This may seem offensive to Westerners (including me!), but Sri Lankans are deeply committed to their culture and the respect engendered by strict societal roles. Children bow to their parents, and fathers bow to monks. In many ways, these people benefit from the absence of the identity struggles so prevalent in Western culture, where we are taught that we can be and do anything. We often translate freedom, our most treasured birthright into extreme independence and a removal from the comforting interdependence engendered by traditional family roles. Sri Lankans take refuge in guidelines that work for them. Many westerners refuse to accept being average and insist on making their own, changeable rules. This lack of role identity can result in suffering.

Outside, Manel has had it. It was her turn to swing even before her dad came home. Wiping her hair back from her face with a sweaty hand, she puts her hands on her hips and shouts up at her younger brother. She is 7 years old now, and she wants some respect. She leans back a little as Neil's belly almost hits her on the swing forward.

"Hey! Let me swing now! You've had that branch long enough!"

"I. Am. Not. Done!" Neil says, enunciating each word with every swing forward. "I. Am. Swinging. As. Long. As. I. Like!"

Manel squints up at him, wiping sweat off her eyebrows as she frowns.

"Listen, little brother, I said get down!"

Neil ignores her, swinging even higher. He is happy, noticing the cool feeling on his belly as he swings faster. Manel wipes more dirty sweat off her cheeks with the back of her hand. She really wants to feel that breeze. Realizing that her little brother is not going to give up his perch without a fight, she decides to act.

When Neil swings back all the way, his hands only loosely on the branch, Manel pushes him in the stomach, surprising him. He shudders and lets go, unable to re-grip the branch. Neil falls and flips over as he tumbles onto his back, scratching his back on a rough patch of jungle floor.

He cries out. "That really hurt! Manel, you hurt me! I will tell father!"

"Don't you dare! You hear me?"

Manel grabs Neil's chin, hard. "Look at me! Do NOT tell father! I mean it!"

Her sweat wet hand slips off Neil's chin, and she stands up, brushing dirt off of her knees, fighting back tears. She doesn't even want to swing on the branch now. She is tired of fighting. Manel turns on her heel and stomps away, frustrated by her little brother's stubborn refusals to share.

There is no way Manel could know that Neil's stubbornness would one day be his greatest asset. He will use it to make his way to America, where he will open a temple in the middle of a small Christian town and become a chief ambassador of Buddhism to the United States.

Little Neil Bandara will eventually travel the world as a famous Buddhist Monk named Bhante Sujatha, spreading loving kindness and generosity everywhere he goes.

Right now, though, Manel is little Neil Bandara's older sister, frustrated with his constant demands for attention and his irritating way of stealing the limelight in every circumstance.

Neil sits up and rubs his eyes, frowning with pain. He is sore and hungry. He already knows that hunger and poverty are not his ultimate destiny, and he wonders how he will survive this hard beginning to his life.

Chapter Three

The Blue Lotus Temple

"But oh how I mourn my sin, ingratitude, vileness, the days that add to my guilt!"

The year is 1867, 100 years before the birth of a boy destined to be Venerable Bhante Sujatha. A young wife pulls her woolen scarf tighter, sitting up straight on a hard wooden pew with a sudden chill. The third hour of the worship service is always hard for her in the frigid cold. She warms herself with a smile, remembering her husband's joke that morning as they walked to the two year old white clapboard church off the town square in Woodstock, Illinois.

"Good thing we are on our way to praise the Lord, my dear. If this cold kills us before we get there, we'll go straight to the pearly gates!"

The Puritan church was built in 1866 by returning Civil War Veterans and local teetotalers, who wanted a proper place to pray and honor the Sabbath. The tall spire on top of the church seemed to connect with heaven.

There was no heat or comfort inside this Puritan worship center. Suffering and self-abasement were considered the sure paths to salvation.

The young wife brushes her husband's hand off her leg.

"You're impossible!" she whispers.

Her husband stares straight ahead, with just a hint of a smile, and raises his voice as he prays the divine mercies prayer with the rest of the church.

"Father, I have sinned, yet still I live and fly repenting, to thy outstretched hands. Thou wilt not cast me off, for Jesus brings me near. Thou wilt not condemn me, for He died in my stead. Thou wilt not mark my mountains of sin, for He leveled all, and His beauty covers my deformities."

The couple moved to Woodstock in 1862, just ten years after the town incorporated as a village. They arrived by train, happy to be out of the crowded city of Chicago, and settled near the cobblestone town square, into a plain house with plenty of room for children.

Thirty years later, in 1895, officials decided to put Eugene Debs, the infamous labor supporter, on a train for the remote town of Woodstock rather than into the labor friendly confines of a Chicago prison. The scheme to stop the socialist fails, and Mr. Debs discovers the readings of Karl Marx in the Woodstock jail. Thousands of supporters gather on the town square to hear him speak when he is released a few years later.

Mr. Debs runs for President against William McKinley and loses, twice.

"Thank the Good Lord Debs Lost!" the wife whispers to her husband in bed. Her husband smiles in the dark and pulls her close.

In 1906, she and her husband enter the new brick sanctuary, shushing their grandchildren, who are whispering about the wild new invention called the radio.

The new sanctuary was designed so that there was a natural separation from the convenient offices and spaces surrounding it. There were folding pocket doors placed so that they could be thrown open to a large empty space perfect for a play or a theatrical depiction of the last supper. With plenty of room for children and

Sunday school, the congregation grew as young families began to join.

Two great grandchildren, barely toddlers, stare up at the yellow sunlight, streaming through the magnificent arched windows, complete with stained glass depictions of Jesus. The husband, uncomfortable with this idolatry, leans over to the toddlers. "Hey, look ahead now!"

It's a cold February day. Bhante and I are sitting together in the temple with some brief sun streaming through the magnificent stained glass windows in the Blue Lotus Temple.

Bhante, will you be replacing these stained glass windows? Aren't these pictures of Jesus offensive to Buddhists?

"Offensive? No! Why would I replace them? They are beautiful! Jesus and the Buddha would be close friends, don't you think? I want people to practice their faith. Here, we are teaching mindfulness and loving kindness, not religion. "

The couples grandchildren grow up fighting over who had to hand pump the bellows for the manual church organ. After World War Two, an electric organ gave the great grandchildren a break from these laborious duties.

In 1932, the wife is proud of her great-granddaughter when she joins in the efforts to save the church by partnering with other Christian faiths. Frustrated by the reluctance of fellow Christians to join together and save her beloved church, the great granddaughter urges her friends to accept the 5000 offered by the Universalists, who want to join the Congregationalists in the beautiful sanctuary space.

When the first Universalist Minister, Reverend Aldridge, assumes the pulpit in 1938, the church changes its' name to the Congregational Universalist Church of Woodstock. The wife is glad for her typewritten journals.

45

By 1922, Woodstock, Illinois produced over half of the world's typewriters, and her children had gifted her with a beautiful model after her husband's funeral. He died with twenty one million other Spanish Flu victims in 1918. She wants her family to know about the beginnings of her faith journey, and the joy that was present, even in the tough Puritanical years.

She dies in 1939, a rare, happy ninety three year old woman.

Reverend Aldridge manages to keep the church prosperous and spiritually grounded for eleven more years, longer than any of his predecessors.

The son of the most generous congregant dies in the Second World War. In his honor, the church established the tradition of carrying a forty-eight star flag to the civil war monument on the town square. This tradition is still practiced today.

In August of 1945, a great-granddaughter sits with her seven-year-old daughter and weeps in the pew as the bombs are dropped on Japan. She becomes more committed than ever to supporting the growing, inclusive, liberal view of her church.

Eventually, humanism and world religion combine with traditional Biblical and Christian sources to offer a refreshing change from the oppressive practices of more traditional religious fare.

In 1957, Reverend Stevens raises the membership to the highest count in decades with his nonstop efforts at attaining high visibility through leadership positions in McHenry Country affairs and generous community outreach programs.

In 1975, Reverend Barbara Wuensch was one of the first women to attend a seminary and receive a permanent position as a parish minister. She uses her natural enthusiasm and generosity to attract many young families back to the church.

It is a hot Monday night in August. I am sitting on a chair in the Blue

Lotus Temple, still uncomfortable with the cross legged position on a meditation cushion preferred by so many of the temple members and the monks. I am a beginner in many ways. Bikkhuni Vimala is leading the dhamma talk. She is a divorced American woman with two children, ordained as a Buddhist nun by Bhante Sujatha a few years ago

I love her presence at this temple. The monks from Sri Lanka have been monks since they were boys, raised in virtual spiritual boot camps. But this nun is one of us, an American woman with all the challenges and flaws of every woman trying to make it in this country. I admire her courage, shaving her head and donning the maroon robes of a monk, letting go of her attachments to vanity. I wondered how she did it with children. One of the requirements for a Buddhist monk is the renunciation of family and I could not imagine giving up my children. Bikkhuni smiled when I asked her this question.

"I said that to Bhante, when he asked me to be a nun. I told him I would not renounce my children. If that was a requirement, I wanted to give up on becoming a Buddhist nun. Bhante told me that renunciation did not mean loving or caring for my children less. He told me in the simplest way."

"My friend, you must love all children, all people as your own children. Renunciation means that you must love everyone MORE, not less. Do you think you can do that? Could you love me and your most difficult person as much as your own child? That is the job of a Buddhist nun."

We both smile silently, feeling the inner satisfaction of women who have found meaningful spiritual centers. I am smitten, falling in love with the middle path espoused by these kind monks. The presence of this American Buddhist nun enhances the experience for all the female members of the Blue Lotus Temple.

Citing spiritual compassion as the reason, the Christian church refused a court order to close its doors to the needy and eventually

47

won the legal right to serve as a resting place for the poor.

Over time, many faiths came to use the church as their worship center. Zen Meditations, Jewish Celebrations, and Christian services created an open atmosphere that attracted people from several different faith practices and locations.

Reverend Dan Larsen took over the church in 1990 as a part time preacher and swiftly restored order to the once again struggling church. He inspired a challenging sanctuary renovation and opened up many creative financial solutions.

Under Dan Larsen's expert guidance, the church established a Peace and Justice Protest during the Gulf War and extended peaceful support and welcome to innocent local Muslims after 9/11. Reverend Larsen's commitment to social justice inspired the creation of Diversity Day as an oppositional response to a Klu Klux Clan Rally on the square in the 1990s.

The church broke the final ties with the United Church of Christ in 2000 and declared itself a Unitarian Universalist church. Bhante Sujatha arrived in Woodstock that same year, and began to lead small weekly meditation classes in the basement.

"I did not know English, but I knew how to smile. I did not think people would come back, but they did so I kept going, smiling and leading short meditations." –Venerable Bhante Sujatha

The beautiful stained glass windows in the social room of the church, designed by Pam Lopatin, depict Hinduism, Buddhism, Judaism, Christianity, Islam, Science, Humanism, and Native American spirituality, surrounding a dazzling Tree of Life whose leaves are made up of the colored glass from each of the other windows. These windows offered a clear view into the future of this inclusive spiritual center.

In 2009, the Congregational Unitarian Church officially changed its name the Unitarian Universalist Congregation of Woodstock.

That summer a church member purchased a large closed restaurant in a rural community near Woodstock and offered it to the church as a new home.

Bhante Sujatha realized his dreams of a Buddhist Temple in the middle of small town America when he and his board, now having led meditation services in the basement for 10 years, successfully bought the church on the first day of the new year of 2012.

The impossible path from a Puritan chapel to a Buddhist Temple was complete.

Chapter Four

My Wish

In 1967, as Lalitha and Heenbanda celebrated the birth of their son, the world was at war. The United States sent an additional 475,000 troops into Vietnam, and Israel launched a horribly violent 6-day war between Israel, Syria, Egypt and Jordan. In Sri Lanka, economic inequality spawned new political parties and violent uprisings, replete with terrorist threats and extreme fear.

Neil Bandara was born into a world that needed him and his message of peace. The astrologer who predicted his ordination could not have guessed at the worldwide impact of this small child.

It is a hot night in early September. 2012. Neil Armstrong, the heroic figure who inspired Bhante Sujatha's childhood name, died on August 25th, 2012. The temple audience chuckles as they learn that Bhante's childhood name was Neil. This humbles me. I am privileged to know so many details of this holy man's life. I have known his childhood name for months.

Both Neil Armstrong and Bhante Sujatha took on a mission to do something that others had failed to do.

In Neil Armstrong's case, the failure before his massive success was catastrophic. The first Apollo spacecraft never made it to the planned launch in February of 1967. A cabin fire during a launch rehearsal test in January that year killed all three crewmembers on board and destroyed the command module.

In Bhante Sujatha's case, the failure was evidenced in wars and unhappiness around the globe. Terrorism was on the rise and the Eastern philosophies of meditation, peaceful discourse and mindfulness were clearly losing ground. Consumerism was continuing its fast paced destructive march, selling cigarettes as a throat tonic and touting the healthy benefits of sugary cereals for vulnerable children. The idea of being kind was buried under the avalanche of capitalistic pressure to strive for more achievement and material goods. Competition replaced cooperation as the way to get ahead, and Americans were being sold en masse on the idea that advancement at any cost was the way to happiness.

Plenty of Buddhist monks moved to North America, settling into Sri Lankan or Tibetan Buddhist communities, providing temple services to people who were accustomed to Buddhist practice. Many of these temples were successful and several are larger than the Blue Lotus Temple, but they were created for people who were already familiar with the Buddhist philosophy, who already practiced meditation and loving-kindness.

Most of these temples existed to support the traditional way of life in their respective home countries. A Sri Lankan community would welcome a monk who practiced Theravada Buddhism (the middle path), a Chinese community would honor a Sufi monk, and Zen Buddhist monks would take up residence in a Japanese Community.

Bhante Sujatha was unique in that he created a temple in a former Church in the middle of a mostly Christian, very American town. He landed on the devastated moonscape of the American mind and quietly but firmly began to teach Americans the value of quiet reflection and self-compassion.

Bhante's mission to teach American's the value of meditation, the effectiveness of loving kindness, and the joy inherent in the present moment with no attachments, is a formidable commitment. He wanted to reach people like me, not people like him.

Bhante Sumana, the youngest monk at the temple in 2012, talked to me about his beloved teacher, explaining that Bhante Sujatha had very simple instructions for the monks at his temple.

"Mary this is what Bhante told me when he invited me to come to America;"

"I will sponsor you to come to America, but you must practice, you must be a good monk and you have to teach Westerners how to smile. If you want to do that, I will help you. Will you help me teach Westerners how to smile?"

Bhante Sujatha is a stubborn optimistic risk taker, like Neil Armstrong. Both went up against seemingly insurmountable odds and succeeded.

As I sit on my chair listening to Bikkhuni Vimala, I am excited to learn more about the life of this amazing man, and I imagine a book paralleling these two famous lives. I still have no idea about the direction of my story. I'm waiting for inspiration about the right way to tell this tale.

I drive Bhante Sujatha to the airport early the next morning, and he tells me about his life mission, discovered when he was a teenage monk. This is when I know. I have to tell his story like a STORY, not a dry biography.

"This is my wish, Mary, I read this sutta when I was 15 or 16, and I knew that this is what I wanted to do with my life."

Bhante Sujatha smiles as he tells me about the ideal of a Bodhisattva, one who has the goal of enlightenment so that he can be of service to others. A Bodhisattva not only refrains from harming other beings, intoxication and other harmful habits; he takes action. Many people describe a Bodhisattva as an enlightened being who chooses to stay in the cycle of existence so that he can help others.

The goal, nirvana, is to leave the cycle of existence, to learn the lessons that you were meant to learn so that you can stop being *reborn. Bhante sends me the Sutta regarding Bodhisattvas and although I can feel and see the beauty in the text, I can't even begin to understand it. It seems endless and impossible to comprehend. I begin to use Google to find interpretations of the Buddhist texts that are written for children.*

I am inspired by the simplicity of the tales for children and humbled by my lack of sophistication and experience. I pray that no one notices; I am a hopeless amateur.

In my journal, I write, "holy crap, I am screwed! I lied to a Buddhist monk!"(when I told him I could write this book) I laugh now when I review my notes, but at the time I was really scared that I had gotten in over my head. I also admire that girl's bravery, whoever she was. I don't feel like the same person that I was at the beginning. I suppose that's the essence of a spiritual transformation, which was unavoidable for me. I was literally immersed into a spiritually based world.

"You see Mary! When I read about this, I know that this is who I wanted to be. Every day I think to myself, I want to be the person in that story!" I shake my head, smiling at Bhante Sujatha, moved by his heart, grateful for his generous sharing of the message of happiness through the practice of meditation.

Later, I learn from an astute temple member that the actual text of Bhante's wish can be found in a famous Buddhist sutta about adopting the ways of a Bodhisattva. To be called a Bodhisattva is a high, rare compliment in the Buddhist community. It is comparable to Jesus in the Christian faith, who chose to leave his seat next to his heavenly father so that he could offer his life to us in the ultimate demonstration of love for humanity.

The translation that Bhante Sujatha calls his life mission is listed on the next page. This is printed in the meditation books at the Blue Lotus Temple, and recited by the Sangha at the end of every meditation service

My Wish

May I become, at all times, both now and forever,

A protector for those without protection

A guide for those who have lost their way

A ship for those with an ocean to cross

A place of refuge for those who lack shelter

A lamp for those without light

And a servant to all in need

By means of this meritorious deed,

May I never join with the unwise,

But only the wise,

Until the time I attain Nirvana.

There are many helpful translations of the original text about bodhisattvas. The destination, or goal of enlightenment in the middle path of Theravada Buddhism is Nirvana, leaving the cycle of existence as a separate being. In Mahayana Buddhism, this goal is considered selfish. These Buddhists believe that being a Bodhisattva, an enlightened being who stays here, is the most worthy goal of all.

Many people describe Bhante Sujatha as a Bodhisattva. This is an honor like no other in Buddhism, trumping all other achievements in the life of a Buddhist monk.

Chapter Five

Water

Lalitha is quiet as she cooks rice milk (coconut milk added to rice) for the family breakfast. Heenbanda left the house at 5 am, muttering about a solution to a broken part on the truck he was driving. Before he left, he issued a command, "My dear, you must stop that road work I insist. You are a beautiful woman, and we have two children who need our care. We cannot risk this hard work with men milling about you. You understand me? You must quit today!"

Although she is grateful to have food for her children this morning, Lalitha is concerned about their evening meal. Neil snores softly on the single bed as Manel shifts her body further underneath the light blanket over her sleeping mat on the floor.

Yesterday, a neighbor told Lalitha about a job in a tobacco company separating leaves for sale as smoking tobacco. The pay there is 35 cents a day, and she hopes Heenbanda will approve. Today she is hoping to leave earlier than usual to walk down the mountainside to catch a bus in Kandy. She will quit her road job, and then take another bus to the tobacco company, where she will apply for more appropriate work.

When I arrive at the hill next to the Mahaweli River, I realize how far Lalitha had to walk, and how far she had to climb up and down the hill to her home. It surprises me. I don't think I understood the hardship faced by the Bandar family, until I arrived in Sri Lanka, where the poverty was staggering.

Lalitha lays the knife down on the wooden pallet and scoops up the onions, mixing them in with the rice milk simmering on the fire. She stirs slowly, lost in thought about her job search.

Satisfied with her progress on breakfast, Lalitha stands up and walks over to the Buddha statue. Lighting the candle near this statue always calms her. She decides to meditate, determined to calm her mind before she wakes the children. It is difficult to leave them so early for work.

Lalitha often comes home to find Neil crying and Manel pouting, angry about her brother's refusal to do his share of the chores or some other offense. She is firm in her resolve to allow her children to work out their relationship on their own, but like any mother, she wishes she could influence their actions and thoughts about each other. Unlike most mothers, though, Lalitha knows she cannot do this; she is only be an example of loving kindness who hopes to inspire her offspring with her steady practice.

As so many thoughts come to her mind, Lalitha expertly arranges her skirts for modesty and sits down in a comfortable cross-legged position on her tattered meditation cushion. Closing her eyes, she focuses on her normal breath, in and out, remembering that her breath is not in the past or the future but only now. She notices the cool air passing over her upper lip as she breathes in and the warmer sensation of the air passing as she breathes out. After fifteen minutes, she is refreshed. She opens her eyes and chants quietly.

"Namo Tasse Bhaghavato Arahato, Sama sam Buddhasa" (I take refuge in the Buddha). After she repeats the short chant three times, she clasps her hands in the prayer position near her chest and bows, her forehead on the floor as she pays homage to her teachings.

Many people think that Buddhists are idol worshipers: bowing before a statue, kissing the ground when a monk shows up in the robes of the Buddha and engaging in other practices with symbols of the

Buddha. This isn't true. Practitioners are not actually worshipping the statue. They are sitting before it to remind themselves of the great teachings. They pay respect to Monks and other Buddhist symbols as a way of practicing mindfulness about their own humility.

Bhante Sujatha smiles as I drive him to a workshop in Chicago.

"You know, we have rituals with the Bodhi tree. We walk around it, chanting and watering and meditating. I think people see us worshipping a tree or something.

"But really, we are just reminding ourselves of our path, which was created when the Buddha sat under this kind of tree and meditated. We use these symbols as reminders. We are not worshipping the Buddha or anything else. We are practicing mindfulness and appreciating the great teachings. The Buddha never said, 'Come and believe.' He said, 'Come and see.' There is nothing to worship in Buddhism. There are only things to see, and practice."

Refreshed from her brief meditation, Lalitha stands and removes her apron. She lays it on top of her sleeping daughter as she begins to shake Manel's shoulder, gently but firmly waking her.

Manel pushes Lalitha's hand away and pulls her cover tight.

"I'm so tired, Momma! Please!"

Lalitha sighs, and whispers insistently. "Manel, I must leave. You need to wake up and finish preparing the rice milk." She needs Manel to get up and start breakfast. She can tell the day will be hot, and she knows her children will want to run down to the river to swim. This worries her, and she reminds herself to ask her neighbor to stop them if she sees them heading for the river.

Manel finally sits up, stretching and yawning. "Oh, Momma, I don't want to get up! "

"I know, sweetheart, but I have to go."

"Can't you stay home? I don't want to watch your little son today. He is so stubborn!"

Lalitha is glad she meditated. She is able to stay quiet and centered.

"Darling, I know he is, but you are my daughter and we must help your father take care of all of us today. It's too much for him to do it alone, and I am going to see if I can find a better job. You want to stay in school don't you?"

This always works with Manel. She is a good child, and her father has instilled a love of learning into the whole family. Her father often tells her that he is only happy today and able to care for his family because he left his farm and found intellectual people to help him learn.

"I know our life is hard, but because I was able to get some education, our lives are getting better. People cannot get away from poverty without education, and poverty is a terrible way of life."

Manel sighs and agrees to watch her little brother again. She hugs her mother tight before she leaves. Lalitha's heart softens, and she wipes tears away as she readies herself for the long walk to the bus stop in Kandy.

Yesterday, Lalitha learned that her father-in-law was hospitalized and she wants her husband to reconcile with his parents now. Heenbanda has not spoken to them since his marriage to Lalitha. They disapproved of the quick decision, and they have never met their grandchildren. Lalitha wants her children to meet their paternal grandparents. She knows that her mother in law will need help at the hospital and at home. Unresolved hard feelings have no place in a Buddhist family filled with a desire for loving-kindness. Lalitha's mother gently encourages her daughter to keep steady pressure on Heenbanda to see his father. Buddhist families are not comfortable with separation, and respect for parents is absolute and unconditional.

Bhante Sumana, a young monk at the Blue Lotus Temple, gives the dhamma talk on his birthday. He has come a long way. Three short years ago when he arrived, he could hardly speak English.

"Oh, I have the greatest mother. She saved my life. When I was a baby, terrorists got on our bus and killed all the children. My mother saved my life. She worked so fast. She threw me in a sack and hid me under her seat. I lived because she was so smart. Now, on my birthday every year, I wake up and meditate for two hours about her, thanking her for raising me, sending her loving thoughts. That's how I celebrate my birthday. In my country, my birthday is not a day for me. It is a day for my parents. Tell your mother you love her. If she has passed or she is far away, meditate and send her loving thoughts. May she be happy. May she be well. May she be peaceful. You will feel so happy if you do this. On your birthday, honor your parents, not yourself. You didn't have anything to do with being born!"

The temple members laugh and shake their heads in amazement at this happy monk and his profound message. I wonder, how can someone be so happy with a past like that? Bhante Sumana assures us: "Practice is the path to happiness. Practice."

Lalitha rarely disagreed with her husband, raised in the Sri Lankan tradition of spousal obedience, but in this circumstance she knew that her husband's family needed their help. It was against the Buddhist teaching of compassionate generosity to refrain from seeing her father and mother in-law.

One night, Lalitha gathered her courage and asserted herself, "It does not matter about the past, my love! I am so sorry, but my mother and I are going to see your father with or without you, I swear. He needs our help, and so does your mother. Please, let's go!"

Heenbanda was surprised at his wife's disobedience, but in his heart he knew she was right. He was grateful for her wisdom and eventually agreed to see his parents. Once the couple was reunited with Grandpa Bandara at the hospital, all was forgiven quickly. Heenbanda's mother cried tears of relief and joy when she realized her grandchildren were back in her life. At last, 7-year old Neil Bandara met his paternal grandparents and saw their beautiful rice farm.

Lalitha reminds Manel of her promise as she leaves. "Be sure to feed Neil when he wakes up and please don't fight! Make sure he has plenty of time to get water for us tonight." She hugs Manel once more, takes a breath and readies herself for the long walk to work.

Manel walks outside after her mother leaves and watches Lalitha walk down the hill, squinting to see the smaller and smaller shape of her as she disappears across the road to Kandy, a small dark spot in the shadows of the city.

When Lalitha is out of sight, Manel takes a breath and walks back into the small house, which is already growing stuffy with the advancing morning heat. The small fire makes it even hotter, inspiring the 9-year old to wake her 7-year old brother early so that they can get outside into the cooler air.

Manel puts on her mother's apron, placing her hands in the pockets. She feels her confidence grow when she touches the mala beads that her mother uses in her meditation. Shaking her shoulders self-importantly and jutting out her chest, she pretends to be a grown up. Standing over her little brother in his bed, she shouts.

"Little brother, it is time to wake up! It's getting hot in here! Let's get our chanting done and eat so we can go outside!"

When Neil hears the word "eat" he opens his eyes. He is always hungry, relishing any chance to fill his belly.

He rubs his eyes and kicks off the light cover, already sweating.

"Okay, okay, I am getting up!"

Manel grabs Neil's cup off the floor and pours water into it from a pitcher set near the door for the chance of a cooling breeze. She walks over with the cup as Neil sits up against the wall, rubbing his eyes. He takes the warm cup from his sister, who puts her hand on the top of it just before it reaches the little boy's parched lips, stopping him from drinking.

"Little brother, what do you say?"

"Oh! I- I- Oh, forget it! Thank you! Thank you! Now can I please drink my water?? You know I am thirsty!"

Manel pulls her hand away, watching her brother drink greedily.

"You like that?" says Manel, "Well, I do too and we will need more. Momma said you have to go get the water this morning."

Neil sighs, shaking his head and wiping his shiny brown hair with his palm, enjoying the feeling of his fingers as he untangles his thick hair. The little boy was gifted with an unusual, brilliant head of hair, and he likes to run his fingers through it whenever he can.

"Oh no. I don't want to go for water. Not today. It is too hot."

Manel feels her irritation start to rise like the heat in the house. She takes a breath and grabs the mala beads, calming herself. She counts 5 beads with her fingers, taking a breath as she feels them one at a time. As she breathes deeply, her anger dissipates. After a few minutes, she calmly suggests that they eat first.

"Well, let's get up and eat. Maybe then you'll have more energy to get the water."

Neil gets off the bed silently. He shoves his little feet into his worn sandals and sits down at the fire.

"Like I said, it is too hot. I don't want to get the stupid water. It is too heavy for me. Why don't you go? Why can't we do it tomorrow?"

Manel frowns as she spoons some warm rice milk into her brother's now empty cup.

"Little brother, I do enough for you. Look, I have cooked you some food. You can go get water. We will run out if we wait till tomorrow. Do you want Papa to be thirsty when he comes home?"

Neil huffs and takes the cup from her. He uses his fingers to start eating. The warm mixture is a little too hot, and he drops the rice back into the bowl, shoving his fingers into his mouth to cool them down.

"Darn it, Manel! This is too hot!"

Neil stands up and dumps his food back into the pot. He doesn't want to hike four miles to the surveyor's house for fresh water. He ignores Manel's insistence that he eat and stomps outside to grab the large clay urn that the family uses to carry water.

His sandals slap on the ground as he begins the journey, balancing the empty urn on his shoulder. After 10 minutes, he holds the sturdy vessel in front of him, banging it against his knees as he walks. It hurts, but the boredom is harder to take than the pain from the bumps on his knees. He picks up a stick and hits the top of the urn, banging loudly as he walks.

"I. Hate. Getting. Water! I. Hate. Getting. Water!"

Inside a small hut, a village woman is just sitting down to meditate. She is exhausted from being outside in the hot sun washing her clothes in the river, and has looked forward to 30 minutes of meditation all morning. Neil's voice is loud as he passes her house, and the woman is startled by the banging sounds. Thinking someone is getting hurt, she gets up from her cushion and runs outside, only to see the little Bandara boy, complaining as always.

"You be quiet already! Some people might still be sleeping!" the woman whispers loudly.

Already irritated from being hungry, Neil lashes out, "Oh shut up old woman! I am just getting our water! Go back inside!"

The woman purses her lips together and narrows her eyebrows.

"You listen to me, little boy. You don't talk to me that way! Who do you think you are?"

"I think I am a good boy, and you don't need to yell at me, so there!" Neil hits the urn hard with his stick, deliberately making a loud, ear-piercing sound to emphasize his point. The woman winces. A baby starts to cry in the distance, and other neighbors come outside to see what all the noise is about.

"Well, little boy, I am telling your uncle about this. We'll see what he has to say!"

Neil's eyes well up. He knows that his uncle will tell his father, who will never take his son's side. Heenbanda and Lalitha always pay respect to the adults, and Neil is forever getting into trouble for his smart mouth. He stops banging the urn and runs in the heat until he is so hot he has to stop. He tries catching his breath, wishing he had brought some drinking water with him. His mouth is so dry that it is painful to breathe.

Sighing as he hoists the urn back onto his shoulder, he quietly walks the rest of the way to the surveyor's house. When he finally gets there, he places his palm against the wall and leans over with his other hand on his knee by the water pump, catching his breath, wishing he never had to get water again. He hopes the old woman will forget to tell his uncle. He doesn't want his father to use the punishment cane hanging on the wall in his house.

Neil takes a big breath and jumps, grabbing the handle and using his whole body to work the water pump, grunting with the effort. Once the water is running, he holds his cupped hands under the flow, using the water to splash his tears away and quench his unending thirst. He is tired of being hot and hungry. He knows that

63

his kamma is better than this, and he hopes that he will see his path soon.

The weight of the urn filled with water slows him down as he walks home. He thinks about his father, and slows down, remembering Heenbanda's lessons about mindfulness.

"Chuti Putha, whenever you are hungry or thirsty, remember, it will pass. I will never let you starve. Remember, I am here for you. The Buddha taught us that all suffering is temporary. Just breathe, and wait. It will pass."

Neil slows down as he walks. He is just a little boy in pain, with the grown up responsibilities so often shifted to children in poverty. Shoulders shaking and covered with sweat and dirt, Neil nervously passes the old lady's hut on the way back. He moves as slowly and silently as possible. He holds his breath, trying to keep the urn steady so the precious water doesn't splash. Mosquitoes and flies buzz around his sweat covered, dirty face. He gets bitten on his toes and the back of his neck as he walks, silent and miserable. He dreads the woman telling his uncle even more than the itch of mosquito bites on his toes, and he breathes in, remembering his mother's admonishments: "Breathe, my little son. Just breathe! You will see that just breathing will make you feel better about anything that happens! Let's practice together. Just breathe."

Thoughts about Lalitha help Neil forget about his pain and his fear. He actually smiles a little and walks just fast enough to get home before lunchtime.

Manel is outside when Neil finally arrives home, hungrier than he can stand, setting the urn down so hard that some of the water splashes out. His sister is playing with the dog, laughing as he turns in circles. She grabs his tail and shakes it in front of the dog's face as he bends his body almost in half to see what's happening behind him. Once he spots his own furry tail, he becomes obsessed, running in endless circles to grab it like a squirrel.

Usually this game makes Neil laugh, but right now he is too hungry to care about the dog and his tail. He needs some food.

"Manel! What are you doing? I got the water. Now I need to eat!"

Neil is used to being hungry, but right now he is actually experiencing the sensations of starving.

Manel is tired of his complaints. She feels unappreciated and angry. She turns away from the dog, whipping her head around and flipping her hair back. "You know, little brother, sometimes you are just too much! I made you rice milk for breakfast! You wouldn't eat! Now we have to wait for mom or dad to bring more food! It's not my fault that you didn't eat!"

"C'mon already!" Neil complains. "Did you give my food to that stupid dog??"

Manel looks down, reluctant to admit her transgression. The dog has become her friend. She can't stand to see it starving.

"Please, Manel! Can't we at least make a little rice?" The tired feeling of hunger settles further into the little boy, making his shoulders droop.

Manel is not mindful in this moment. She tries her best, but the young girl is challenged constantly. She sees a bothersome little brother rather than a hungry, exhausted little boy. She and her little brother have grown accustomed to being left alone, and Manel just wants to relax.

"You know what, little brother? I've had it! You are always complaining! I already told you! We have to wait for mom or dad!"

Neil finally gives up, certain his belly will never be full. He looks down at the ground, holding back his tears. Using his snout to push Neil's hand off his thigh, the dog begs for a scratch.

65

Neil pets the dog halfheartedly and stops, walking away to sit down and bury his face in his arms. He wants the comfort of solitude, so he can imagine his mom's voice comforting him and telling him it will be okay. "It will be alright, my little son. Don't cry. Just breathe. I will help you. Just breathe."

Sometimes Neil feels like he can never please anyone—always having to do such hard work and hardly ever getting help. More than anything, he is sick and tired of being hungry. His stomach growls to remind him of his plight, and he starts to cry into his hands.

Chapter Six

Destiny

Sitting on the ground, Neil pulls his knees up close, crosses his forearms and puts his head down. He watches the dirt grow dark with his tears and wishes that his destiny would come to him already.

After a few minutes he sniffs back his tears as he hears footsteps coming towards him. Neil blinks his eyes as he turns his head, rubbing his nose and his cheek on his shoulder. He peeks out to see who is coming.

He sees small lady's feet, with no sandals, and rubs his eyes as he hears Mrs. Attharangama, one of his favorite women from the Subodharama Temple, the spiritual home for the Bandara family.

The temple, located about 3 miles east of the Bandara family home, was started almost 100 years ago by a tough young monk called the Venerable Ganalankara Maha Thero. As Bhante Thero aged, he grew stricter and stricter, respected because of his wisdom and feared because of his disciplined ways of teaching. He preferred his temple quiet and clean and had no desire for too much company.

Bhante Thero's protégé, the Venerable Bhante Dhammawasa, was his teacher's gentle opposite. Bhante Dhammawasa wanted the company of many noble friends at the temple. He intended to start a school for young monks as soon as possible.

The Sangha benefitted greatly from the contrast between these two teachers. It was a wonderful environment in which to practice Theravada Buddhism, also known as the middle path. The Bandara family attended services at the temple frequently and helped out in many other ways.

As Neil watched Mrs. Attharangama approach, he thought about becoming a monk for the first time. This unbidden, inspired thought immediately soothed him and he started to feel better as his destiny came closer.

"Oh," he thinks, "maybe she will help me! Maybe she wants me to be a monk."

Mrs. Attharagama leans down and gently lifts Neil's chin, looking at his dirty face with compassion. She knows life in this village is hard. She sees him collecting the water for his family and breaking up rocks for building materials for his dad, living the hard life of the poor.

She smiles at Neil, conveying her deep compassion.

"Would you like to come to Sunday school?"

The temple furnace kicks on loudly, reminding me that I am in the middle of an Illinois winter, not warming myself in the jungles of Sri Lanka. I am getting lost in this story. I smile at Bhante Sujatha as he tells me about Sunday school so long ago. Of course it is not called Sunday school in Sri Lanka, but Bhante Sujatha always makes sure to tell me his story in a way that is easily translatable to Western Culture. He is a man on a mission. He wants Americans to understand the value of practicing loving-kindness and engaging in meditation. He wants Americans to be happy.

"So this lady, she asks me, would I like to go to Sunday school? I say yes, yes, yes, I would really like to and she tells me I must ask my parents. I ask them and they say, "No, you are a bad boy!" Bhante Sujatha is animated as he talks about his first desires to be a

monk. His face literally lights up. It is inspiring to see the effects of a dream realized.

I am surprised that his parents said no. Later, when I get the transcripts from the interviews with Lalitha, I learn that she wanted Manel to go to Sunday school, convinced that her son would be too much trouble with his smart mouth and his stubbornness. Bhante makes a joke of it.

"You know, they are joking! They are making fun. I am eventually allowed to go to Sunday school, and I am the first student there."

"Bhante," I say, "Are you sure you want me to tell this story? I mean, I am not a practiced Buddhist, and...."

The little monk laughs, "Neither am I. We are all beginners, you know."

I smile, thinking about his lifelong education in Buddhism.

Bhante continues. "You are the one to write this book. You see, my friend, I don't need you to be experienced. I need you to write a book that will fill people with joy when they read it, okay? That's all."

Bhante Sujatha's life is about teaching Westerners to be happy, and I am one of the lucky recipients of his efforts.

Later I learn that a board member at the temple wants to know if Bhante Sujatha has seen my credentials or my work.

"No, my friend," he said, "I checked her heart, not her brains. I considered her love, not her experience. She is the right one. I am sure."

I ask Bhante about his greatest gifts.

"I am, how do you say it, I have charm?"

"Bhante, you have charisma. You are charismatic."

"Ah, yes! That is my gift! And I can see people right away. I can see what they can do before they can! I remember watching people walk down the hall to my first temple here in Illinois, in my small apartment. Right away, I would notice their gifts. Somehow I get to see what's possible for people. I can use these gifts to help people. My teachers at my temple in Sri Lanka did that for me. They knew I should be a monk."

His happy face softens, and I see the furrowed brow of a concerned man.

"You know, Mary, there are so many people to help. I have these gifts. I have to be so mindful of my ego and make sure I use my gifts to help people, not boost my ego."

"Bhante, how did you choose me to write your story?"

"You smiled so kindly while I told you the beginning. You brought a beginner's mind to my life. And you have a good heart. I knew you could do it."

I think about how we operate in the West, always checking credentials and setting expectations.

What if we were all like Bhante, checking each other's hearts instead of our brains? What if we just asked each other to do our best and then let it happen? Maybe we investigate skill sets too much and hearts too little. What if we saw possibilities in a person rather than probabilities based on their past? What if we judged our capacity for loving kindness as the thing to expand, rather than our wallets or our status? What if our children were taught to practice extreme kindness? What if self-compassion beat out self-esteem as an essential skill for a happy life?

In Buddhism, practicing loving kindness is a way to earn merits. It is beautiful way to view life, seeking opportunities to earn merits

70

through acts of loving kindness or generosity rather than chances for our own advancement in this society.

Earning merits ensures that your kamma will improve as you go through your lives. Short term, self-centered solutions are rarely seen as opportunities for karmic improvement.

In Bhante's philosophy the results of our actions are indicative of our motivations, our thoughts and our practice. If we are not practicing loving kindness towards ourselves, we cannot extend loving kindness towards others. If we are not practicing meditation, we cannot detach from our emotions and remain calm and centered in the most stressful of circumstances. If we are motivated by greed rather than giving, or competition rather than cooperation, merits, the ultimate prize, are likely to remain out of reach, no matter how much worldly success we experience.

When Lalitha gets home, a boy who has started down his karmic path greets her. Neil runs up to her as she nears the top of the hill, almost knocking her over with a hug.

"Momma! Momma! Can I go to Sunday school! The lady asked me today! Can I go??"

Lalitha plants her feet, digging her heels into the dry ground behind her. She knew this would happen one day when the astrologer predicted that her son would be an ordained monk.

"Little son, settle down! What's this? Sunday School? Manel, did Mrs. Attharangama come by today?"

Manel rolls her eyes as she answers. "Yes, momma. Yes, she did. She asked Neil to go to Sunday school."

Lalitha looks down at her little son, already squirming away from her, ready for his next adventure. She shakes her head as he starts to ask about eating, as always.

"First of all, Chuti Putha, we need to get ready for the New Year celebration at your grandparent's house tomorrow.

Neil talks louder, sensing his mother's distraction. "Momma, before we tell Poppa, can I eat? I am so hungry! Manel did not feed me enough, and I got the water right away!"

Manel stomps her foot in frustration. "Oh, you little brat! I fed you! You complained and stormed off! Momma, it's no fair! He always gets his way! Always!"

Manel unties Lalitha's apron, yanking it over her head and throwing it on the dirt in front of the house. She walks over to the swinging tree to cool down in the shade, picking up a stick and drawing a little girl who is happy—unlike her, she thinks to herself—squinting with frustration.

Lalitha knows that one of her children will go to Sunday school and become interested in ordaining as a monk. She thinks back to the astrologer, surprising her and Heenbanda with the news that their baby boy was destined to be a monk.

Is it possible that he was wrong?

Neil is so stubborn and always getting into trouble. Her brother-in-law stopped her on the way home to tell Lalitha that the neighbor was complaining that Neil used bad language and bothered her with loud noises. Lalitha worries that her little son might be in trouble. Men in her village were tough, and children were beaten for disrespecting adults. Monks could be also hard on disobedient children, and Lalitha did not want Neil to be punished in this way.

As a poor family in Sri Lanka, the Bandaras expected their son to marry and help his parents. Heenbanda could not work hard forever, and Lalitha did not even know if he would let her work at the tobacco plant. She saw the scars on his hands and the fatigue on his face at the end of a day of hard labor, and she knew they would need Neil and his future wife and her parents to help them. Lalitha

72

made up her mind to convince the temple to take Manel to Sunday school.

Manel, named after the beautiful blue lotus flower, obeyed her parents, usually without an argument. They could survive without her if she joined the temple. Lalitha had no way of knowing that Neil was going to Sunday School and becoming a monk no matter what his parents or anyone did or said. Her little son was already tough enough to work through any obstacles in the way of his dreams.

Lalitha loved to help Mrs. Attharagama prepare the meals for temple celebrations. One hot day in July, Lalitha uses a thick handful of coconut hair to slowly scrub a counter in preparation for the villager food donations. She breathes mindfully as she uses the familiar rhythm of cleaning to gather her thoughts. She repeats three words to herself, "Buddha, Dhamma, Sangha, Buddha, Dhamma, Sangha." This simple chant reminds practitioners that they possess the happy Buddha nature, the simple teachings of the dhamma, and the support of like-minded individuals even in times of hardship or challenges.

As Lalitha cleans mindfully, she takes a final deep breath, closes her eyes and repeats her short chant one more time, slowly. "Buddha," she whispers, smiling slightly as she imagines a happy calm presence within her. "Dhamma," she sighs as she feels gratitude for the people who have protected and shared the profound message of the dhamma for countless lifetimes. "Sangha." Lalitha feels the supportive community surrounding her as she stands up straighter and wrings out the coconut hair in the crude temple sink.

She turns to Mrs. Attharagama, who is busy sweeping the kitchen floor, distracted by thoughts about the upcoming celebration.

Lalitha speaks. "My friend, I know you have invited my son to go to Sunday school with the venerable Bhante Dhamawansa, and I am grateful."

Mrs. Attharagama stops sweeping and turns to face Lalitha.

73

"Yes, he is meant for this education. I can see his nature."

Lalitha takes a breath.

"He is precocious and precious to me, of course. But he has a stubborn, disrespectful nature, and I fear that he will endure too many punishments here."

Monks demonstrate the ultimate practice of loving kindness and discipline. The young abbot of the temple, Bhante Dhammawasa, was a gentle teacher, but he allowed the monks who taught and helped at his temple to practice discipline as they saw fit. Many monks practiced severe physical discipline to keep their young charges in line, and Lalitha feared for her son's safety. In addition, although her practice prohibited her from voicing this, Lalitha did not think she could bear the heartbreak of living without her only son.

Mrs. Attharagama reassured her dear friend.

"Lalitha, you will see. Neil is meant for this life. He is too smart for the schools in your village. His stubbornness will serve him well if he chooses the path of ordination as a monk. Bhante Dhammawasa agrees with me. He is inviting Neil to Sunday school, not Manel."

Lalitha speaks firmly, failing to hide her growing anxiety at the thought of Neil becoming a monk.

"No, I will not allow it. He is my only son. We need him and he needs us. Manel is far better suited for the temple life. She is quiet and obedient. She is skilled in cooking, cleaning and serving. Please, reconsider."

Mrs. Attharagama pauses, allowing the silence to calm her mind. Lalitha remains quiet, doing her best to focus on her breath.

"My dear friend, I cannot agree with you. I am so sorry. I would ask of you the same that you are requesting of me. Please reconsider."

The women know they have arrived at an impasse. They practice a faithful acceptance of uncertainty. Neither of them speaks as they quietly resume their cleaning tasks.

That night Lalitha defers to Heenbanda's insistence that they accept the choice made by Bhante Dhammawasa.

"We must accept this invitation for Neil, my dear wife. I will not allow disagreement with a senior monk."

Lalitha looks away, blinking back tears, sure that her Chuti Putha is starting down an irreversible path.

When his parents tell him they are allowing him to attend Sunday school, Neil claps his hands and shouts with delight, "Thank you!"

The week before Neil starts his temple education feels like the longest week of his life. He anticipates his Buddhist education as eagerly as an American child waiting for the day she leaves for Disney World. Finally, the big morning arrives, and Neil wakes up before anyone else. He jumps out of bed with excitement, dancing around like a joy bomb. "I am going to Sunday School! I am going to Sunday School!"

Heenbanda stirs, blinking his eyes in the early morning darkness. "Chuti Putha!" he whispers loudly, "What are you doing? We are sleeping! It is not a work day today!"

Heenbanda is concerned for his wife who has been working at the tobacco plant this week separating leaves from stems until her fingers are sore. She needs her rest. He is fiercely protective of her.

Heenbanda sits up and rubs his eyes, careful not to disturb his wife, sleeping quietly beside him on the sleeping mat.

Neil jumps up and down, landing with a thud on the floor. He is filled with happiness. Today is the day he is starting the journey to his grand destiny. Heenbanda is happy to see his son so pleased, but he is determined not to wake his wife or his daughter. He whispers quietly, knowing his son will settle down to hear him.

"Little son! Shhh! I have an idea! I will let you come with me to take the dairy cows to the river if you are very quiet!"

Neil stops his antics and closes his lips tight. "Okay, daddy," he whispers, "I will be as quiet as a mouse!" Neil is grinning, stopping his giggles with his hand. He loves going with his father down to the river. Heenbanda is proud of his dairy cows; they provide milk for his family and others. He donates all he can to the monks at the Subodharama Temple.

Neil's father is teaching his young son the value of generosity. The Pali word for generosity is caga, which can be interpreted as letting go. Being generous weakens attachments, a primary cause of suffering. Generosity through giving was the first lesson the Buddha taught after he was enlightened.

Heenbanda takes a small drink of water from his cup, left near the cook fire the night before. Neil is already outside in the dark, where the sun is just starting its rise over the Mahaweli River and the hills and jungles of Peradiniya and Kandy. Birdsong and distant monkey caws complete the early morning experience as stars disappear into the increasingly bright sky. Heenbanda loves morning time, and he takes a big breath when he walks outside, smiling at the countryside. The cows start to rustle, curious about humans being awake so early in the morning.

One cow is particularly stubborn, and she backs up further into the corner of the fenced area where the dairy cows are kept, doing her best to avoid contact with annoying homo sapiens today.

Heenbanda and Neil walk together towards the fence where the cows are kept. This feels like the best day of Neil's life. Being with his father, swimming with the dairy cows, and going to Sunday school are the greatest activities he can imagine.

Neil eagerly accepts Heenbanda's offer of a loving hand to hold, slowing himself down as he walks with his father. He hears Lalitha's gentle voice, reminding him; "Slowly is holy. You have so much energy—you must learn to use it wisely. Always slow down when you think you need to speed up. Always."

Heenbanda smiles. Neil's pent up energy is palpable, and Heenbanda takes pity on him. He decides to let his son move.

"Would you like to run, Chuti Putha?"

"Yes! I'll beat you to the gate! If I win, can I ride it? Can I?"

Heenbanda opens his hand and nods in response, laughing as Neil takes off, shiny hair blowing in the breeze as he escapes constraints and expresses his unbridled energy. Arriving at the crooked wooden gate, he stops and inhales, enjoying the sweet pastry smell of his beloved cows.

"Go ahead, Chuti Putha! Jump!"

"Okay daddy!"

Neil laughs as he jumps up to the second rung of the wide wooden gate, hanging on skillfully as he leans forward with his waist on the top rung, feeling like the king of the world. He spreads his little arms wide, ready for flight, and shouts, "I'm ready!"

Heenbanda grunts as he lifts the gate and shoves it open, looking over at his little son. Neil enjoys the effort it takes to balance with his arms out, daring himself to keep letting go as the gate swings wide, throwing him backward and forward as it moves.

"Wheee!"

The gate comes to a fast stop, and Neil is thrown backward, landing in the dirt, laughing. "Daddy that was fun! Can we do it again? Can we??"

Heenbanda shakes his head.

"No, of course not! Remember, we are here to feed our family! Noble service is more important than a ride!"

Neil smiles. "Daddy, I want to be noble like you. I want to be a monk."

Rubbing his forehead to hide unbidden tears, Heenbanda admonishes his son. "Chuti Putha, you will be educated. You will go far. You don't have to leave us and be a monk. Do you understand me?"

Neil is quiet as Heenbanda gently prods the cows, moving them towards the open gate. The low mooing and restless snorting of these gentle giants joins the distant monkey caws and the cacophony of bird songs. A dense jungle of comforting sound surrounds this humble father and his stubborn son.

Dust is kicked up as the cows paw their way through the sandy grass, staying close together as they begin to move towards the cool river.

As usual the stubborn cow doesn't move, digging her hooves into the ground and snorting in defiance of any human influence. Her nostrils flare as she lowers her head and swings, threatening anything close with her 30 pound, rock hard head.

Heenbanda tells Neil to watch the eleven cows that are gathered together for the hike to the river while he carefully approaches the stubborn cow.

"Now settle down, my stubborn one. Settle down."

The cow stops swinging her head and moos, loudly, staring at Heenbanda, daring him to come closer. She lifts her head and kicks a milk bucket over with her back leg. The clanging pail startles the cow and Heenbanda, who both stop for a moment.

Heenbanda sees his opening and moves in quickly to the right of the cow. He knows that once he gets on her right side and strokes her hide she will cooperate. Cows like to be stroked firmly and tight spaces comfort them. When Heenbanda moves in close and takes charge, the cow naturally submits. Neil's father is an observant man, and he has spent hours studying the habits of his cows so that he can more easily manage them. They are large animals and they can easily injure an inexperienced person. Heenbanda makes a mental note to remind Lalitha to stay away from this dangerous cow. He takes a breath to help himself remember.

Neil watches the other cows as they form a group and move down the familiar path to the river. He is fascinated at the way the cows move towards each other, protecting themselves from the heat, the cold and the predators by sticking close to one another.

"You know, Mary, people can be together and help each other like the cows, but being alone, like the stubborn cow, is real freedom. I love being lonely. It means I am free."

He smiles broadly as I tear up. I just told him I am struggling with loneliness.

"Can I tell you a story, my friend?"

"Yes, please," I say, eager to get the words to share with Westerners about how to overcome the dark days of loneliness that befall most of us at one time or another.

Bhante Sujatha takes a sip of tea and tells me the tale of the Buddha as a young prince:

"Siddhartha was the future Buddha. His father, the king, wants his son to be happy and is overjoyed when Siddhartha meets a beautiful young woman and marries her. Soon they have a son, and the whole kingdom celebrates. Siddhartha, wanting to see the world, has visited different parts of the villages around the kingdom. He purposefully removed his grand clothing for these tours and wore

79

the simple robes of a peasant so that people could interact more easily with him. He saw death, illness and poverty. He wondered how people could stop suffering with all this misery in life, and he questioned the way of life he was leading. The richness of the palace and the beauty of his wife and child were not the answer. He saw that every living being suffers and dies, and he was compelled to seek the answer to this dilemma.

"How can people ever be happy in the midst of so much suffering? The Buddha realized that he could only find this answer if he were alone. He wanted to learn how to end suffering for people in this world. He wanted to teach people how to be happy.

"On a moonlit night, lying in bed next to his wife and child after a wonderful celebration in the palace, Siddhartha realizes that he must leave his family. He cannot be comforted by their presence if he wants to solve the puzzle of suffering. With a heavy heart, he decides to leave while they are sleeping. He knows that his wife and son will be cared for at the palace.

"As soon as he makes his decision, his heart grows lighter. The Buddha is not pained as he leaves; he is happy. We are happy when we finally go within ourselves and love ourselves, even when that means letting someone or something go. This is his first step on the path towards enlightenment."

Bhante Sujatha continues:

"I was kind of like that when I left to become a monk. I was happy. My family was so sad, but I was happy. You see, loneliness, when it comes to you, is a gift. Loneliness is one of my favorite feelings. Loneliness is freedom. Meditation is lonely. But when you meditate you get to know yourself, so you have yourself, like your own best friend, all the time. Before you practice meditation, you don't know yourself like this. You are unhappy and dependent on other people for your happiness and you don't know why.

"I love loneliness. I smile when I feel it and see that I am free in that moment."

Loving loneliness. I am looking at my own life as Bhante Sujatha speaks. I can't help but think the Buddha was selfish. I do not understand how a father can leave his family. I know there is a deep message in this teaching. I think about the Western view of loneliness; the encouragement to overcome this valuable experience. I wonder if we are on the right path.

Could Westerners learn to see loneliness as part of the formula for true freedom? To see that until they are lonely that they do not know themselves? That we can be our own best friends? That we must be our own best friends?

Bikkhuni Vimala says it frequently; you must be your own best friend. Loving yourself is a big challenge. Send kindness and love and serenity to yourself. As I practice, I notice the emergence of a reassuring voice within. I stare at my reflection in the morning, unhappy with myself and I hear it; you are beautiful. You are loved. All is well. I am actually becoming my own best friend, always wanting the best for me.

"Wish the best to yourself. Send yourself a message to have a wonderful day!"- Bikkhuni Vimala

Heenbanda is tough. The stubborn cow knows she is no match for his insistence that she come along for the walk. He walks straight at her and reaches for her nose ring. She backs up and gives a defiant snort. Neil watches his father and wishes they could just leave the cow alone

The little boy is relieved when the cow gives up and moves forward, walking with her head held high like a queen. Neil hates it when his parents get rough with the stubborn cow, or any animal.

Neil and his father walk down the hill to the river as the sun starts to peek over the horizon. The sight of the water excites Neil. Quickly forgetting about the stubborn cow, he runs ahead, eager to jump into the cool water of the Mahaweli River, the longest river in Sri Lanka.

The great Sandy River is 208 miles (335 km) long, rising on the Hatton Plateau on the western side of the island's hill country, flowing north, providing much needed irrigation to the tea and rubber growing regions of Sri Lanka. Near Kandy, where the cows will be drinking and swimming soon, the river is close to its principal tributary, the Amban Ganga. The water is especially fresh at this juncture, and the river provides wonderful solace from the heat.

As Neil and Heenbanda walked down to the Mahaweli River in 1975, the World Bank was exploring the tributary as a possible resource to generate electricity and irrigation for the inhabitants of Sri Lanka. Neil's life is composed of so many stark contrasts between poor and rural; rich and developed. In many ways, he lives in the middle of the east and the west without knowing it. His life is an example of a middle path from the day he was born.

Neil skids to the edge of the sandy bank, stopping himself to wait for his favorite cow. When she enters the water, he turns to his father, still making his way down the hill with the last few cows. "Daddy! Daddy! She's in! Can I jump now? Can I swim?"

Heenbanda nods his assent, wondering where in the world the astrologer got the idea that this little boy was destined to sit in meditation for hours every day as a monk. He watches his little son flash a jubilant smile and jump off the bank, grabbing onto a cow's neck as it leads him further into the river. Neil is fearless, treating the cows like an amusement park ride. He could easily fall and be crushed under a cow's weight, but Heenbanda knows his Chuti Putha is safe. Neil uses his small size to scramble off and on or around and under any cow with lightning fast speed.

Neil jumps off of one cow and dives under the water, swimming underneath the belly of the stubborn cow, feeling like a brave explorer in the deep sea. The little boy stands on a slippery cow, shouting. "I jump NOW!" as if he is a king. He pretends like the cows are listening to him as he darts back and forth, taking deep breaths before his jumps and coming up breathless after making it safely under another huge animal

Too quickly, his lips are blue and his skin is wrinkled with water and cold. He follows the last of the cows reluctantly out of the water, climbing up onto the bank and flopping down in the muddy sand.

"Little monkey, you will be dirty! Get up!" Heenbanda shouts as he herds the cows together for the trip back up to the house. Heenbanda wants Neil to stay clean for the temple festivities.

He knows that Lalitha will be grateful if Neil has had a swim and is clean for Sunday school. It is still too early to awaken his wife, so Heenbanda decides to clear some land while they stay outside. He was granted land in Peradiniya through his work with a construction company in Colombo. Unfortunately, working in Colombo is getting more dangerous as terrorism grips Sri Lanka, making it difficult for Heenbanda to go to the construction sites without risking his safety.

As Heenbanda waits patiently for the cows to finish climbing out of the water, he thinks about his land. He was granted a small plot near the river, and he imagines building a workshop where he and his son can repair machine parts and earn real money. He furrows his brow as he considers Neil's new adventure in Sunday school.

What if Neil chooses ordination? Then what will become of their dreams?

Neil and his father finish the hike up the hill and herd the shuffling cows back through the gate.

Heenbanda speaks. "Chuti Putha, I will build a workshop for us! Come, you can sit near the river and watch me hack down the grass. We will create a space for our business!"

Neil shakes his head with delight, water droplets flying off his shiny hair in the sun.

"Well daddy, you know I want to be a monk, but Yes, oh, yes! I like that! Can we bring some vade (bread)?? Can we? Can we eat now?"

Heenbanda shakes his head and tousles Neil's wet hair. "Yes, my little son, yes. Wait here and be quiet!"

Neil is left outside in the new dawn, listening to the weak wind rustle the tree leaves, smelling the cook fires starting as he breathes in the clean air of the jungles in Sri Lanka so long ago.

So much of the area where the little monk grew up is deforested now. I ask him about this.

"I am happy. I like the sun."

"But isn't so much of the beautiful jungle gone? Don't you feel for the young people there now without the magic you experienced?"

"Magic? You mean the jungle, my grandparent's farm?"

"Yes, you see, don't you? The unrepeatable time that you lived there?"

"Well, we all have that, don't we, my friend?"

"Yes, yes, I guess we do." And I think back to my own childhood, in a suburb of Chicago with vacant fields everywhere and no cell phones. I realize that I have some magic to remember too.

"So, you see, my friend, we all have magic as children, even the children in Sri Lanka now. They have more sun than I did, that's all."

Later, I ask Lalitha about the deforesting of her homeland and how it has affected her. She says she is sad to see people suffering, but that is the nature of people and conveniences. "More conveniences mean more suffering". When she and her family were poor, they had less to worry about, really. "Now people have so much. It is

84

hard to have so much."

More conveniences mean more suffering. It is hard to have so. This is difficult to assimilate into my Western mind. More conveniences mean more suffering. Maybe because we think we need these conveniences now more than we need each other?

Neil takes the bread from Heenbanda and tears into it hungrily as they walk back down the path to the spot that Heenbanda has started to clear near the riverbank.

The little boy acts as he walks, puffing out his chest and pretending to be various adults.

"Look, Daddy, I walk like a soldier," he says as he marches along, wielding the stick like a rifle.

"Now I am an old woman!" With this, Neil bends over and uses the stick that was just a gun as a cane, walking in wobbly slow motion.

"Now, I am a monk!" Now Neil slows down and folds his hands in the prayer position near his chest, chanting softly and bowing to the trees as he walks. He turns to one tree and pretends to hold out an alms bowl.

"Why, hello, old man, I am here to visit you today! Do you have food for me?"

He takes the stick and fashions it as an umbrella, held over his shoulder just like the monk that visited their home for alms yesterday. Turning to his father he says, "My friend, Heenbanda Bandara, how can I help you?"

Heenbanda smiles but inside he is afraid, seeing this obvious evidence of his son's destiny.

He is proud that his son might be a Buddhist monk, but his wife is against the idea, afraid her little son is too young; she is unable to bear more hardship and poverty when her only son leaves the home. Heenbanda is also concerned about Neil leaving, but as the man of the house he knows he must honor the path of ordination if it is offered to Neil. He is a faithful husband, and he will honor his wife, but his choice must be in line with the temple's teachings, which are not changeable because of emotions, even if Heenbanda shares many of those feelings with his beloved wife.

"That's funny, Neil, but let's get going now!"

Neil stops his antics and runs down to his "special resting place," a clearing in the grass where he can lay on his back or sit and watch his strong father swing the scythe through broad swaths of jungle grasses and weeds. The little boy loves watching his father's strong arms wielding the scythe, and he muses to himself about big battles as he sits in the clearing. His eyelids flutter as he yawns.

Suddenly a cobra comes out of nowhere and passes over his legs. Neil is unable to speak for a moment, opening his mouth, certain the cobra has bitten him. After a few seconds that seem like an hour, his voice comes back in a loud scream.

Heenbanda turns to him, startled. "Little son! Little son! What is happening!

"I am bit! Father! I will die! I am bit! I will never be a monk!"

"What?? Bitten by what?" Heenbanda's face is flushed from working in the jungle heat, and he wipes his nose with the back of his hand, looking down at his son, trying to see what or who might have bitten him.

"Father, it was a cobra! A cobra! Oh no, I am not a mongoose! I will die!"

Snake venom cannot paralyze and suffocate a mongoose as it does in humans. Mongooses have receptors on their muscles that are shaped so that the active ingredient in the venom cannot attach and

86

block acetylcholine. This blockage of acetylcholine receptors in the muscles is the mechanism used to paralyze and suffocate humans in less than fifteen minutes.

"Little son! Settle down! Settle down!" Like any parent trying to get work done, Heenbanda is frustrated and wonders if his son is just trying to get his attention. He holds the scythe down by his side and looks at Neil, furrowing his brow so his son knows he is serious.

"Now, what is this about a cobra?"

Neil starts to cry. "Father, why won't you listen to me? I am bit! I am dying—I will never be a m-!

The cobra appears again, sticking its head out of the tall grasses inches from Neil, hissing a threat. Heenbanda reacts immediately; raising his scythe, he cuts the snake's head off in one swing. Neil shrieks and scrambles like a crab, scuttling back on his hands and feet as the creature's head falls to the ground.

"See?? There it is! The same snake that momma had to fight! He came back for me and bit me!"

"What? What are you talking about? Your momma does not fight snakes! And you are not going to die! Here, I will check you!"

Hot breezes rustle through the grass, bringing irritating throngs of mosquitoes into the clearing. Heenbanda swats the bugs away from his head and Neil's leg. He sits on the ground holding his young son, checking him all over for snakebites—now concerned about the mosquitoes, knowing they can also bring deadly sickness. The cobra body lying next to them is one more reminder of the constant dangers of life in the jungles of Peradiniya.

Heenbanda sees no evidence of snakebite. He sighs with relief.

"You are not bitten, Chuti Putha! Settle down!" Neil stubbornly insists that he is going to die.

"I don't care what you say! I know I was bit! I know it! And I am not going to live now! I will not be able to go to temple and be a monk!"

Neil's eyes are red with tears, and Heenbanda knows his son is really frightened and not vying for attention. He wants to comfort his son, but as his father, he must be tough. If Neil is to grow up into a man, he must learn not to overreact. He must learn to think of others and not so much about himself.

"Little son, I tell you, you are not bitten! You are frightened, which can feel as bad as being bitten. But you are not dying now, and you can still go to temple! And no one has given you permission or invited you to become a monk! Stop talking like that!"

Heenbanda stands up with Neil in his arms, leaving the scythe and the cobra on the ground, sighing as he realizes he will have to make the trip back down the mountain to clean up the mess after he takes care of Neil.

As a Buddhist practitioner, Heenbanda knows it is wrong to harm an animal, but as a father and a man, he knows he must protect his family. Buddhist rules are not dogma. The word practice is an important distinction in Buddhism, allowing the faithful to interpret the teachings and follow them as best they can. Some practitioners believe that eating meat violates the precept about doing no harm, and some believe that culling herds of deer by hunting is a noble service, leaving more resources for the remaining animals in a herd. Heenbanda feels it is necessary to kill the cobra to protect his child. This is his way of practicing the dhamma. Buddhists *practice the rules, where many religions require their faithful to follow the rules.*

As Bhante Sujatha often reminds his temple community, Buddhism is not a religion. It is a philosophical way of dealing with our minds, our emotions and our life. Taking the Buddhist precepts, the vows to abstain from harm, gossip, sexual misconduct and other hurtful behaviors, simply means that the practitioner will do the best they can to live up to these promises. They are promising to practice, which implies a sincere admission that they know they will not be perfect in their practice of these vows.

Leaving the clearing task incomplete, Heenbanda carries Neil up the hill to the mud house, determined to bring Lalitha's son to her for comfort.

The little boy starts to squirm in his father's arms, and Heenbanda stops and puts Neil down on his feet. For a moment, Neil, still crying, starts to walk forward, thinking his father is letting him walk back on his own. He squares his shoulders and takes a breath, trying to stop crying and be brave. Heenbanda surprises him by grabbing his shoulder and whispering, "Stop, little son. I can help you." Neil turns back to his beloved father and sniffs, half smiling with relief, feeling joy from his father's attention mixing in with his fear.

Heenbanda leans over, bracing himself on the steep path as he hoists his young son up in the air, letting Neil wrap his legs around his waist and his arms around his neck. Feeling his son's wet face against his neck, Heenbanda squares his shoulders and starts the climb to his home, frowning as he considers the impossible task of educating and feeding his boy while he and Lalitha are climbing out of poverty.

Neil rubs his nose on Heenbanda's neck and peeks over his strong shoulder, watching the unsteady landscape as he bounces along, feeling safe at last. The river sparkles in the sunlight, and Neil is present to the magic of his young life and his beautiful home country.

Inside the tiny house, Lalitha and Manel are up, preparing rice milk and vade for breakfast before they go to the temple. Manel rolls her eyes as Heenbanda lets Neil down. "A cobra scared him," says Heenbanda. "Please tell him he is okay."

Lalitha immediately puts down the bread patty she was forming and wipes her hands on her aprons, telling Manel to keep working on breakfast.

"Let me see you," she says to her precious son.

Neil feels the force of his mother's love and his eyes well up with tears.

 "Momma, I was so scared! I think a cobra bit me! If I die, I will not go to temple; I will not be a monk!"

Heenbanda purses his lips together, feeling anger at his son's insistence on being bitten. He notices Manel, who has stopped working on breakfast, looking meanly at her brother.

"Manel! This is not your concern! We must get breakfast ready, or we will be late!" Manel is surprised by her father's reproach and swallows her hurt as she goes back to the task of forming the vade patties for breakfast. Heenbanda is tough on his family, taught by his father how to handle the vast responsibility of a family.

Lalitha hugs Neil to her, stroking his beautiful soft hair and telling him that he is all right.

"You are all right, my little son, you are okay. You can relax." Lalitha's meditation practice helps her to stay calm and breathe in and out slowly, knowing her calm energy will be transferred to her son as he cries in her arms.

Neil is soothed by the rhythm of his mother's ribs, as she breathes steadily, slowly, and deeply. He sniffs a final time. "Momma, I just want to be a monk."

"Shhh…you are too young to be thinking about that." Lalitha looks at Heenbanda with worried eyes as she rocks back and forth with Neil in her arms, stroking his cheeks and his hair.

As they connect with each other across the space between them, Heenbanda receives Lalitha's unspoken concern about Neil and his desire to be a monk. He takes a breath and turns away, picking up the machine part he left on the floor that morning. Heenbanda studies the part, hoping for a distraction. He cannot imagine how he will prevent his son from leaving the family to become a monk.

As Heenbanda stares at the machine part, his mind clears. Although he does not practice meditation in the same way as Lalitha, he disciplines his mind in other ways, setting it free to work on a mechanical problem so that he can stay centered. Like his wife he was raised with the belief that he must take care of his mind, much like Westerners care for their bodies.

Bhante Sujatha is talking to a group of beginners at the temple; explaining the concept of a wounded mind:

"You see, friends, we all have wounded minds, and meditation is the only way to heal these wounds. With regular practice over time you will see that you can heal. You really can. It is important to care for our minds; to cultivate mindfulness in our lives."

The more I learn, the more it astounds me that meditation is not taught in every school in this country. Our minds need care and exercise, just like our bodies.

"Neil, come with me and we will get the milk ready for the monks," Heenbanda says as Neil grabs some rice from the bowl on the counter. "Let's leave your mother and Manel to their work."

"But I want to eat! "OH, we will have plenty of time for eating today. First, we must get milk for the monks remember? You can have some milk for yourself, too. It will make you feel better."

The promise of the warm sticky sweetness of fresh cow's milk is enough to convince Neil, who stuffs some rice in his mouth and follows his father out the door to the cow enclosure.

Heenbanda and his son sit close together on a small stool on the ground beneath a cow. Neil's father reminds Neil to pull the teat this way and hold the bucket that way, teaching him the art of milking a dairy cow. They milk two cows—gathering a full bucket, enough for

91

three bottles. True to his word, after Lalitha has boiled the milk for a while, Heenbanda gives Neil his very own bottle, which Neil greedily drinks down, rubbing his belly and smiling after he takes a long swallow.

"Save some for Manel, now."

Manel is pleased when Neil hands her the half-full bottle, telling her that he is offering it to her in thanks for breakfast, as his father instructed.

The family eats together around the fire, enjoying a rare, relaxed moment together. Neil flashes his broad smile and Manel laughs. Lalitha and Heenbanda feel grateful for their family, safe and happy in this moment.

When breakfast is finished, Lalitha and Manel wipe out the bowls and the cups, placing them back around the cook fire; ready for the next meal. The family members slip into their respective sandals, gathering at the door for the 15 minute walk to the temple.

Chapter Seven

Sunday School

The family walks a mile or so along the Colombo-Kandy Road to the path that leads to the Subodharama Temple. Neil is thrilled to be the first student in the Sunday school, which was being started by the Venerable Bhante Dhammawasa, a kind monk who is committed to educating children and ordaining monks in the teachings of the Buddha. Buddhist monks are not evangelical; they are more interested in the practical applications of a spiritual life. The Subodharama Temple offers a refuge from searing poverty and Bhante Dhamawassa recruits monks and nuns in an effort to alleviate the suffering in his community.

Feeling his shoulders go weak with the effort of holding the milk bottle on his head as he walks, Neil removes it from the top of his head and clutches it to his chest like a present. Lalitha reminds him to put it back on his head, where the intermittent breeze might cool it, away from her son's warm body. "Chuti Putha, we want the milk to be cool for the monks! It is hot today!"

Neil reluctantly lifts the bottle back up on his head, doing his best to steady it there as he walks. Heenbanda smiles at his son's awkward gait. Neil sways side to side as if he is going to fall over with the effort of balancing the milk bottle on his tiny head. The bottom of the bottle is surrounded by Neil's extraordinary, shiny brown hair—smoother than so many of the people in Sri Lanka, with their coarse short hair that is impossible to control.

For the first time, Heenbanda has the thought that his Chuti Putha will have his head shaved if he becomes a monk. He is silent as he squeezes Lalitha's hand.

As they walk along the Colombo-Kandy road, a few cars pass and Manel watches as a bus stops to pick up a young girl and her mother. She wonders where they are off to, imagining herself on a trip with Lalitha. Manel wants out of the cycle of poverty and hunger just like her little brother.

For some reason, I never considered the personalities of people in poverty. I don't consider myself prejudiced, but I can see now that I had painted starving people, especially children, with a broad brush. As I learn about life in Sri Lanka and other poor countries, I realize that these people are not satisfied with their lot in life. Just like us, they want more. One or two dollars a day is not enough anywhere. I am beginning to understand Bhante's mission to help. There are so many people in desperate poverty. Just like us, they are happy, sad, frustrated and funny. When I see a woman covered in boils, sitting on a city street in Sri Lanka, I feel shame about my lack of understanding prior to my visit. Later I regret not talking with her.

The 9-year old girl's thoughts turn to excitement as she and her family arrive at the path to the temple lined by lush jungle plants alive with the buzz of insects and birds. Manel feels the hint of coolness offered by the denser foliage, and she and Neil skip up the hill together, thrilled to be arriving at one of their favorite places. Somehow Neil keeps the bottle in place on his head while he skips with happiness. It seems to him that everything is easier at the temple.

The Subodharama Temple is truly beautiful. Every monk I interviewed remembered the big mango tree, the large Buddha statue and the gorgeous Na tree. This tree is the national tree of Sri Lanka, dripping with large white flowers and heavenly smells. No matter if they had tough times as a young monk at this temple; they were unanimous in their descriptions of the richness of the place.

When we drive up the road to the temple the summer this book was published in Sri Lanka, I am pleased to see it is as beautiful and lush

94

as I could have possibly imagined. The monks got it exactly right. The sight of so many monks, talking, meditating, sweeping and relaxing takes my breath away. I honestly couldn't believe I was there.

Breathless from skipping, Neil is anxious to hand over the milk bottle and start his favorite temple activity. He takes the milk bottle off his head and puts it down in the shade of the mango tree, wiping his mouth with the back of his hand. He wants to be clean and presentable for the monks. Bhante Muditha, a visiting teacher from a nearby monk school in Kandy, walks up to Neil and asks him if he brought milk for the monks.

 Neil bows to the ground and smiles, nodding his head to the monk as he grabs the milk bottle after bowing and hands it to Bhante Muditha.

"Thank you, my little friend. Now, I hear from a temple member you have been climbing this mango tree like a monkey?"

Neil looks up at this senior monk, who at 30 years old seems ancient to the little boy.

"Well, you know, I am hungry. Bhante Dhammawasa lets me climb and pick a mango to eat every Sunday. I have to share it with my sister."

"Hmmm," says Bhante Muditha, wondering about his brother monk's permissiveness. "Perhaps climbing the tree and picking a mango is not excessive if you are hungry. If you were not hungry, I think I would stop you from climbing the tree, as it is really just a distraction from your practice. Since you say you are hungry, go ahead and have some fruit. This can help me with my loving kindness practice."

Neil stands still for a moment, not sure if it is okay to climb.

"Really, my little friend, go ahead and climb. Enjoy a piece of fruit while I take this milk to my brother monks."

Surprised by the tough teacher's permission, Neil scrambles up the tree as fast as he can. As always, his small size enables him to move quickly. Neil is always the winner in any climbing contest. Bhante Muditha smiles as he watches the little boy clamber up the tree like a monkey.

Neil sits on a branch, pressing his palms down hard and rocking back and forth vigorously. The movement causes a big ripe mango to fall right in front of his waiting sister. "Catch, Manel!"

Manel expertly grabs the mango, sinks her teeth into the juicy fruit to cause a rip and starts to peel the thick skin back with her teeth, eager to taste the succulent fruit.

"Use your hands! I don't want your mouth all over my half!"

Neil jumps down in front of Manel, making sure she complies. They walk together to the cool shadow of the Buddha statue, leaning against the base of it as they split the juicy mango.

The children do their best to keep the sticky juice from staining their clothes. They are very careful with their clothing. Each one of them just got a new outfit at the Buddhist New Year Celebration with Heenbanda's parents. The children receive one new outfit a year at the New Year Celebration. Heenbanda and Lalitha buy themselves new clothes only once every two years.

Heenbanda and Lalitha walk up together, stopping to bow three times to the ground before Bhante Dhammawasa. Heenbanda and Lalitha bow to demonstrate their respect and adherence to the Buddha, the Dhamma and the Sangha. They bow before the senior monk to demonstrate their respect for the robes, which represent the Buddha and his teachings.

"Okay," says Heenbanda, "Now it is time for Sunday school, my son! Let's go!"

"Bhante, can you tell me, is it hard here in America, where people

don't bow to you?"

Bhante Sujatha smiles.

"No one ever bows to me. Mary, they are bowing to the robes. As a young boy, it was hard at first; people bowing to the ground before me three times. My ego would be awakened, you know? But as I grew into a mature monk, I became used to this. People are bowing to the teachings, to the Buddha, to the dhamma, to the sangha; never to me.

In Sri Lanka, these robes separate me from people. I am respected, but separate. Americans, unfamiliar with the meaning of these robes, are not respectful, but they are also not separate. They are able to be more familiar with me. They hug me and shake hands with me and walk alongside me. In Sri Lanka, we are comfortable with the respect, but we are sometimes lonely and not able to reach people like we can here. I like both cultures, but I enjoy Americans so much. They are so open to sharing personal experiences; I really appreciate that."

A temple member interrupts our interview, asking Bhante to come and answer a question from a newcomer. While Bhante goes to speak, I reminisce about a bike ride through a beautiful hilly park with one of the younger monks.

It was a beautiful summer day. As the monk took off ahead of me on his bike, I followed close behind, nervously anticipating riding alongside him. I didn't know what I would say. When we finally hit a wide path, riding next to each other, I made small talk

"So, what would this be like in Sri Lanka? Would I have to ride behind you?"

The monk laughed. "Um, no. We would not be riding bicycles in Sri Lanka, and even if we did, you would certainly not be riding with me."

97

It hit me when he said this. We were really really lucky.

"Mary," says Bhante as we sit in the temple basement," I never say no to a newcomer who wants to speak with me. It is my favorite part of being a monk."

I smile. "I bet. Now, we were talking about your robes."

"Oh yes, my robes. I wear them on purpose, you know. I adjust them just so, and people notice me. These robes are a gift, especially where people don't know what they mean. One time I was waiting at the gate at the airport for a flight and the announcement came over the . . . over the… what do you call it?"

I am reminded that Bhante has only learned English in the last 10 years, and I wonder how he has done so much here.

"The intercom?"

"Yes, yes. You know, Americans do not like this when they say on the intercom the flight has been changed to later. And we must all go to a different gate. I see people start to argue with the lady at the counter. One man I notice is very upset. I just pick up my book and walk to the other gate. It is a long way and when we get there, we all wait for an hour. Then the lady tells us that the flight has been cancelled and now we are to go to a different gate, again far away. I am lucky, you know? As a monk I don't have much stuff to carry with me, and I watch the people struggling with their children and so many belongings. I am glad I wear the robes; it makes my life so much easier. Even I am bald, you know? I don't worry what I look like."

He smiles.

"Actually, Bhante, you look pretty good," I say, and he laughs.

"So I walk back to the different gate, and I think to myself, well, maybe I will just walk and walk today. I can feel some, some bothering, you know?"

"But I just smile. I am happy." He shrugs his shoulders. "Why not? Why not be happy, my friend? Why not?

I am in the middle of a challenging circumstance at work. I realize that until this moment I did not think I could be happy at work with these challenges. But when I ask myself the question, "Why not be happy?" I have a hard time coming up with a good answer.

"So the man, I notice him again, he is walking back and forth, what do you say—pacing— and I just stand there, smiling. He looks at me and hangs up his phone. I wonder if he might be angry with me. He comes right up to me and says, 'How can you be like this? Why are you smiling?'

'Well,' I say, 'how can you be like that?' Why are you angry?" This stops him for a minute. I think he is surprised when I say this. So I say it again. 'How can you be like that?' Then he gets a little upset I think.

"I'm normal, you know? I am upset! I mean, how many gates can they make us walk to? What do you do? Why are you so happy?'

"When he asks me this, I smile at him. 'I am a Buddhist Monk. I practice being happy.'

"Then I say, 'Well, why aren't you happy?'"

As Bhante shares his story, I realize that in the West we say this frequently. We are sold on the idea that we must have a reason to be happy; that to be happy is the result of some outside circumstance working out well. In Bhante Sujatha's life, happiness is a chosen way to live, not a destination.

Of course, I am new to the practice; I don't yet understand that Bhante's messages have more than one part. I have a hard time understanding the Buddhist concept that all life is suffering. Bhante

99

tells me the middle path of Buddhism offers us a way out of the trap. We can let go of suffering in the same way that we let go of our thoughts. Suffering, unlike pain and loss, is always optional and temporary.

"Anyway, the man and I, we end up talking for 45 minutes about the practice of meditation and the way it helps us to be happy. I tell him about the Metta Sutta, the loving kindness meditation. I tell him that if he takes even 5 minutes to wish himself and others to be happy, well and peaceful, that he will be happier. And so you see, my friend, without my robes, this man would not have noticed me. I look different. It makes people curious about me. I like it when they ask me what I do. I like to tell them I am a Buddhist monk, and I am happy without money, and I am happy when I am lonely and I am happy when I am sick. I am happy."

"You see, I know that I can pay attention to my breath; I can smile. I can practice compassion and be happy. Even if someone is very upset, or crying to me, I am not upset, you see? Americans, they need this. They want to be happy. That man, yelling on his cell phone, he saw me, just smiling, and he wanted that, you know? It is simple, really."

"Just accept and let go. Accept and let go. Don't tolerate. To tolerate means you are angry, saying to yourself, "Well, I will just put up with this as long as I can, and then I will be happy again.""

When you tolerate something, you are disappointed, and usually when you are disappointed, you know you are angry really. Disappointment is another way to say "I am angry that things are not going my way." You can't be angry and happy.

"Bhante," I ask, "do you think that all negative emotions are mixed up with anger?"

"Yes, yes, that's right. Most negative emotions happen when we don't get what we want, you know?"

100

I do. I know.

Bhante Dhammawasa motions for Neil to come along with him to his first day of Sunday school, and Neil very happily follows, thrilled to be going with the teacher monk; already knowing he belongs at the temple. Today he is not going into the main temple with his family. He is walking past the Na tree, past the large beautiful statue of the Buddha, towards the Dhammasalawa, the practice room and schoolroom where the experience of Sunday school waits for the little boy who is soon to be the little monk.

One day, along with Bhante Dhammawasa and Bhante Muditha, he will transform the Subodharama Temple into a respected school for monks. Through a series of serendipitous events, he will end up here, near me, in McHenry County, Illinois, asking me to write a biography for his celebration in Sri Lanka as an ambassador of Buddhism to the United States. As I write this, it is still hard for me to believe that I got to meet a chief sangha patron of North America here, in McHenry County, Illinois.

Time at the temple is soon Neil's favorite activity. He is an eager student, learning quickly, and his Sunday school teacher, Bhante Dhammawansa, appreciates the young boy's natural charisma. Neil Bandara rapidly becomes a star in the dramas, regularly put on by the Sunday school students.

One Sunday, the students are acting out a Jataka (children's) tale about power. It is an exciting day for the little monk, who is playing the lead part. The little boy fidgets as Bhante Dhammawansa helps him with his fake long beard, crafted to help Neil look like the old man in the story.

"Ohhh," says Neil, bending over slightly and holding a cane. "I am so old! I must rest!"

His teacher smiles and reminds his student that he must be mindful of his ego. "Remember, no ego, my student, no ego."

"Yes," says Neil, "no ego."

Bhante Dhammawansa is already a wise teacher even though he is still a young man, not even 25 years old. Bhante Muditha and Bhante Dhammawasa are also young, although all these teachers seem very old to Neil Bandara. These men entered monasteries as young boys and participated in the strict schedules and practices of adult monks with years of experience. Running a monastery, teaching complicated Buddhist philosophy, and starting schools for monks seem like impossible accomplishments for such young men until one considers the years of training and schooling they receive by the time they are 20.

Neil's acting skills and his compassion thrive under the gentle tutelage of Bhante Dhammawansa, a Sunday School teacher who was truly dedicated to enriching the youngster's world with the teachings of the Buddha.

In this Jataka tale Neil plays an old man with a son and a beautiful young wife. People thought the old man was lucky to have such a beautiful wife, yet the old man was worried.

Neil squinches his brows together, acting like an old man lost in thought.

"Oh, no! I cannot always trust my beautiful wife! When I die, she will waste all my hard earned wealth! She and my son will end up poor! Poor! How can I protect my wealth?"

Neil paces back and forth, stroking his fake beard and trying his best to look worried. This is difficult for the 7-year old boy living his dream. His natural charisma and joy shine through any sadness he tries to convey.

"Aha!" says Neil, standing up and raising his cane in the air, momentarily forgetting that he was a crippled old man, "I have a good idea. In fact, I have a great idea!"

"I will bury my wealth and tell only my trusted servant the secret location! Then when I die he will not disclose the location until my son has finished his education and can support the whole family! There! I have solved it!"

The people in the audience smile at Neil, who, obviously remembering that he is playing an old man, puts his cane back down and leans over on it, talking more quietly:

"Okay, now I am sick, oh! I do not feel so well! Nanda, come and help me bury my wealth in the secret spot we picked out!"

The student who plays Nanda, the trusted servant, comes on the stage with a shovel. He and the little monk act out burying a pile of money, throwing papers into a hole. Patting the fake dirt down on top of the mound, the child playing Nanda smiles.

"Master, I promise with all my heart, I will not disclose this location to anyone but your son!"

"Thank you, my trusted servant," whispers Neil, sounding ill. "Now, I am very sick and I must die."

At that moment, the little actor has no trouble acting sick because he is starting to feel feverish. His face, where the beard is fastened by tape, is starting to itch. He closes his eyes as he falls onto the ground, taking one last deep breath before he dies on stage. There is muffled laughter from Lalitha, who loves watching her little son at his dramatic best.

Lying on the ground, Neil blinks his eyes, feeling tears start while his face seems to heat up. He remains as still as he can while the other students finish acting out the Jataka tale.

The wife, played by an adorable young girl with crazy curly hair, runs onto the stage and speaks to a boy older than her playing her son. She looks up at him, trying to act like a mother.

"My son! Your father has wisely hidden his wealth, so that we cannot squander it. Now that you are educated you can ask Nanda, his trusted servant, to show you where the wealth is buried, and then you can support us!"

Nanda comes back onto the stage, and he and the son walk a few steps to the hole. Nanda stands on top of it and says, "I will not tell you the location after all! You are the son of an old man who married a young woman! You do not need this wealth; you will probably waste it!"

This happens two or three times while Neil's face grows hotter and hotter. The son finally goes to the old man's wise old friend who tells him to watch where the servant stands when he will not tell the son the location of the wealth.

"Dig the dirt right where he stands. He is being stubborn and abusive because he is not accustomed to power."

Sure enough, the son goes to the spot where Nanda stood and finds the wealth.

"You see," says the wise friend, "power is bad if your mind is not trained to handle it. You must practice mindfulness with power. It can affect us and make us unhappy. We must grow accustomed to it over time or avoid it."

By the time the lesson of the Jataka is complete the glue in the tape used as beard adhesive has turned the little monk's face as red as an apple. He struggles to stand up and bow gently with the other student actors.

The audience gasps at his appearance. Bhante Dhammawansa and Bhante Muditha rush up to the little monk, grabbing his face in their hands.

"Oh, my! " cries Bhante Dhammawansa, "What is happening?"

"I..., I don't know!" says Neil, the feverish feeling made worse by the fear. "I think it's the beard! Get it off of me!"

Bhante Dhammawansa yanks the beard and the mustache off a little too quickly, causing the little monk to cry out again in pain.

Bhante Muditha runs outside and breaks open a branch on a succulent plant, rubbing his hands in the salve before he runs back in to the temple. He uses his fingers to rub the salve into Neil's upper lip and chin until the cooling sensation provides relief for the little boy.

"Oh, yes, if you look, you know he still has a burn from it," says Bhante Dhammawansa, now living in Florida, talking with me on the phone about his former Sunday school student and good friend, Bhante Sujatha.

Bhante Sujatha smiles as he remembers dramas.

"Oh, I really loved acting and singing! My, um, my charisma? As you say, this is my gift, you know. I must not use it for my ego. I must use it for good. People are attracted to me, so I tell them about meditation and the middle path, and I show them loving kindness. But sometimes they still get attached to me, and they think, oh, if Bhante leaves, we will be sad; the temple will not be all right, but I remind them, no, you can do it! You can! It is not me that is making the difference for you. It is your practice!"

Bhante Dhammawasa observes Neil's happiness when he is at the temple. The venerable teacher decides that this little boy will be a monk. For his part, Neil does everything he can to please the monks: going to the temple whenever he can; bringing them milk and watching them meditate; feeling his heart grow heavy when he has to leave.

Bhante Muditha laughs as he shares one of his favorite memories of Bhante Sujatha. We are sitting in the temple basement after a big temple celebration. Several monks are visiting to chant and take part in a celebration of the Buddha's birth. Temple members line up to bathe a small statue of the Buddha. Two by two, they step up to the small Buddha resting on a beautiful bowl with lotus flowers and use golden ladles to scoop up water and bathe the statue. This practice is meant to remind people about the magical circumstances of the Buddha's birth when even the rain was more gentle than usual, separating into twin streams of cool and warm water. It also demonstrates the idea while it is easy to wash away physical dirt, it is far more challenging to wash away the "inner dirt" of anger, greed and ignorance. Traditional Buddhists silently wish themselves free of greed, hatred and delusion as they bathe the statue. Bhante Sujatha allows for a Western interpretation at the Blue Lotus Temple, encouraging people to think about letting something go and taking on a new, better practice. As I ladle water on the statue, I think about letting go of fear and practicing courage as I nervously anticipate my interview with Bhante Sujatha's teacher after the ceremony.

"Oh, I remember him as a little boy! He was so funny! One time he came to the temple, you know, when were chanting and meditating. He came early with his milk for us. He was always bringing us milk from his generous father. We enjoyed that milk so much, you know. It was so good, so refreshing."

Bhante Muditha laughs again. He has a face that looks so serious, and I am surprised by his levity. So many monks have told me about his strict discipline. He is visiting the Blue Lotus Temple from the Great Lakes Buddhist Vihara Temple in Canada where he is now the head monk.

I am excited and nervous when I meet him at the Blue Lotus Temple on a Friday night. We sit together in the basement after a beautiful celebration in which the members of the temple community and their families take turns bathing a small beautiful statue of the Buddha who sits in an intricately designed bowl near the front of the temple. Bhante Sujatha smiles as he stands at a podium. The crowd is so big that people are standing in the back. Bhante instructs us to think about something we want to let go of and something we want to take on for the coming year. "We are washing away the past," he says, "and creating something new."

I decide to imagine the successful completion of this book, a book that will do justice to this monk who has done so much for my world. Bhante's simple message of being happy, peaceful and well is working. I can see it tonight. I am honored to be included in this group of people, meditating and trying to be kinder and more compassionate. Our goals are private—but common—in that we are all committed to our inner journey to peace and happiness regardless of what is happening in the outside world. Our shared ambition is to become kinder and happier. It's a beautiful space to occupy in a world where this is not commonplace.

"So, Mary, oh my gosh, this is so funny."

Bhante Muditha laughs, a deep wonderful heartfelt chuckle. "Oh, he took some milk to the temple you see? And he came when we were meditating, and instead of leaving the milk there, he just stood in the front waiting for us to be done with the milk on his head like this, you see?"

Bhante Muditha holds a cracker above his head with one hand. He raises his other hand to hold the other side, making a circle with his arms around his head.

"You see, my shoulders get tired like this right? And here is this little boy, standing there for an hour waiting for us to be done meditating so he can give us the milk. We love him, you know? We want him to be with us! Of course we do!"

I smile as I imagine the scene, the monk I have come to respect so much, as a little boy, standing for as long as it takes; holding a milk bottle; patiently waiting in silence, not even considering disturbing the sacred time of meditation and chanting. This is another lesson for us in the West. It is a good idea to keep some sacred time in your life, some activity in which you engage in where others just know not to disturb you. For many of us this is meditation. Sacred time allows us to get to know ourselves, to consider our thoughts, *and to gain awareness about the patterns of thinking that empower us or disable us. We must learn about ourselves to love ourselves*

Not engaging in self-reflection and meditation is essentially you ignoring you. I imagine a child trying to speak with me while I stare past her. I'm continually surprised by the benefits of this simple practice.

Chapter Eight

The Stubborn Cow

Eight-year old Neil steals handfuls of rice from the cook pot while Lalitha is outside tending to the stubborn cow whose udder is hot and swollen with milk. Heenbanda warned her to stay away from the cow, but Lalitha is confident in her ability to handle the animal, and she does not want to leave this time consuming task for her hard working husband. Before she went out, she admonished her son to stay in the house. Manel is with Heenbanda, helping him with clearing down by the river.

"Stay inside, Chuti Putha. That cow can be a little crazy. I'll be right back to feed you."

Food is scarce in the house lately, and Neil's sandals are uncomfortable and worn down to holes beneath the balls of his feet. He can feel the uneven ground as he nibbles on the rice, and he wishes he could have some new shoes. The bottoms of his feet hurt.

Neil knows that taking his share of the family food before a meal is disrespectful, but he is so hungry that he cannot help himself. He is about to push another finger-full of rice into his mouth when he hears the clanging of the milk bucket as it falls on the ground. His precious rice falls from his hand when he hears his mom cry out "Stop! You must stop!"

He wipes his mouth with the back of his hand and runs outside to see his mom lying on the ground with the stubborn cow rearing back, looking ready to kick her. Neil runs past his mother and pushes the cow right in the chest. "You stop! That is my momma! Stop! We must milk you!"

The cow responds by lowering her huge head, using it like a 30 pound wrecking ball, swinging it back and forth, hitting Neil in the forehead and knocking him down. As Lalitha pushes her self up, the cow leans into her and swings her head, hitting Lalitha's cheek, causing her to shout out in pain.

Neil scrambles to a semi-upright position on his hands and knees. Raised by Heenbanda, a fiercely protective husband and father, Neil knows he must protect his mother.

He spies the big stick that Lalitha dropped in her struggles with the stubborn cow. The weapon is on the ground, in the middle of the small herd now crowded together to protect themselves from the crazy cow and her dangerous head.

Using his small size as an advantage, he gets up and runs over to the herd, squeezing his way in between their hot oily hides as they expand and contract with heavy bovine breaths. He grabs the stick and raises it over his head shouting, "Get out of my way! Get out of my way!"

The cows shuffle and snort and move awkwardly, bumping into each other as they part ways so the little boy can run out of the middle of the herd to save his mom who is being knocked down by the stubborn cow every time she tries to get up.

Neil raises the stick up high, imitating his father with the scythe, and yells, deepening his voice as best he can. "Leave my mother alone! You hear me! Leave her alone! Let her be!"

He hits the cow all over, aiming for her nose but frequently missing the mark. He reaches up as high as he can and still falls short of reaching the stubborn cows head. Neil is trying his best to remember how his father gets through to this cow. His fear about not being able to protect his mother interferes with his mindfulness.

He cannot remember his father's instructions. The stubborn cow is now lifting her chin high to avoid his blows, growing more and more agitated as Neil hits her with the stick.

Lalitha is lying on her side, almost unconscious from the force of the cow's blows. She watches helplessly as Neil grabs the stool she was sitting on when the cow started her violent protest and places it right underneath the dangerous head.

Trying to tell Neil to be careful—not to stand on the stool when the cow is swinging her head like this—Lalitha feels her throat constrict. She can only whisper while she watches her son climb onto the stool right next to the stubborn cow, who snorts meanly as Neil gets closer.

Neil surprises the cow and Lalitha when he raises the stick up and slams it on the cow's head so hard he falls off the stool. Neil lies on the ground, trying to catch his breath as Lalitha turns toward him. She rolls herself over on top of her son, trying to protect him from being trampled.

Lalitha smiles weakly as she sees the cow's hooves moving away, heading back towards the herd, satisfied that she has once again taught these humans not to mess with her. Neil is laying face down underneath her on the ground, covering his head with his hands, waiting to be trampled. Lalitha shakes her head a little, wincing as she does so, but still smiling at her son's bravery. She thinks to herself that the astrologer could not be right. Surely this beloved, brave little boy is not meant to leave his family for the monastery.

A needle pierce of grief causes Lalitha to gasp, as she shuts her eyes tight, blinking back tears. As a practicing Buddhist, she accepts impermanence as a way of life, but the reality of losing her son seems far beyond the comfort of the dhamma.

Neil's kamma seems to be leading to the path of husband and father with his determined actions in the pasture today. Kamma is not the same as fate in Lalitha's Buddhist teachings. (Theravada Buddhists like Lalitha, who practice the middle path, use the Pali word Kamma for the Sanskrit word Kamma.) Lalitha understands Kamma as meaning the choices one makes; the volitional or willful actions they take. She knows that the things her little son does or says or thinks, all of his daily choices, set his destiny into motion. The law of kamma, as Lalitha and other Buddhists practicing the middle path understand it, is the law of cause and effect.

Many people mistakenly use the word Kamma to mean the result or the fruits of Kamma. In the Buddhist middle path, Kamma is complex, action-based and changeable. There is a sense of destiny, especially in the astrological readings, but there are still endless choices to make on the way to the right path. This is part of the nature of suffering, when human beings and animals make the wrong choices and resist the path set out before them.

Neil's actions, his kamma, do not seem to be leading to monkhood. Manel, on the other hand, with her quiet calm disciplined nature, seems to be better suited to the serious practices of Buddhist monks and nuns.

Heenbanda arrives home to find his wife and son in the house resting on the sleeping mats. Lalitha's face is bruised and her hair is a mess. Neil's eyes are swollen almost shut from crying. Heenbanda is concerned again about his family's welfare when they share the happenings of the day with him. He watches them and thinks about the safety of his parent's farm.

As the man of the house Heenbanda must listen carefully for danger at night. As he lay next to the love of this life that night, he hears a monkey too close to the house and the scurry of a rodent outside the door. He leans up on one elbow, ready to spring into action when he hears a scuffle between the wild dog, sleeping near the house as always, and the rodent, who limps off after the tussle. Heenbanda listens to the monkey's caw as it runs away from the dangerous canine threat.

The tired father feels gratitude for the dog who will stop at nothing to protect his adopted family. Sitting up in the dark, waiting for his eyes to adjust, Heenbanda remembers an important lesson that Bhante Dhammawasa taught last week at the temple:

"Know well what leads you forward and what holds you back and choose the path that leads to wisdom."

This is the way that Heenbanda makes his choices. Like many Buddhist practitioners, he considers his internal experiences as he walks his chosen path, rather than an outside result, which is a secondary consideration for him.   It is painful to imagine life without his Chuti Putha and even worse to admit that he has failed in his efforts to provide for his loved ones, but he knows that the path to wisdom and peace does not involve his attachment or his pride.

Later that night, Lalitha turns toward him in her sleep as he muses. Heenbanda observes her beautiful bruised face and calloused hands. She needs a faithful husband, a devoted father and a humble servant to the Dhamma. Heenbanda realizes that giving up control in this way, by sending his precious son to live with his once estranged parents on the farm he left at such a young age, is the path that will leave him wiser and more competent to care for his family in the future.

He takes a deep breath, relieved by the lightness of his once heavy heart. A man who chooses a path that leads to wisdom rather than control or worldly success has earned the right to be a family leader in the Buddhist spiritual practice. Choices guided by spiritual discipline rarely leave practitioners with heavy hearts or second thoughts. Choices guided by fear, impatience or ignorance usually attract unhappiness to our lives.

Buddhists believe that with a mind trained in the practice of loving kindness and meditation a person can trust their center, the small, quiet, inner voice that we all possess. Without steady spiritual practice this voice is hard to hear, and so we operate in life without our most valuable resource, the calm reassurance of a healed mind. Heenbanda's heart is light because he trusts the path to wisdom found through a lifetime of disciplined adherence to the Dhamma.

The nun at the temple is explaining the Buddhist concept of self as I listen with rapt attention. I am someone who struggles mightily with being still and at peace with myself.

"We are not our thoughts; we are not our bodies; we are not our minds, so who are we?"

Until she said this, I subscribed to the notion that we are our thoughts, or at least the thinker behind the thoughts. Vimala went on:

"Friends, you are like a clear sky with nothing to distract from your pure eternal unchanging essence. Out thoughts, our experiences, even our breaths are just clouds in that sky, coming and going. Black clouds threaten storms and white clouds give us something beautiful to look at, but who we are never changes. Enlightenment reveals that clear sky. There is no way to create that sky. It existed before you were born, and it will continue forever after. The goal of spiritual practice is simply to see that sky and rest easily in its perfection.

Bhante Sankicha, a highly educated wise monk from the temple in Michigan, explains this further in my interview with him.

"Mary, I encourage people to be as still as possible during meditation and to pay careful attention to the small silent space between an exhale and an inhale. I want them to find their still point. That is where who they are emerges. That is where enlightenment starts."

With diligent spiritual practice, Heenbanda found his still point. He made the choice to send Neil to his grandparent's farm and slept peacefully beside his beloved wife, who smiled in her sleep as her husband put his familiar protective arm over her waist.

Chapter Nine

Hungry

Hiking up the hill from a full day at school, Neil Bandara sighs as her hears the sound of hammering. Near the mud house, Lalitha, Manel and Lalitha's mother use heavy mallets to break large rocks and pieces of concrete into tiny pieces suitable for use in Heenbanda's growing construction projects. Neil tries to control his frustration as he approaches his mother, who is wet with sweat from her work.

Lalitha looks up and smiles, using the heel of her hand to push her matted hair from her forehead.

"Hello, little son!"

Manel and Neil's grandmother don't look up from their work, lost in concentration as they use smaller mallets on broken pieces of concrete. They are careful not to smash their fingers as they break the concrete into the smallest pieces possible. Manel winces as she hits the mallet against a stone hard piece, feeling the reverberations through her wrist all the way up to her shoulder blades.

When Neil enters the house he sees that the fire is out, and there is nothing in the pot. He becomes a little panicked, feeling so hungry that he is dizzy.

He walks outside, calling to his mother.

"Mama? Where is the food? Isn't there any vade? Where is the stew?"

Lalitha is distracted, tired from breaking up the rocks. "Oh, honey, we didn't have time. We will make something in a little while."

"But, mama I am so hungry! I think I will die if I don't eat!"

Neil's grandmother, feeling that her daughter is working too hard, speaks up. "Little boy, you can wait! Can't you see your mother and your sister are working so hard?"

Neil is really hungry. He is not joking when he says he thinks he will die. His stomach hurts and he cannot believe there is no food for him.

"I am so hungry!" he yells, stomping back into the small mud house, completely losing his mindfulness.

He grabs the empty cook pot, picking it up over his head and smashing it on the floor. He kicks it, so hard he hurts his foot, grabbing his toes and sucking air through his teeth, tears of pain springing to his eyes.

"I have to eat! Why can't anyone see this!" he yells as he kicks at the pot and sweeps a plaster vase and a cup off the shelf near the door; not caring as they break into sharp pieces on the ground. "I will die! I swear! I will die!"

He kicks the pot and the broken pieces of plaster out the door, crying as he runs after them, clanging down the path to the river.

Lalitha watches helplessly, unable to navigate the gulf between her compassion and her anger. She understands the pain of hunger all too well, and she knows Neil cannot help himself.

Lalitha's mother stops her work and puts her hand on her daughter's shoulder.

"Khanti, my darling. Khanti."

Lalitha lets her tears fall and allows her mother's hand to connect her to the dhamma lesson about patience, one of the ten perfections in her Buddhist tradition. There are ten perfections in the Buddhist tradition, listed in the appendix at the end of this book.

"Oh mother, when will our lives get easier? When?"

"Darling, the Buddha taught us all life is impermanent. Your circumstance will change. In the meantime, we can practice khanti."

In Buddhism patient forbearance or khanti, refers to the idea that we can be mindful about our pain. If our home is burning, or our loved one is dying, or our child is hungry, we can practice awareness of our minds, and our tendency to internalize external events. With practice, we can be calm and effective even in the midst of tremendously painful events. Khanti is not tolerance. Patience is a gift given to a practitioner that they can use to move closer to nirvana and lessen their suffering.

Neil ends up near the river, sobbing into his hands. Heenbanda comes across his precious son as he makes his way home from 8 hours of hard labor. He sits on the riverbank near his Chuti Putha, offering silent, solid support. When Neil is ready, he and his father begin the muddy climb back up to the house.

The time has come. Heenbanda must send Neil away for the summer so that his young son will be cared for properly. Neil might even remember what it was like before he wanted to become a monk, and go back to being a son on his way to marriage and a family. Heenbanda holds out hope that time on the farm will help his young son lose his desire to leave the family and become a monk.

That night, lying on their sleeping mat, Heenbanda tells Lalitha that they must send her little son away for at least the rest of the summer, so that he can have enough food and enjoy his parent's farm in the country. Lalitha gratefully agrees, hopeful that a stay on the farm will help her precious son.

117

Two weeks later the whole family makes their way to Kandy to catch the bus to the country, standing on the crowded bus in the heat as it bounces over the rutty road on the way to the paradise of the farm in Gale Gadara, a few hours away.

"Bhante, when I was young, I can remember the feeling of scrambling out of the cold pool in my parent's backyard and running through the open gate to the blacktop driveway in the summer. I would lie down in my bathing suit on the warm asphalt in the sun, and it would feel so good. It is one of those magical childhood memories. Now I sometimes think to myself, 'How in the world did I ever think it could get better than this?' Is there anything you can remember that's like that? That's so good when you remember the feeling that you can't believe you ever thought it could get better?"

"Yes, Mary, yes, I do! It was on my grandparent's farm! I was so happy there! I would just run and run!"

He smiles broadly. "Oh, those soft rice fields! Oh my goodness, the country! I was so free! Can you imagine? I did not have to work there like I did at home, and you know, my grandparents; they spoil me! They have so much food! Oh, it was wonderful!

"But didn't you already live in the country?"

"No, you see, it is funny. I know when I say mud house or the mountains you think, oh, Bhante lived in the country. But no, my friend, you see we lived in the city; for us, it was the city.

"My grandparents, I don't know, it was wonderful, you know? The freedom?"

I do. I know.

Neil spent a year at his grandparents' house, attending third grade there while his family worked hard in Peradiniya, making their home life better for their beloved Chuti Putha.

Chapter Ten

Determination

Lalitha is standing in her mud house holding a basket of laundry. She is hot and flushed from the hike up to her home. She thought that her son might lose his desire to be a monk in the year at his grandparent's farm. Nothing of the sort happened.

Neil's desire to be a monk grew even stronger while he stayed with his grandparents. He would imagine climbing the mango tree while he ran in the rice fields. He carried a little bowl in the fields and practiced begging for alms from the farm animals and the plants. Neil's grandfather was regretful that he did not spend more time with this remarkable boy when he was younger. Obviously, he was on his way to greatness.

Destiny is hard to resist, and Neil Bandara was born under the auspicious horoscope that leads to ordination as a Buddhist monk.

Neil resumed his temple studies at Sunday school when he came back to Peradiniya that summer. Bhante Dhammawasa began to talk seriously with the little boy about being ordained as a Buddhist monk. The little boy was so excited when Bhante Dhammawasa first brought up the possibility of monkhood that he yelled "Yes!" in the middle of the quiet temple. He couldn't help himself. He knew that he belonged there.

Lalitha's heart sank when her little son came running into the house that day after Sunday school. She and Manel were home working long hours to be sure there was enough food prepared for the

119

celebration of Vesakha day. Manel was chopping about 100 sweet potatoes after Lalitha's mother peeled them, throwing the peels into a bucket for Neil to bring out to the cows later.

The little boy leaned over with his hands on his knees, catching his breath while Lalitha threw another handful of sweet potatoes into the steaming cook pot.

"Momma, momma, Bhante asked me to become a ...."

Lalitha rebukes him. "Chuti Putha, you know better than to come in and pay no respects to the Buddha! Light the candle, say your chants!"

"But momma, I have to ask you! I want to become a monk!"

Manel sets her knife down and sighs. "Well, little brother, you might want to start by paying your respects to the Buddha."

Lalitha admonishes her daughter. "Manel, this is not your business. Little son, please. You cannot become a monk. Now light the candle and say your chants."

Neil glares at his sister. "You know, Manel, you should stay out of it!"

Lalitha's mother pipes up at this. "Little son! That is enough! Now pay your respects!"

Neil purses his lips and breathes out. "Okay, okay. If I do the chants, then I can be a monk, right?"

"Little son, please!"

"Okay! Whatever!" Neil stamps his feet as he walks across the dusty floor to the Buddha statue, grabbing a piece of small kindling from the shelf and lighting it with the cook fire. He lights the candle, quickly bows and then says the chant, "Namo Tassa Bhaggavato, arahato, sama sam buddhasa" (I take refuge in the Buddha.)

Neil says his chants so fast that they are unintelligible."NamotassabhagghavatoarrahatosamasambuddhasaN amotassabhagghavatoarrahatosamasambuddhasaNamotassabhag ghavatoarrahatosamasambuddhasa."

He runs the words together, thinking about how to convince his mom to let him become a monk while he chants. He surreptitiously peeks up at the Buddha, silently pleading for help. His mother must see that being a monk is his kamma.

When he is done chanting, he whispers, "Please help, Buddha, please, I must become a monk!" as he bows to the ground.

 Heenbanda walks in to see Lalitha doing her best to keep cooking while her young son pesters her ceaselessly. "Momma I will do all the potato cutting; I will give half of my share to Manel; I will carry the milk AND the cook pot to the temple. Just say yes to me! Let me be a monk!"

Heenbanda's face is flushed as he corrects his son. He knows he is losing control.

"Okay, okay, little son, I have already said this! Stop pestering your mother! You are not becoming a monk! You are too young to leave us! You are our only son! Now come with me for milking! We have to get back to the temple quickly! Mrs. Attharagama is waiting for the stew!"

Neil knows he must listen to his father, and he reluctantly follows him out to the pasture. As soon as they sit down to milk the stubborn cow, who is, as usual, swollen and cranky, Neil asks his father if he can be a monk."

"So, father, don't you think I could be a monk?" Neil asks innocently as he holds the bucket under the cow teats while Heenbanda squeezes and pulls.

The milk makes a tinny sound as it hits the bucket and Neil waits

121

until the bucket is filled up enough to silence the spurts. "Did you hear me father? I want to be a monk! Bhante Dhammawasa says I can be a monk and live at the temple!"

Heenbanda ignores his son, sighing as he stands up with the milk bucket. The little boy is finally quiet, sensing that he might have gone too far. Heenbanda is a tough man who was raised by a strict father and he will, just like his father, swat his son when he has had enough. Heenbanda's silence can be dangerous, and Neil wisely decides to wait to ask him again.

Bhante Sujatha asks me to please, just fill people with joy. "Do not talk so much about the negative. See people with loving kindness." I agree, and it is not until later that I notice my attachment to a "tell all" book. I want to be a realist, a famous truth teller, rather than a faithful servant to the dhamma. I reconcile these feelings with my understanding that this is not my book. This is Bhante's book, and I will honor all of his requests. I notice that it feels good to do this, rather than succumb to my craving for fame and gossip. I am aware of my suffering diminishing as I let go of my selfish desires. I seem to be acutely aware of my inner experiences as I write this book. I don't even use the word yet, but I am becoming more mindful.

Neil puts the milking stool back outside the gate and grunts with the effort of pulling the wooden fence post on the gate up and out of the rut so he can push the gate closed. His father has always helped Neil with this task, but today Heenbanda is angry, frightened by the prospect of losing his Chuti Putha. He leaves his son alone with the hard work of closing the gate.

Today, the family will join other family members and members of the temple in celebrating Vesakha Day (Buddha Day). In one day, they celebrate the birth, the enlightenment and the death of their beloved Buddha. Neil and Manel are very excited as they skip and run alternatively along the path that leads to the temple.

It is the first full moon of May, a month that the whole family enjoys. There is always plenty of rain with the monsoon season fast approaching and Neil breathes in as he runs, enjoying the fresh smell of wet foliage drying in the sunshine. He stops himself abruptly and pushes off his back leg, leaping as far as possible, trying to beat his older sister in an impromptu skipping race. He spies a mongoose and swears he sees the tail of the cobra it is chasing. The water, the plentiful greenery drenched with fruit and nuts, and the lush grasses perfect for nibbling always bring out the wildlife in the month of May.

Neil and Manel are thrilled when they spy or think they spy yellow eyes in the bush as they pass. Even spiders come out and play, extending their webs at several places across the path, feasting on a plethora of insect life. Heenbanda relaxes as they walk, laughing at the children skipping, brushing webs out of the way for Lalitha, and reassuring her that the webs were just what they needed to stop the crazy bad mosquitoes at this time of year.

Neil takes a big breath and smiles as they come upon the temple with the large statue of the Buddha glistening with rainwater in the sun. He rests under the mango tree, staring up at the shiny branches heavy with ripe mangos. "I am finally home," he thinks to himself as he skips over to a group of monks near the Na tree, gorgeous with rain soaked green leaves and lush white flowers.

Monks have come from the main temple in Colombo to help celebrate the big day. They are joking about collecting alms in the rain. A young monk is telling his story about an old man that ran out of his house in the storm to tell the monk he had some good food for him if he would just wait a minute. The monk followed the man up to his door to go inside the house, but the man did not invite him in. He closed the door and left the young monk standing in the rain— thinking about whether he should stay or go.

This young monk's teacher takes over telling the story, laughing as he describes the young monk returning in soaking wet robes with watery rice and beans in his bowl. "Oh my gosh, we had terrible food that day!"

The young monk smiles at his teacher as he chimes in, "Yes. I waited for the man for 20 minutes. I got so wet, and I still waited."

"Well," says his teacher, "Why didn't you ask to go in the house?"

"You know, my teacher, I did not want his house to get wet."

All of the monks burst into friendly laughter, imagining the young monk, just standing there patiently, blinking the rainwater out of his eyes, waiting. Neil feels pulled by his destiny as he watches a little monk take his teacher's hand, leaning against the older monk as if he was his father. Neil wants that with Bhante Dhammawasa.

He wants to be his first student learning to be a monk. The little boy is always surprised at how good he feels when he thinks of this. He loves his family, but his heart lives at the temple with the monks.

Bhante Dhammawasa smiles at Neil as he tells the other monks that the story reminds him of the young boy standing next to him.

"He wants to be a monk, you know? And so he likes to bring us milk, as much as he can."

A monk from Colombo with a large brown face smiles down at him. "Why, little boy, where do you get your milk? Do you have cows?"

Neil smiles. "Yes, yes we do! My daddy has 12 cows! And, yes, I want to be a monk! Do you want me to get you some milk?"

The monks all laugh and smile at Neil. Neil looks up at them, feeling intoxicated by their attention, wanting more. Neil follows his Sunday school teacher, as the monks part ways, walking out to greet their various communities in the crowd. Bhante Dhammawasa stops and turns to look at his young student.

"My little friend, you shouldn't go with me, right? Aren't your grandparents here with your parents and your sister? Go, be with them today."

They are now standing in the cool shadow of the Buddha statue. Neil swallows a lump in his throat. He shuffles his worn sandal in the dirt and sways a little as he talks, looking down at the ground so Bhante Dhammawasa doesn't see his tears. "But, Bhante, I want to stay with you. I want to be a monk. I want to live here."

Bhante Dhammawasa is a compassionate teacher. He doesn't want to see the little boy suffer, but he knows that his parents must give their permission for Neil to be a monk. "Little boy, I will ask for your horoscope. If I see that your astrology is correct for becoming a monk, I will ask you to join me at the temple."

Neil enjoys the relief from the heat and the sun in the shade of the Buddha statue.

"Thank you, my Buddha," he whispers. The Buddha statue, so serene and beautiful, seems content to just sit, letting the little monk bask in his shade as long as he likes.

Bhante Dhammawasa smiles "Well, my friend, let's go see your parents and eat!"

"It is possible!" thinks the little boy, as a smile broadens across his face. "I will be the little monk!"

Neil is dizzy with happiness when Bhante Dhammawasa takes his hand as they walk. Soon they see Heenbanda who waves them over to the table with the rest of the Bandara family. As Neil sits on the ground to eat, he pretends to be pushing aside robes, and he keeps his distance from his family, already knowing that he has found his real family with the monks at the temple.

That night at home Lalitha realizes the truth. Her ten-year-old son is not giving up his idea of being a monk. In fact, he is more persistent than ever.

Neil is causing a scene, pestering his mother about becoming a monk.

Lalitha loses patience. "I already said no! You will not leave us to be a monk! Heenbanda, please! Help me!"

Heenbanda is busy twisting the gears of a sprocket just so, fixing a machine part for his neighbor. He is sitting cross-legged by the cook fire, and Manel is practicing her meditation in the corner by the Buddha. Neil is taking full advantage of this opportunity to pressure his mother.

"Heenbanda, please!"

Heenbanda puts the machine part down, hard, on the packed mud floor and stands up, towering over his little son. Now Neil is standing in the hot shadow of his angry father, wishing he were standing in the cool shadow of the Buddha statue with his teacher.

"Listen, Chuti Putha, you are staying with us, you understand? We think you are too young to join the temple. You are staying here!"

"But, daddy, I-"

"Stop it! That is it! I won't hear of this anymore! You understand me?? No more!"

Neil thinks fast.

"Then, then I will throw myself into the river! I will jump off the bridge! I will die! I want to die! If I cannot be a monk, I want to die!" He runs out the door into the dark night. Lalitha starts after him, but Heenbanda stops her. "No, no, let him go! We have to let him go!"

Today is the big day. Venerable Bhante Sujatha is being honored as a Chief Sangha Patron (Sanganayaka) of North America for his tireless efforts to share the path the dhamma with Americans. The three-wheeled taxis in Sri Lanka are all plastered with his picture, and thousands of people line the streets for a glimpse of the little monk. I am uncomfortable in the heat, which turns out to be a gift. Without the discomfort to manage, I don't think I could have handled my nerves.

I stop with the rest of the parade on the bridge over the Mahaweli River. Michael Fronczak, Bhante's noble friend, turns to me and speaks. "Mary this is it. This is the bridge."

I am standing near the edge of the road over the river. Bhante Sujatha's childhood threat was not whimsical. The young boy would have died if he jumped off this bridge. He could never survive the fall, and even if he did, swimming against the rushing current here would be impossible.

I look down as Michael stands near me, patiently waiting for my response. "I see," is all I can muster, imagining the fear Bhante's parents must have felt.

The whimsical descriptions of Bhante's childhood are a child's view. As an adult, I can hardly conceive of the stress of raising children in the jungle while I struggled with starvation level poverty. I admire Bhante's parents for their ability to teach their son about mindfulness in the midst of such challenging circumstances.

"Yes," Michael says, observing my understanding. The loud traditional dancers start up again and we being to move, walking towards the Subodharama Temple for Bhante Sujatha's ceremony. The crowd grows even thicker as we approach the temple.

Manel opens her eyes, giving up on her quiet meditation. For a minute she and Lalitha think Heenbanda is saying that Neil has to go to the temple. Heenbanda sees the surprise and fear in their eyes and quickly reassures them. "No, no, I mean we must let him cool off from his anger outside. He will not jump in the river; he wouldn't dare!"

All three of them are silent for a moment, and Heenbanda breaks the silence. "Yes, well, yes I'll go and make sure he does not jump in the river, of course." Wishing he could leave his son to learn his lesson, Heenbanda stands up and sighs, ready to go and find Neil so that Lalitha and Manel can be at peace.

Lalitha sits down near Manel and lets her daughter rest her head on her shoulder. Manel feels sweet love as her mother puts a protective arm over her shoulder and holds her close. They rock gently together, thinking about Neil and his future, wondering what it will mean for them.

Heenbanda walks down the familiar path, not slipping in the dark since he knows every step. He finds Neil standing in the shallow water at the edge of the river, his sandals and his mala beads left on the bank.

"Chuti Putha! No! You must get out of the water!"

Neil turns to his father in the dark, silhouetted against the murky water. His beautiful hair shines in the moonlight. Trees and bushes line the banks, ruffled by jungle breezes. Something howls in the distance, and Heenbanda hears the chatter of a monkey nearby. Neil is already becoming a monk. He is calm and quiet. He is mindful beyond his years. In the moon lit darkness, Heenbanda finds himself imagining a monk's robes on his precious son.

"Chuti Putha, come now. Let's get out of the water. Come."

As if he is just waking up, Neil shakes his head and blinks. His thick eyelashes flutter in the dark.

"Father, you don't understand. I am going to be a monk. It is my kamma. I will not live if I am not a monk. I am already a monk, you know? I was born to be a monk."

Heenbanda looks down, humbled by his son's commitment to his destiny. "Please stop saying that you must become a monk. You are too young. Stop saying you will jump in the river and that you want to die. You are breaking your mother's heart."

With the thought of Lalitha, the little boy slowly turns and makes his way back up the riverbank, accepting his father's hand extended to help him. "Father, I will not break momma's heart. I will be a monk and a good son. I will."

Something rustles in the bushes, and Neil and his father quickly move back up the path back to their home.

The women sense the change when Neil and Heenbanda walk into the small house. Lalitha wants to ask what happened, but when she sees Heenbanda's eyes, she senses that it would serve her well to keep quiet. Manel starts to say something and Lalitha gently hushes her, keeping peace in her small family.

Chapter Eleven

Honoring his Parents

Early the next morning Neil brings milk to the temple, anxious to ask Bhante Dhammawasa how he can be a good monk and a good son. He thinks that if he can answer this question he can finally convince his mother to let him go home to the temple where he can at last fulfill his kamma. Neil arrives in the middle of meditation practice. He keeps the milk cool on his head, balancing it carefully as he slips out of his sandals and walks like a bride, one careful step at a time, making his way slowly to the front of the temple. Standing in front of the Buddha, the little boy waits patiently, hoping the monks will be done soon and open their eyes. After 15 minutes his shoulders start to tremble but he hangs on, remembering his mother's admonishments about keeping the milk up high so it can stay fresh. His mother would have told him to just put the milk down now, of course, but at ten years old Neil is still young and not able to understand everything.

When Bhante Dhammawasa and Bhante Muditha open their eyes, they both smile at Neil Bandara, standing there with the milk.

"Well, hello little friend? Have you brought us some milk?"

"Yes!" says Neil, "Yes, and I came here to ask a question, a very important question!"

"Okay, my friend. You can ask us your question."

Bhante Muditha uncrosses his legs and stands. "I will take the milk. Please give my blessings to your parents for this. Okay, so, what is this important question?"

"I have to know, Bhante, if I become a monk, is it true that I must renounce my parents; that I can no longer care for them?"

"Yes, my little friend, it is true. You must renounce your parents, your sister and all your family when you take your vows. But this does not mean you cannot care for them. Let me tell you a story:

"Once a young boy like you wanted to be a monk, and his parents were concerned, as he was their only son."

"Like me!" says Neil, eager to hear what the Buddha said about this.

"Well, the young boy convinced his parents to let him become a monk. So he left them to become a forest monk, dedicating his life to meditation and poverty. His parents grew old without him, and they became poor and sick. One day they were robbed, and they eventually became beggars. When the monk heard about this, he decided he had to leave the life of a monastic and take care of his parents."

Neil is paying close attention to his teacher.

"That, my little friend, is called filial piety. Can you say that?"

"Fi-li-al P eye iti."

"Exactly! Good job!"

"Well, one day the monk saw the Buddha at a temple where he stopped in to practice for a moment before he went to help his parents. 'Buddha,' he cried, 'I have an important question for you. My parents are old and need my help, but I am an ordained monk! How can I help them and honor my renunciation vows?'

"My friend,' said the Buddha, 'it is a meritorious act to care for your parents. You must continue to care for them and still practice the beautiful life of a monk. How can you do this?'

"The monk decides that he will collect alms for his parents and himself, first collecting and delivering food to his parents and then collecting for himself. The Buddha agrees that this filial piety is a meritorious act and perfectly in line with his monkhood."

"Were you married when you decided to become a Buddhist nun?"

"Oh no," says Bhikkhuni Vimala. We are sitting in the now familiar basement of the Blue Lotus Temple.

"If I was married, I would have had to obtain permission from my husband to leave the marriage. You see, renunciation is a pretty serious part of the vows that we take. I asked Bhante if I had to renounce my children, and I told him that if I had to do that, I did not think I would take on being ordained. I would not give up my children."

Bhante Sujatha smiled at Vimala when she asked this question.

"No, no, my friend,' he told her, 'you only give up attachment. When you accept ordination as a Buddhist nun, we are asking you to love every child just as much as your own children. We are asking you to love and care more, not less. More."

Bhikkhuni and I smile at each other. Love more. Everyday Bhante Sujatha awakens with this mission. Add more love to the world.

"We can smile. We can practice loving kindness. This generosity can change the world. Smile. Add more love. If we keep adding love we will obliterate hate. We can do this in one generation. Crowd out hate with love."-Venerable Bhante Sujatha

Chapter Twelve

The Storm

After Bhante Muditha tells him this wonderful story, Neil decides to run all the way home, thrilled that he can give his mother this good news. He slows down when he hears the rumble of thunder. Monsoon season can be a dangerous time.

The wind starts high above the trees as the little boy walks down the path near the Colombo Kandy road. He sees a bus sway with the force of the wind before he feels it hits him, a tremendous gust that knocks him back into a thorny acacia bush. As he falls back into the bush, he sees a duck flailing in the wind above him. Even though he is scratched and bruised from his fall, his natural affinity and sympathy for animals bursts forth, and he silently wishes the duck well.

Soon, all is chaos. Neil is hanging onto the bushes as he makes his way against the wind, closing his eyes against the stinging rain, trying to get to the duck that has fallen onto the road and is pinned underneath a tree branch. The little boy wants to help the duck.

"Hey! Hey! Get away from my duck!! Get away!"

The bellowing voice sounds far away in the storm, and the little boy, who is naturally sensitive to emotions, feels the anger gathering around him like the dark storm clouds above him.

"That is my duck! I saw him and now, I am taking him! Get away!"

Neil turns and sees a man approaching him. He can hardly see the man, but he is not afraid. He recalls the teachings of his beloved Buddha about compassion and wisdom.

Here in the West, we are taught that wisdom (panna) is primarily intellectual and compassion (Karuna) is emotional. Many times we believe that compassion actually gets in the way of wisdom. Neil has been raised in the Theravada Buddhist tradition. He is taught that being compassionate is wise. Insight, or understanding the Buddha's wisdom, most especially the teaching of no self (in Pali, anatta), is attained through the practice of meditation and study. This wisdom leads to compassion. Conversely, practicing compassion enhances understanding and wisdom.

Lalitha reminds her little son often, that to see the path to nirvana clearly, the little monk must use the two eyes of Panna and Karuna.

"You see, you cannot attain the happiness of enlightenment without seeing through two eyes, Chuti Putha, like this." Lalitha smiles and holds her right index finger and her pinky finger up to her face, folding the middle two fingers down under her nose as she points at both of her eyes. Neil always laughs when she does this and then tries to do it himself, always getting mixed up, using his index finger and his middle finger, not understanding how to fold the middle two fingers down.

Lalitha usually laughs as they smile at each other, holding their hands up to their faces. She makes sure that her little son gets this lesson, one of the most important lessons in all of Buddhism.

"See how happy we are? How we are laughing? This is because we understand the paths of karuna and panna, you see? We see through both eyes."

"And, my son, the very good news is that when you are kind, you actually become wiser. You see? So if you are kind, you become wiser. If you are wise, you become kinder. Isn't that beautiful?"

Neil loves this teaching and tries to practice it whenever his young mind remembers. Neil thinks that he must save this duck as part of his loving kindness practice. As the wind howls, he grabs the branch that is trapping the duck. His neighbor breaks into a run, slipping on a wet pile of leaves blown into the path by a gust.

"I will get you for this! That duck is mine! Mine! My family is hungry! Get away!" he shouts as he pushes himself up off the dirty leaf pile, red-faced as the rain pellets sting his eyes.

Neil uses all his strength, shaking as he lifts the heavy branch and sets the duck free—who limps a bit, then trots, and finally turns around and takes off flying with the wind, crazily spiraling up into the air. The poor animal is unlikely to survive this storm, but Neil Bandara thinks he has earned merits for his compassionate act, and he is happy for this.

The neighbor stops as he watches his meal fly away, shoulders drooping in the storm. "You little brat! I said that duck was mine!"

The little boy hoots at him. "Ha HA! The duck got away I guess! HA!"

Neil points at the man. "That duck knew you were going to kill him and now he is free!"

Heenbanda comes into view, out of breath with worry and exertion.

"Chuti Putha, what are you doing? What are you saying? We must get out of this storm!"

Just then, the rain seems to come down in a sheet, soaking all three of them. The little boy's sandals get blown off as he is knocked back down to the ground in the rain.

Heenbanda ignores the neighbor's angry threats as he picks up his little son, tears in his eyes, hardly noticing the violent storm, while his precious Chuti Putha tells him that he saved a duck to earn merits and that he is becoming a monk.

"Chuti Putha! This has to stop! You are not becoming a monk! And that man was hungry. He wanted to feed his family!"

Neil buries his face in his father's shoulder, closing his eyes against the pelting rain. He doesn't care if the man was hungry. He is only 10 years old, and he just wants his precious duck to be safe.

The storm causes damage everywhere, and Neil practices filial piety, helping with the mess and knowing he is earning good merits for his kamma. It is not until after the clean up is finished that he lets Lalitha know the good news: he can still care for his parents after he is a monk and that the Buddha actually recommended this course of action to a forest monk.

As Lalitha listens to the story about the forest monk, she realizes that her little son is on the way to fulfilling his destiny. As much as she sees his stubborn willfulness, his disrespect to any adult who dares practice injustice or cruelty, his fast chanting and scant bows, she hears in the story her little son's monk-like compassion and wisdom. He remembers details that other children leave out. He gets the message about the middle path, and most importantly, he shares that message effectively with others. Lalitha knows in her heart that her little son is leaving her soon; he is going off to live out his destiny predicted at his birth.

The next week at a family dinner, sitting on the ground in the sun, sharing a big bowl of stew prepared by Lalitha and his grandmothers, Neil is surprised when his father stands up and announces to all, "My little son is going to live at the temple! We will call him the little monk now! Chuti Putha, you are going to the temple!"

Neil drops his food, stands up, and runs over to his father, not even noticing the pain from the cuts on the bottom of his feet, injured when he stepped on brambles during the storm. He yells "Yay!" and runs over to his father, stretching his arms around Heenbanda's legs, trying to get close. Neil's father stands up straighter and backs away, staring at the cows, thinking about how to fix the lock on the pasture gate. He is determined to let go.

Chapter Thirteen

Love

Later that night, as they lay together under the light cover on their sleeping mat, Lalitha whispers in the dark to her husband. Something howls in the distance and they hear the crackle of a distant fire outside.

"My love, why? Why did you say our precious Chuti Putha could go to the temple?"

Heenbanda pushes himself up onto his elbow, resting his head in his hand, staring at his beautiful wife—watching her lips move in the dark, seeing her white teeth and appreciating her loyalty to him. He leans over and silences her with a kiss.

Lalitha closes her eyes, feeling tears slide down the sides of her cheeks, vulnerable before her husband.

"My darling," whispers Heenbanda, "our son was never meant to stay with us. He was born to be a monk. We don't really have a choice, you know? He doesn't either. You know you were born to be my wife as I was born to be your husband. We are all linked together, you, Manel, our Chuti Putha, and me. We must honor his path to becoming a Buddhist monk. It is a great honor, you know. We can be happy that our son is choosing this path."

Lalitha smiles through her tears, so grateful to have this man as her husband. She is comforted by his wise words and reminded why she fell in love with him the first time she met him. She takes a deep breath as Heenbanda leans over and kisses her slowly and surely, letting her know she is engulfed in his love even in her grief.

John Bardi, a philosophy professor at Penn State, shares a story that Bhante tells his students when they ask about love:

"I sit and watch my students watching Bhante. They are being exposed to a rare example of loving kindness in action. His presence captivates them. These kids don't know it, but they've been waiting for this message of unconditional love and acceptance their whole life. Bhante teaches that happiness really originates inside of us. It's not out there, no matter how much stuff you buy or accolades you collect. This talk about love is one of my favorites and I'll tell you what he said:

'You know, my friends, love is like a sandwich. One piece of the bread is love and desire, which is the easiest part. But one piece of bread does not make a sandwich, does it? We need another slice of bread and this slice is called loving-kindness. Then of course we need something in between the two slices of bread, and that magic ingredient is respect.

'So you see, if you want to have a relationship with someone, the question is not do I love them, or do I feel a certain way? No, it is this. Can I treat this person with great kindness and respect? Can I maintain my loving kindness practice in this relationship? If you can do that, you can practice love, you see? You can be happy in this relationship.'

I am moved by the concept of practicing love. I am starting to ask myself, "Can I practice love here?"

If I cannot, I want to change the circumstances. I know I can practice love anywhere, but I am learning about the benefits of building a life that supports the practice of loving kindness and nobility. I am attracting noble friends and kind souls. A year after writing this book, I notice that my life is filled with kind people and inspiring circumstances. I don't think of this as luck. I see it as the result of the practice and my fortunate immersion into a spiritual life.

The next morning, Neil wakes up before everyone else again, thrilled that he is going to the temple. He tries to be quiet as he tiptoes outside. Lalitha is sleeping lightly, anxious to see her son before he leaves for his first temple stay. She sits up and brushes her hair off her face with her hand, stretching her neck and sighing, willing herself to get up and start this sad day, knowing that for her Chuti Putha it is a day of celebration.

Smiling on purpose, she walks outside in bare feet, shivering a little in the early morning air, seeing her young son standing near the stubborn cow. Neil strokes the cow's neck, unafraid. Her little son has the kamma to be a monk, she realizes, and in the next heartbeat she notices his gorgeous shiny hair.

Lalitha breathes in sharply, stunned at her grief, as she thinks about someone shaving his gorgeous head. "My lord," she thinks, "how can they do that? What will they do with his beautiful hair? What will become of my beautiful son?"

Neil turns when he hears his mother gasp. His compassion is already growing, and he sees her shoulders slump with grief.

"Stay strong and gentle," he whispers to the stubborn cow, as he pets her neck one last time and walks over to his mother.

Neil wraps his arms around Lalitha's small waist

"Don't worry, my beloved mother, it will be alright. I will still be here. It will be alright."

140

Chapter Fourteen

Leaving

The next morning the whole family walks down the hill to the Colombo Kandy road. When they come to the crossing point, Lalitha lets go of her son's hand. Neil looks up at his mother quizzically "Momma, aren't we crossing?"

"My Chuti Putha, you are wanting to be a monk now. If you choose this path, you know I will not be with you. You will be crossing roads and learning about life without me. You will not be able to hug me or stay in our home. I want you to cross this road alone as practice for the life you w Neil looks over at this father standing with Manel and holding her hand, waiting to cross the road. Heenbanda does not return his son's glance. Neil takes a breath, squares his shoulders and steps onto the dusty road only to jump back as a careless bus driver swerves to avoid a rut in the road. The family can feel the wind of the bus as it passes, and the diesel fuel makes all of them cough. Heenbanda coughs a little longer than the rest of them, masking a sob of sadness about his Chuti Putha.

"Momma, please! I am almost hit by that bus! Didn't you see me? I do not want to die! I just want to be a monk!"

"My precious son, being a monk means you are renouncing me, you understand? You will not receive my help!"

Some people from the temple community walk up to the Bandara family and say hello. Neil takes advantage of this other family's presence and grabs his mother's hand, knowing she will not rebuke him in front of the Sangha. He mutters to himself, "Sanghang sarranang gachami" (I take refuge in the Sangha), smiling at his cleverness.

The family walks together safely across the street. Manel and Neil break off and running ahead just after they start up the path to the temple. Manel wonders what it will be like for her, all alone with her parents on Sundays.

Chapter Fifteen

The First Temple Stay

After the meditation and the dhamma talk, Neil hugs his family good bye. His mother is crying a little, and her little son pats her back as they hug. "Mama, I will be back so soon! Don't be sad! I am only here three weeks!"

He backs up, separating himself from her at last. Lalitha moves forward, but Manel grabs her hand and Heenbanda puts a strong arm around her, holding on tightly to her upper arm, guiding her to turn around and leave their son.

"Our only hope of keeping him is to let him go, my darling. We must let him go." Heenbanda almost lifts his wife off the ground with the pressure of moving her towards the temple door.

After the last of the Sangha leaves, Mr. and Mrs. Attharagama stay and help clean up the temple while Bhante Dhammawasa sits on his cushion on the raised platform in front of the Buddha statue. He directs Neil Bandara to sit directly in front of him so that they can talk. Neil nervously stands up from his cushion, missing his mom. He walks up to his teacher and sits down, keeping his head lowered so his teacher does not see his tears.

Bhante Dhammawasa gently explains that pain is caused by attachment to others and the desire for things to stay the same.

"My little friend, do you notice that the more you think about your wish to be with your mother, the more pain you feel? Do you want to feel worse, my friend, or better?"

Neil sniffs and wipes his eye before he looks up, his shiny hair illuminating his eyes rimmed with sad emotion. "I want to feel better, Bhante. I want my mom to feel better. I want her to still help me cross the street and be with me at night. But I want to be a monk. I am sad, since to be a monk means I must renounce my mother."

"Well, you know the Buddha taught us about suffering. He called it Dukkha. And we have learned from our great teacher that all dukkha originates in our minds. It is your mind that is causing the suffering of missing your parents. This is the second noble truth, that the root cause of suffering is mental clinging or desire.

Can you sit with me, and close your eyes, and feel your aloneness now, which is how it has always been? Can you see that you can let go of your attachment, even to your mother, as a clear pathway to happiness? Let's meditate together."

Neil sniffs and smiles as he closes his eyes, realizing he is in the middle of his first lesson as a young monk.

Of course, the little boy's mind is not trained. He thinks about his mom for a few seconds, wondering how he can practice nonattachment with her, and then forgets all about why he is meditating and starts to shift around, wanting to get up and go outside into the sunshine.

 Bhante Dhammawasa is a gentle and wise teacher, and he knows that the young boy cannot sit too long. He opens his eyes after only 5 minutes, laughing softly as he watches Neil uncross his legs, scratch his nose, cough into his hand and open his eyes. He is surprised when he sees his teacher watching him and afraid of a punishment, but Bhante Dhammawasa just laughs.

"Can I go outside and play now? Can I climb the mango tree?"

"Yes, yes you can." Bhante Dhammawasa nods his assent vigorously, enjoying the young boy's energy. Neil jumps up and quickly makes his way to the door outside, tired of the dim temple. Once outside, he looks to the left and claps his hands in happiness at the sight of the sparkling Buddha. He looks to the right and laughs at the luscious Na tree, saying, "and Hello beautiful flowers! I am staying with you now!"

Then he looks down the hill at the path through the jungle to the Mahaweli River and Kandy. "People!" he yells, "I am going to be a monk! I will stay at the temple and climb the mango tree as much as I like!"

He shrugs his shoulders and giggles, running over to the mango tree and grabbing a branch. He pulls his hand away when a splinter cuts into his palm, and for a brief moment he thinks of the smooth spot on his swinging tree.

"No," he thinks, "I must let go! I am happy to be here!"

Neil uses his mind to lessen his suffering. He lets go of his worry, recognizing it as just a thought.

He grabs the branch again, ignoring the splinter as he swings up into the tree. He climbs as high as he can, scrambling up the trunk, resting near the middle of the tree, afraid to go much higher where the branches look thinner. At home he was not allowed to climb this high and their swinging tree was not as big as this mango tree. As he sits in the beloved mango tree, he can see the Mahaweli River. He wonders if his father will be bringing the cows home soon.

Bhante Dhammawasa, a wise teacher, lets Neil play as much as he wants. He wants his first student to fall in love with life at the temple. He knows that it is sometimes hard, and he often hears Neil crying in the night in the sleeping area for the young monks.

"You know, Mary, I was so young. I was used to sleeping with my whole family. If I woke up in the middle of the night, you know, my

145

mom, she would always help me. I was happy at the temple during the day, but at night I would be hungry because we could not eat after lunchtime, and so sometimes I would wake up with hunger pains. It was darker there, in the jungle. Our house was in a lighter spot. I was afraid of this dark. I would feel so lonely. I would cry and feel terrible. My teacher would hear me sometimes and come and walk with me to the bathroom, but he wasn't like my mom, you know? He was not like her."

"Bhante," I ask, "If there was something you could say to that young boy now, crying by himself in the temple; if there was a lesson you could tell him that might make him feel better, could you share that with me? Because so many people here in America are suffering, waking up in the middle of the night and worrying about money or their relationship or some sickness, or maybe just worrying about being awake! Is there something I can put in the book that might be helpful to them?"

Bhante smiles, sitting back in his battered chair. For the first time, I notice a small grimace as he shifts his hips back. I wonder if he is in pain.

"Well, my friend, I guess I would whisper to him, 'Just wait. Just wait.'

"Because, you know, in the beginning it was so hard, but then in six months or so, I am happy, you know? I am happy!

"So let's tell those people that are awake in the night, 'just wait.'"

I nod my head and smile. I notice him shift painfully again.

Just wait.

Back at the little mud house, Manel was very happy to have her parents and her tree to herself. The first few days she ran up the hill after school, jumping up on the branch, swinging as long as she liked and resting happily with no worries about her turn to swing.

She drew in the dirt leisurely, making pictures of her new family of three, with her little brother way off on the side, looking out through a temple window. On the fourth day, Manel grabbed the branch and heard the silence around her. She let go without swinging and sat down to draw. The little mouse that Neil chased away all the time skittered across the ground in front of her.

She sighed. "I don't want to draw," she thought, and now that my little brother is not here to chase the mouse, I have no need to protect the little creature." Manel feels the beginnings of her grief.

At the temple, Neil Bandara is sitting down to eat the delicious food prepared by a generous member of the Sangha, who always cooks fresh coconut rice for the monks. He is learning to eat mindfully. At home, Neil liked to talk while he ate. Here at the temple the monks are teaching him to eat mindfully and silently, looking down at his bowl and carefully eating. At first the delicious food is enough to keep the little boy happy. But, after a few days, he grows tired of the same food; he is finding it hard to eat mindfully. He wishes he could go home and talk to his sister.

Bhante is giving the dhamma talk at the temple.

"On my last trip to Sri Lanka, I could not wait to get out of the cold here, you know? I wanted to be warm, to wear my sandals and my robes with no coat. I wanted to see my family and the Subodharama temple. I am tired of Americans always worrying about time. Then after I am in Sri Lanka for a few days, I am tired of sweating. I wish they had more air conditioned buildings like here. I want to see my brother monks at the Blue Lotus temple. I miss my friends in the Sangha here. I wish that my Sri Lankan friends would be on time for once."

The Sangha laughs.

"When the day comes to leave Sri Lanka, I am so happy to be coming back here. Then I get to O'Hare and I think to myself, 'Oh, I miss Sri Lanka, where people bow to me!' I go outside to see if my

brother monk is here to pick me up. It is so cold when I walk outside that I shiver. I wish it were warmer. Bhante San is in a hurry to get back to Woodstock in time for the meditation that night, and I wish we could relax and visit more. I wish Americans weren't always so careful about time.

"Think about it. You look forward to coming here, you know? You are stressed maybe with work or your kids? Then you sit down to meditate and you start to wonder when meditation will end so you can get back home.

"This is the nature of things, you know. This is a cause of suffering, always wanting things to be different or better. Even when we are happy, we start to worry that it won't last or we become attached to whatever it is out there that is making us happy.

"This is why we must practice meditation, so we can cultivate mindfulness about this. We can be happy in Sri Lanka and happy here. I can be happy warm, and I can be happy cold. I can be happy with you and happy with my family. I can be happy running around in a hurry here or relaxing in Sri Lanka, you see?"

I laugh, wondering how he knew about me, realizing that my mind is just an average human mind—always scanning the horizon for the new and improved thing, constantly seeking ways to cause suffering by convincing me that it could be better. It can't. The present moment is all we ever really have. And the present moment is beautiful. This is why we focus on our breath in meditation. "Our breath is not in the past or the future. It is only now."

Bhikkhuni Vimala tells us about FOMO, the fear of missing out. When I hear this phrase, I am surprised at the prevalence of this feeling in my life as I rush from one situation to another. Rushing is a sure sign that I am suffering from FOMO.

Chapter Sixteen

Meditation and the Owl

Bhante Dhammawasa is shaking Neil awake. The young boy looks out through tired eyes, dried tears on his reddened cheeks from crying himself to sleep the night before. As the teacher's voice grows a bit louder, it comes to Neil that he is here now, in his dream. The little boy is starting to notice the feeling of being present.

Neil Bandara has finally come home. He has taken the first real step on his way to fulfilling his destiny. A real Buddhist monk at the Subodharama Temple is waking him up!

Of course, Neil has no idea of the rigors of an ordained monk in training. None of that matters now, though. He sits up and yawns, pushing back his thick hair, shining in the early morning starlight. He feels like he is alive in a dream.

"Little monk, wouldn't you like to come and practice with me? Wouldn't you like to learn to chant and meditate?"

Neil loves being called a monk. He graces Bhante Dhammawasa with his smile, slowly spreading across his young face like an early morning breeze in the grasses near the river. Bhante Dhammawasa's heart skips a beat as he takes a sharp breath, realizing that this precious child, Lalitha's son, with his famously gorgeous hair and stubborn, wonderfully compassionate personality, is now his to teach as a monk.

In a way, Neil has come to teach the older monk too. The abbot of the temple is aging, and Bhante Dhammawasa suffers from grief. Seeing the little monk's joy at taking part in the simple tasks of a monk's life reawakens Bhante Dhammawasa's heart, filling him with joy.

Neil is so happy as he comes fully awake that he sits bolt upright in the bed and laughs, clapping his hands together as he exclaims, "Oh, teacher! Yes! Yes! Let's go! I want to be a monk! Yay!"

"Okay, my little friend, okay! Let's go to the temple!"

And so Neil Bandara begins his first day of his dream, living at the temple with Bhante Dhammawasa. They sit together in the temple and meditate, and the little boy can feel the Buddha's compassion as he sits in the temple. Bhante Muditha and a novice monk sit with them.

The two monks and their students bow three times, touching their foreheads to the floor as they kneel down, signifying that they are taking refuge in in the Buddha (the teacher), the dhamma (the teachings) and the Sangha (community). Bhante Dhammawasa uses a wooden tool and circles the outside of a golden bowl he holds in his lap. Neil is excited to feel the effects of the ringing bowl so close to him. He imitates the older monks, looking serious and closing his eyes as they start their silent meditation.

Neil knows that he should quiet his mind, but he is not sure how to do that. He wonders if he will learn. He thinks about his sister and wonders if she is swinging on his tree right now. He swears he can hear a stick scratching the dry dirt into a picture and feel the breeze on his belly as he swings in the tree. His stomach rumbles, and he notices that he is very hungry. He wonders if there will be rice with coconut milk for breakfast, and he finds himself imagining Bhante Dhammawasa collecting the best alms for breakfast, specifically the food from his mom.

Lalitha is actually wiping tears away as she separates stems from leaves at the tobacco plant, feeling a little less hopeful that her son will stay with his family. But Neil, being a ten-year-old child, imagines his mother at home as he meditates. He wonders if his dad is fixing something. He notices his stomach again. He remembers he is supposed to focus on his breath, and he tries his best to notice the air passing over his upper lip as he breathes. He feels like he can't get enough air when he does this and gives up. He shifts his legs a little under him, feeling numbness in his right foot, and thinks that maybe being a monk won't work for him. Maybe he can't sit this long and be quiet. He wonders when the meditation will be over. He wishes he were home. He misses his mom. He feels sad. Then he remembers that this is his kamma, and feels some peace settle into him for a moment. Then his mind goes back to thinking.

He wonders if Bhante Dhammawasa or Bhante Muditha knows that he is not doing well at meditation today—that he is thinking so many thoughts that he can hardly sit still. He shifts again and opens his eyes just a crack to make sure the older monks are still there. They are, sitting absolutely still, a half smile on their faces. The little monk closes his eyes again and wonders how they stay so quiet and happy.

He notices that he feels really eager to get up and move around. He thinks maybe he is too young to stay here for three whole weeks, and then he misses his mom again. He wonders why monks have to meditate so much and hopes he will be able to do it. He feels bad because he is thinking and tries to breathe deeply, taking in a big loud gulp of air that gives him the hiccups. His teachers both smile at the sound of the little boy's hiccups, which he tries to stifle with his hand.

The little monk worries about his teacher getting angry at him for making noise during meditation and thinks about how his father would scare the hiccups right out of him. He opens his eyes, uncrosses his legs, hiccups loudly and re-crosses his legs the other way. He sighs with boredom as he closes his eyes again. He counts to himself, hoping his teacher will use the wooden tool to make the beautiful golden bowl ring. This is one of the Neil's

151

favorite parts at the temple, watching a monk expertly use the wooden tool to make a bowl ring with a soul penetrating sound. He thinks to himself that he might not see this now that he is meditating with his eyes closed. He really wants to learn how to make a bowl ring to signal the end of meditation. "When will this end?" he wonders. Then he wonders if his dad ever got that hole in the gate fixed. Will ever really be a monk? He misses his mom.

"Rinnnnnnggggg."

Bhante Muditha rings the temple bowl. Neil smiles with relief as he listens, knowing that soon he will be able to open his eyes and chant.

A Sangha member sitting next to me asks Bhante how to calm his mind. I can't wait to hear. I want to know this. During meditation today, I could not stop myself from one thought after another. I felt agitated after we meditated rather than calm. It didn't seem to be working for me.

Bhante Sujatha smiles. "My friend, you cannot do it. You cannot quiet your mind. Our minds are always thinking, you know? That is the job of your mind. If you are not thinking, you are dead."

I laugh. The temple member asks another question. "But isn't the point of meditation to quiet your mind? Aren't you supposed to have some kind of amazing moment of presence or something?"

"No, no. Westerners confuse meditation with relaxation, but that is not what we are doing here. We are cultivating loving kindness and mindfulness. There are three important goals. The first is to become present or aware, the second is to stop judgment and the third is to practice compassion for yourself and others. We are observing our mind so we can practice more compassion, you see?"

Bhante Dhammawasa is a gentle teacher. He knows that this little boy is restless. The wise monk uncrosses his legs, surprising Bhante Muditha who has already begun to chant.

"My friends, let's go to the Bodhi tree. Let's walk around that as we chant."

Bodhi trees are lush banyan-like trees with thick leaves that provide refuge from the hot sun. The Buddha sat under one of these trees until he attained enlightenment. In the Buddhist traditions, the Bodhi tree is treated as an especially powerful and significant symbol of enlightenment.

Monks often circle a Bodhi tree as they chant to remind themselves that they are on the path to enlightenment.

I ask Bhante if Buddhism is a religion.

"You know, Mary, when people see us chanting, they think we are religious. But we are not a religion. We have no conflict with any religion. We have our weekly practice here on Saturdays, so people can go to their Christian church on Sundays. If I was in a predominantly Jewish community, I might have the temple services on Sunday.

"I really want people to know that they can practice meditation and their religion. I don't want anyone left out of this message. I really want them to know about meditation, especially the loving kindness meditation. If Americans meditate and cultivate a practice of loving kindness, we can get to world peace, you know? We can make a loving kindness force, like your armed forces. We can be the loving kindness forces. We really can."

The little monk's hair sparkles in the sunshine as he runs ahead to the Bodhi Tree. Bhante Muditha shakes his head and smiles, wondering how this restless little boy will adapt to monkhood. Bhante Dhammawasa raises his voice to his young student.

"Hold up little monk! Let's pay our respects."

Neil hears his teacher and stops so fast that he slips in the grass and falls forward, catching himself on his arms and finding himself

153

face to face with an owl. For a moment he feels confused. It is morning, a time when owls should be asleep high up in the trees.

"Bhante!" he whispers loudly, still raised up on his arms in a pushup, afraid to let go and disturb the owl.

Bhante Dhammawasa, lost in conversation with Bhante Muditha about the idea of a new school at the Subodharama temple, doesn't hear the little monk's pleas for attention.

Neil's arms are shaking as he keeps himself from falling on the little owl, who is staring up at him with her enormous eyes. How can there be an owl on the ground in the morning? Don't they live high in the trees and come out at night?

Finally the young boy takes a breath and pushes down hard, managing to spring to his feet without hurting the owl. Bhante Dhammawasa and Bhante Muditha are closer now and Neil shouts out. "Bhantes! Bhantes! There is an owl! How can there be an owl!"

The teacher monks calmly proceed up the path until they come to the injured young owl, now trying to fly, flapping one wing and skittering in the dusty ground.

"My little friend, this is very interesting!" says Bhante Dhammawasa.

"Very!" says Bhante Muditha.

The little monk is concerned that the owl might need some water. "Teachers, can we help the owl? Can we help her?"

Bhante Dhammawasa smiles down at the little boy standing before him with tears of compassion running down his dirty cheeks, some shiny hair stuck to the side of his face with sweat and dirt.

"Well," says Bhante Dhammawasa, "you know owls are very wise. Her big eyes are windows of compassion and wisdom. She does not make much noise, you see? She is gentle and quiet. When she

154

hoots at night, it is for a purpose, not just to make noise. She shakes her head frequently. We can use this motion when people are talking with us, letting them know we are listening and reassuring them we are not arguing. When someone speaks to us about outside subjects, things we cannot influence in the moment, we can listen and gently shake our heads. This will be a compassionate service to that person. You can earn merits for this."

The temple laughs as Bhante Sujatha tells us that he used this technique of shaking his head and smiling as he listened to his friend go on and on about politics. At the end of an angry rant about a politician, the friend looked at Bhante and stopped, noticing that the monk was silent.

"I'm sorry, was I talking too much?"

Bhante Sujatha smiles as he answers. "Yes, yes, you did, yes. You talked too much."

The Sangha laughs, some of us thinking about Bhante nodding and smiling as we were talking.

Bhante Dhammawasa continues. "As far as helping this owl, she does not need our help. She is young and her mother is nearby, waiting for us to get out of the way so she can help her youngster. You see, little friend, sometimes the most compassionate action is to step aside and let another person or animal help with the problem. Our egos are strong. You will notice that you want to be the one to help, to get the good feeling or earn the good kamma, but it is often wise to let someone else have that feeling and earn those merits. Do you see how we collect alms from your mother in the mornings? We do not say thank you. She does not expect our gratitude. Of course we are grateful, but we know she is earning her merits, just like us. So we practice no self, the ideal called Dana Paramita. Can you say that word back to me little friend?"

The young boy says "Da-na Pa ra mi ta," getting it right the first time. Both teacher monks smile at Neil's obvious intellectual ability.

"Yes, exactly, very good. So you see, in our practice, with no self, there cannot be another. We are one. There cannot be a giver without a receiver. By walking away from the owl, you are earning your merits by giving the mother owl the chance to save her youngster. By accepting her help, the little owl is also earning merits. Your mother could not earn her merits by giving us alms unless we stand at her door with a bowl for the alms. So you see— the giver and the receiver create each other. We cannot separate the two. One is not better than the other. We can appreciate poor people and injured animals as important receivers, to be respected equally with the givers.

"Receivers make giving possible. Remember that. To be a receiver is a meritorious act. To give is also a meritorious act. You allowing me to give you this lesson, you are allowing yourself to receive this lesson, and the baby owl can be a receiver who is also giving me this lesson.

Neil is quiet, collecting his thoughts. He walks with the teacher monks and does not look back at the injured owl. He does not run ahead anymore. He is a small boy walking between two wise men, slowing down to learn on the way to becoming a monk.

Chapter Seventeen

Becoming a Monk

At 4:30 am, each day during the first three weeks at the temple, Neil is awakened by the gentle voice of Bhante Dhammawasa. He participates in the meditation and the chanting with his teacher monks and a teenage novice monk, a student from a nearby school run by Bhante Muditha. The novice monk is 16 years old and Neil is happy that he is with him, especially at night, when they sleep in the living room of the temple.

Bhante Dhammawasa talks with Bhante Thero and Bhante Muditha. He meditates on the possibility of inviting the little monk to stay for three months, so that he can make an informed choice on whether or not to be ordained. One day, as he observes the little monk carefully walking around the Bodhi tree, singing the chants so beautifully, stopping to patiently water the tree as proscribed in the temple practices, he knows that he will ask Neil Bandara to join him as his first student at the Subodharama temple.

The next morning, Bhante Dhammawasa visits the Bandara household to talk with Lalitha and Heenbanda about Neil's possible ordination. The little boy has done well in his first three weeks, and Bhante Dhammawasa wants him to stay.

Lalitha breaks down and retreats into the house, sitting before the Buddha statue and thinking about life without her son. She buries her face in her hands and cries, while the Buddha statue sits serenely above her, unaffected by her sadness.

157

Bhante Sujatha smiles as I explain my struggle.

"You know, Mary, when you are upset I am still smiling. Do you see that? I stay in my boat, you see? I know that there is only enough room for you in your boat. If I jump in with you, we will both drown. Pay attention to yourself. Cultivate mindfulness through the practice of meditation. We are helpful only when we are mindful. If you are not mindful, you will jump into my boat, and we will both drown."

Heenbanda runs his hand through his coarse hair, and as he pulls out a knot roughly, he thinks of Neil's shiny hair, so soft, unlike any hair Heenbanda has seen. The thought that he might never ruffle his little son's hair again forces him to look down while Bhante Dhammawasa is talking about the horoscope and the little monks kamma. He watches a tear fall to the ground, helpless to stop himself.

Lalitha breathes and composes herself. She comes back to pay her respects to Bhante Dhammawasa, who has honored her son with the opportunity of becoming an ordained monk. Lalitha and Heenbanda are still saddened and against the idea of their only son joining the monastery, but they respect the Buddhist teachings more than their own attachments. They would never complain to a senior monk. According to their spiritual practice, this is a great honor and so they are silent about their misgivings, gathering Neil's New Year clothes, knowing he will not be with them this year to celebrate. Their grief is private.

Lalitha wants to give the monk Neil's favorite sleeping cover, tattered from so much wear. She knows she cannot, as her son is beginning a new life at the temple without attachments from home. She notices a shiny hair on the blanket as she picks it up and loses her composure again, glad that her back is to her husband and Bhante Dhammawasa.

Heenbanda and his wife bid Bhante Dhammawasa goodbye and watch him as he disappears down the hill, taking their precious little son's only belongings with him. "Oh, Chuti Putha," Lalitha whispers quietly to herself, "my Chuti Putha."

"You know, Bhante, that's something that is so different here, you know? The way that your parents still respected the monks at the temple and brought milk and donated food when they did not want you to join. The monks kind of talked you into it, you know? Here in the West, we might object. Parents call teachers and yell at them if they discipline their children. They burst into an army recruiter's office and yell at the recruiter if their child joins the army. What do you think of that?"

Bhante tilts his head, thinking.

"Hmmm… I don't know. You know, I think we have respect for our temple. My parents, even though they are sad, they have respect. They do not blame the temple. They know that their unhappiness is with MY choice. They trust that the temple and the monks are doing their best. We don't ever blame our teachers. We are grateful to them. "I pause to think about this for a moment. I consider my own reaction to things in my life. So often we feel justified in our anger, and we rage against the one we feel is the cause of our pain or loss.

Bhante continues. "Maybe here, you don't respect your teachers so much? Or you try to protect your children from their lessons? We believe in kamma, remember. Our children are taught from a very young age that they are responsible for their choices. Parents do not disrespect adults unless there is a really clear wrongdoing. Even when I was starving, my mother did not respect me when I kicked those pots down the mountain.

"Children bow to their parents in my country. It is okay with us if our children do not like what the adults do. We do not expect them to allow our children to practice any disrespect, and we trust that the adults want to help our children. I think here you think that maybe adults are not all so good, you know? I love your freedom, but sometimes I think children are confused, you know?"

Yes, I know.

Chapter Eighteen

The First Three Months

Neil is in the mango tree when Bhante Dhammawasa returns, happy to see his young student eating a mango and enjoying himself. He greets the little boy as he passes under the tree, smiling up at him and waving. The little monk sees that his teacher is carrying his clothes, and he feels a lump in his throat, remembering his mother and wondering what will happen to his sleeping cover. He thinks about the mouse that lived under their swinging tree. "I wonder if Manel has seen that mouse," he thinks to himself. These thoughts are painful.

In these first three weeks, Neil Bandara has practiced meditation and learned a little about the suffering caused by attachment. He sits in the mango tree, holding a half eaten mango with juice dripping down his arm mixing with his sweat, and breathes. He pays attention to the way the breath feels going in and out of his nostrils, enjoying the little breeze on his upper lip. After a few minutes, he smiles to himself, thinking that he will enjoy being a monk.

A few days later, Bhante Muditha, not Bhante Dhammawasa, comes into the living room to wake the little monk and Upul, who was up late talking with Neil about the experience of getting his head shaved.

I am with Bhante in the basement of the Blue Lotus Temple and he is telling me about his friend, Upul. When I listen to the interview on tape, I wince as I hear myself asking him to repeat that name.

Did you say Paul?

160

No, Upul. He is a meditator.

Upaul??

No, no my friend. Upul. Upul.

Now I know that Upul Gamage is actually a famous meditator, who was taught by Godwin Samararatne, another famous spiritual teacher who ran the Nilambe Retreat Center in Sri Lanka. Upul took over the retreat center when Godwin died, and I am completely humbled when we arrive at Nilambe in Sri Lanka, and I meet Upul. Unfortunately we don't have time to talk, but he gives me his phone number and asks me to please call him. Writing My Wish is such an honor. I joke with people that if you want to write a biography, pick a kind Buddhist monk. You'll meet the best people in the world, and everyone is patient and supportive. It's quite remarkable.

Upul reassures Neil about his hair. "Oh, it will be alright, you'll see, simple, and easy, see?" Upul runs his hand over his head, smiling. "Now I can rub my head anytime to remind myself that I am a Buddhist monk. It's very handy for mindfulness."

As he falls asleep that night, Neil rubs his soft hair, wondering.

"Time to get up!" shouts Bhante Muditha in his booming voice. Neil rolls over on his sleeping mat, too tired to sit up. He waits for his teacher's gentle voice. He feels a cool breeze as Bhante Muditha yanks the covers off of his little body.

"Oh!" Neil says as he curls up into a little warm ball, willing himself invisible.

Muditha will not tolerate sloppiness or lateness. Neil doesn't understand that there are different rules from different monks, and Upul feels sorry for him.

"I said, time to get up!" Bhante Muditha claps his hands loudly. "Up!"

161

Upul is already up, cleaning up his sleeping area and donning his robe, swinging the fabric over his bare shoulder expertly. He feels compassion for his young friend, who doesn't know the rules here. He tries to help.

"Bhante, can I help you wake the little monk?"

"No, no, that's okay. I got this. You go and get the water, please. We practice at 5 sharp."

Upul raises his eyebrows and purses his lips, sucking air in through his teeth, sorry for the little monk, who has not experienced a tough teacher or the actual life of a monk in his first three weeks. Quickly slipping on sandals, he starts out for the water pump.

Bhante Muditha grabs Neil's ear, pulling hard.

"Ow!" says Neil. "Ow! That hurt!"

"Yes," says Bhante Muditha, shaking his head and smiling. "Yes, it hurts when you are late!"

Neil sits up, leaning back on his arms, shrugging his shoulders and rolling them back. He scratches his head and wishes for the millionth time that his mom was here.\

"Okay, okay, I am up. I am up."

"Here," says Bhante Muditha as he throws a folded bed sheet at Neil. "You can practice donning your robes."

Neil stands up and yawns. He rubs his ear, feeling the hot spot where Bhante Muditha pinched it. Frowning, he unfolds the bed sheet, holding it up in front of his face.

"Bhante, how do I do this? Bhante?"

Neil lowers the sheet and sees that Bhante Muditha is not there. He takes the unwieldy fabric and tries to drape it over his shoulders and walk. His feet get tangled and he trips, falling forward and hitting his forehead, unable to free his arms to stop himself.

He twists himself out of the sheet and holds it together around his neck like a cape, dragging it behind him on the ground as he slowly walks around the sleeping room with an imaginary bowl, pretending to be a monk collecting alms. He is determined to get this right.

When the practice bell rings, Neil folds the sheet as best he can, and runs out to the join his soon-to-be brother monks.

Bhante Dhammawasa, Bhante Muditha and the novice monk are all sitting quietly, waiting to begin their practice. Neil slows himself down as he enters the space, feeling for the first time like a real monk. He sits on a meditation cushion next to the novice monk and smiles silently.

Bhante Dhammawasa rings the bowl and the monks slowly close their eyes and breathe. Neil is alone with his thoughts. He tries his best to practice the metta sutta, the loving kindness meditation taught to him as a very young boy in Sunday school. He wishes himself to be happy, well, and peaceful. Then he wishes his mother to be well, happy, and peaceful. Then he starts to think about Lalitha and remembers that she will not help him cross the Colombo Kandy road. He wonders if he will cross this road alone after collecting alms, and he hopes there are no crazy bus drivers out there when he collects alms. He does not want to get hurt. He really likes to run. He wonders if he will be able to run when he is a monk. He remembers that he is meditating on loving kindness and goes back to wishing people happy, well, and peaceful. When he has thought about the well being of everyone he knows, he wishes the animals and all sentient beings happy, well, and peaceful.

"May they be happy, may they be well, may they be peaceful," he thinks to himself silently.

He thinks of the little mouse and his family cows. He wishes he could see his father. The little boy stays seated for the whole hour of practice. He shifts his position several times, but he is happy. For the first time, he is able to practice like a real monk. When Bhante Dhammawasa rings the bowl, he opens his eyes and smiles, happy to be in the temple with the monks.

Bhante Dhammawasa begins the chanting, his low and melodious voice being joined by the loud bass tone of Bhante Muditha, then the higher pitched clarity of the novice monk. Finally, Neil joins in. All three monks blink in surprise at the beauty of the little boy's voice.

Neil knows he will need to memorize many chants as a monk and he is happy that he knows these chants, hearing them since he was a young boy.

The little boy grows restless and tired after 15 minutes of chanting. He hopes Bhante Dhammawasa will stop the chants early like he did the day they saw the owl. Then he remembers that this is practice at being a real ordained monk, not a little boy visiting the temple. He shakes his shoulders a little, straightening up and pressing his hands together hard in the prayer position, determined to be strong enough to handle his dream of becoming a monk.

After 90 minutes of chanting, the novice monk gets ready to collect alms. He disappears underneath the robe, holding it over his head, somehow twisting it just so to form a collar and pins it under his right arm. He drapes the front of his robes over the alms bowl, making a cover to keep the elements out of the food.

Neil watches as the novice monk leans over and grabs an umbrella to keep the hot sun from burning his bald head. He notices that the novice monk keeps his right arm pinned to his side, his elbow holding the robe firmly in place.

I tell Bhante Sujatha I want to learn how to wear the robes formally as they do for alms collection. "Okay!" he says enthusiastically as he quickly unfolds his robes, disappearing as he holds the material high over his head and begins to twist it together making a beautiful collar and drape. I don't even try to imitate him. It seems completely beyond my abilities. I have so much to learn.

Next, Neil cleans the sleeping area. He takes a broom from the closet and methodically sweeps the floor, humming a chant as he sweeps. Simple cleaning tasks feel good to the little boy. He likes the way he can hum, think or meditate as he works, and he loves the feeling when his space is nice and clean.

An hour later, the novice monk and Bhante Muditha return with alms for the breakfast meal. The three monks and their young student sit against the wall in the dining hall, not looking at each other, cross legged on the floor, eating and drinking mindfully. Neil stares down at his food, trying hard to concentrate while his youthful mind wanders around with thoughts about how nice it would be to talk while he eats.

After breakfast, Neil cleans the kitchen. He gathers coconut hair together into a rough sponge and rubs the hair on a bar of soap. As he scrubs the bowls, he hums some more, enjoying himself. Neil loves to clean. This trait gets him far in his monastic life. He will always be welcome in any temple as a monk who rolls up his sleeves and does the work.

Bhante Sujatha smiles at me as we sit in his condominium talking about his experiences at the Subodharama Temple. "You know, Mary, I just do it. I never expect my students to do something that I will not do. No matter what, even the toilets, I just say, 'Well, here, I will start, you see?' Then I am doing it, and I think the student monks, they feel like I support them. I always do the work. I don't care. I never mind the work. I say, 'I will start and then the monks I am teaching join in.'

"Always, I say, we must demonstrate responsibility before we get to teach anything. Responsibility before rights. That's what I say. I don't think I have the right to tell monks in training what to do unless I take responsibility. I will take out garbage or clean the floor. I will do whatever I am asking them to do. Responsibility before rights

you know?"

Eleven-year-old Neil becomes familiar with the rhythms of the temple life. His loneliness fades as he engages in the busy life of a monk. He has the hardest time with eating. He wants to talk as he eats, and he is so hungry in the afternoons. After their early lunch, Buddhist monks did not eat until the next day. Neil's hunger keeps him up at night, which makes the loneliness even worse.

 Somehow, with great effort and determination, Neil stays at the temple for 90 days, not seeing his parents even at the Saturday services. Bhante Dhammawasa knows that it is best for the little monk to rely on his wise teacher and seek advice only from him. When Neil is ordained, he will renounce his family.

The time for that choice comes quickly. Bhante Dhammawasa sits with the little monk after practice on the last day of Neil's visit and talks softly with him, telling him the day has come for him to go home and say goodbye to his family.

"Tomorrow you will be ordained, and then to go home and live you must disrobe and no longer be a monk, do you understand?"

Bhikkhuni Vimala smiles at my question about disrobing.

"Actually I ask myself these questions every day. Is this lifestyle still for me? Is it still in line with my practice? As long as my answer is yes, I will keep practicing as a Buddhist nun. But I think all of us ask ourselves every day, is our practice okay? You see, it's very personal.

"In Theravada Buddhism, disrobing is not shameful and no one is ever shunned from a temple community if they change their minds and decide to stop practicing as a Buddhist monk. Of course, it is not good to disrobe in that people sort of wonder what happened. Why you would disrobe? But a disrobed monk is still a practicing Buddhist, still a community member, still deserving of respect and kindness. It is hard enough to make the choice to disrobe. No one

166

would want to make it worse by shaming the person or something."

Neil Bandara is certain that he wants to be ordained. He looks in the cracked old mirror above the sink in the kitchen that afternoon after meeting with Bhante Dhammawasa. His hair is especially shiny today. Neil knows it is ego to think about this, but he is still attached to the way he looks, and he is more attached to the wonderful compliments he receives all the time.

"Oh Chuti Putha, your hair looks wonderful!"

"Lalitha, your little son has the most beautiful hair!"

"O my gosh, little boy, I love your hair. What a handsome little boy."

Neil thinks about how it felt when Heenbanda rubs his head, ruffling his soft hair and sometimes commenting, "My Chuti Putha, your hair is just wonderful! Just wonderful! Why one day a girl will love this hair, and you will have the most beautiful children, won't you?"

As Neil stares at himself, he can almost feel his father's hand, and he wonders what it will be like, to never have that feeling again. He swallows and thinks about his mother. He wants so badly to hug her right now, and he whispers to himself, "You will be okay little monk. This is your kamma. You can do it. You can."

For me, one of the most profound unexpected benefits of my meditation practice is this natural inclination and ability to reassure myself.

Closing his eyes, Neil imagines the next day, seeing his entire extended family. His grandparents will be so proud. But he will never again be with them like he is now. He will be a monk at the temple. They will bow in front of him. For a few minutes, Neil breathes in and breathes out, lovingly and mindfully. He extends compassion to himself, wishing himself happy, well, and peaceful as he says goodbye to his family.

"You can be your own best friend. Extend loving kindness to yourself. Treat yourself like a best friend would treat you. If you are making a choice, ask yourself, 'What would my best friend tell me?' and go from there. If you love yourself well, you can love others well too. That's the way it works. You can't really love unconditionally until you love yourself unconditionally."

I smile as I listen to Bhikkhuni Vimala speak at the temple. Being my own best friend. This idea can change your life.

Neil opens his eyes, feeling better, ready to go home and say goodbye to his family. He turns from the clean dishes to go to tell his teacher, and he is surprised when he sees that Bhante Dhammawasa is standing there, watching him.

"Oh my little monk, I remember the day I went home to say goodbye. It is such a big day for you. It is a sad and happy day. You can use your practice to help you. Remember we are seeking enlightenment; we must work to attain nirvana. I will be with you as your teacher. I will take care of you and guide you in your young life so that you earn many merits. We are happy as monks. Our lives are simple. We do great service. When you go see your family, you will see if you are ready to make the choice to be ordained. Go and be open. Love your family. Be sure you are ready for tomorrow."

Neil puts down the coconut hair he was holding as he stared in the mirror. "Okay, Bhante, I am ready."

Chapter Nineteen

The Goat that Wept

For the last time as a layperson, Neil Bandara travels the familiar path from the temple to his house. He starts by walking around the grounds of the temple, up the hill to the house where the laypeople sometimes stay and around the dhamma hall, remembering the first time he went there as a young boy so many years ago. He walks over to the big Buddha statue and remembers standing in the cool shade, talking with Bhante Dhammawasa and wanting so badly to be with him.

He looks at his beloved mango tree and feels so sad that he and his sister will never climb together again. Finally, he goes over by the Na tree and remembers standing with the monks and the novice monk, wanting to be one of them. Now he is on the eve of that dream. He sits under the Bodhi tree and thinks about his favorite Sunday school lessons when the students would sit outside and listen to Bhante Dhammawansa tell so many wonderful stories.

Neil smiles as he remembers his favorite story from the Jataka tales, The Goat that Laughed and Wept:

A farmer tells some children to bathe a goat in a river so that it is ready for sacrifice. As the children wash the goat, it laughs, making a sound like a pot smashing. Then it weeps loudly.

(Neil and his friends would laugh about this part of the story and imitate the goat's sounds, trying to cackle loudly like a goat to each other as they acted out the story. Each time they would try and laugh like a goat, everyone would laugh so hard that tears would

come to their eyes. Then someone would say, "See, now we weep like the goat," and their bleating sounds would make them laugh even harder.)

In the story, the goat tells the farmer that he laughed with joy because he knows this is the 500th and last time he will have his head cut off. 500 decapitations are karmic retribution for cutting off the head of a single animal as an offering for the feast of the dead, just like the farmer was about to do to the goat.

The goat talks to the farmer. "Then, master, I wept, knowing you will also be doomed to lose your head 500 times. I pitied you."

Neil sits quietly underneath the Bodhi tree, remembering. He is grateful that he was naturally compassionate to animals, avoiding the terrible karmic retribution that befalls cruel people.

The farmer decides to protect the goat, who shakes his head sadly as he speaks, "My deed, cutting off the head of an animal for sacrifice is very evil and your protection is weak. We cannot avoid this."

Shortly after uttering those words, a lightning bolt hits a rock. A sharp piece of the rock flies out, neatly cutting off the head of the goat. The animal is finally released from his endless cycle of existence as a sacrificial being.

In the story the Buddha tells the people, "If people only knew that the penalty would be rebirth into sorrow, they would cease from taking life. A horrible doom awaits one who slays."

Buddhists are not all vegetarians. I was surprised to learn that the choice of how to practice the precept of doing no harm is very personal. Buddhism is like that; people can make their own choices about the best ways for them to practice. Dogma, although I find it when I search, is not in the center of Buddhism.

Soon, Neil will be teaching young children about the dhamma. He wants to be a teacher who reminds children that if they follow the teachings of the Buddha and do meritorious acts, they can better their kamma and create good lives for themselves.

Neil stands up under the Bodhi tree, already feeling like a monk, wondering about the celebration his family is planning tonight. He crosses the busy Colombo Kandy road with confidence, surprised by his lack of fear. He cannot imagine needing to hold his mother's hand.

Bhante Sujatha tells me about confidence as we drive to a meditation in a neighboring town.

"You know that is an effect of meditation. You get more confident as you practice. It is so difficult for most people to meditate. When you practice and you can sit for 30 minutes or more, you feel better about yourself. You also get to know yourself. You can trust yourself. I mean if you don't know yourself, how can you trust yourself? Also, when you have the thought, 'Oh I cannot do this, or that is impossible,' you recognize those thoughts as just passing thoughts in your nonstop thinking brain, you know? You can accept them and let them go. Then you can do that thing that you thought you could not do. You can do anything really."

I smile at the little monk, pleased to be around his good kamma, feeling happy that my life intersected with his.

Neil passes by the familiar path up to his beloved childhood home and walks over to his special resting place near the Mahaweli River. He sees that his father has cleared more bushy plants, making Neil's special spot hard to find. He stands for a moment, observing. With a calm mind, Neil's spots a small piece of skin from the slain cobra. Neil walks over to the place where the terrifying cobra passed over his leg and sits for a while meditating on his father's kamma. He knows that his father had no choice but to kill the cobra, which was so dangerous to his son. Neil reassures himself that Heenbanda will not suffer the same fate as the goat slayer.

Finally, the young boy starts up the rickety steps to the small mud house. He can hear voices and smell wonderful curry and coconut rice milk cooking. His stomach rumbles with hunger, and he has to stop for a moment, standing against the same tree that Heenbanda leaned against as he wrestled with raising his children in poverty. Neil thinks about his father's struggles as he leans against the tree. He hopes his parents will be happy that he has chosen to be ordained.

Lalitha and Heenbanda are actually reluctant as they plan the celebration, hoping their precious son will change his mind and return to their family.

As Neil leaves the shade of the tree and walks up the hill, he pushes his hair out of his eyes, hot with sweat now, wishing he had some shade from the sun and smiling when he realizes that tomorrow he will have an umbrella, just like a monk. Tomorrow he will be a monk. His bright smile at this thought could light up a town.

Chapter Twenty

Saying Goodbye

As Neil approaches his family home, his cousins and friends run down the hill to greet him, excited that he will be ordained and asking him all kinds of questions about being a monk.

"Will they really shave your head? Can we touch you tomorrow? Aren't you sad to leave your parents? How much do you study? Have you learned new chanting? Is Bhante Dhammawasa nice to you? Is Bhante Muditha mean? Is it hard to get up so early? Do you like the alms? Do you like to eat mindfully? What will your name be? Are you nervous?"

Neil smiles and answers their questions patiently. He is acting like a monk now.

"You know Mary, I remember seeing a billboard in Las Vegas about a car. It said 'Excite your Senses.' Why would anyone want to do that?

It takes me about a year to understand this. As I practice meditation, I grow to prefer quiet contentment. I don't notice this change, or any of the other changes, while they are happening. When I meditate, I am not striving for anything; I am just trying my best to sit still and keep my focus on my breath and loving kindness. As time passes, though, positive changes are happening.

173

Lalitha gasps with relief when she sees her son. She runs down the steps to greet him, hugging him and pushing him away, holding his shoulders and looking at him, crying as she holds his face in her hands, pulling him close and stroking his beautiful hair.

Manel runs up behind her mom, awkwardly hugging her mom and her brother, flooded with hope that her little brother will stay. She asks him to come swing in the tree.

"I have left it just so for you little brother. You can swing all you like." Neil smiles kindly at her. "Thank you, my sister, but you know I am here to announce my ordination. I don't think swinging in a tree is a good idea, do you?"

Manel's heart hurts as she realizes that her little brother is becoming a monk for real. She reaches out to hug him, and he backs away, letting her know that he is serious about renouncing his family. Manel hangs her head as Lalitha looks on, quietly counting her breaths.

Heenbanda walks over to his little son and ruffles his hair. He squats down in front of him, speaking softly. "My Chuti Putha, you know the family is here to celebrate your ordination, but we do not even care about that. Your mother and I want you to know that you can change your mind. You can cancel tomorrow. No one will be mad. We will love to have you back with us, living as our son. Please, my little son, listen to me."

Neil Bandara is not easily swayed, of course. He has grown to know himself as a monk in these three months. Life at the temple is his dream.

Neil is silent. Heenbanda sees the resolve in his son's eyes, and he fears he has lost this battle. He stands up and walks away, going to his wife for comfort.

Soon it is time for the big meal, and everyone is sitting around a special cook fire on the ground outside. When everyone has settled

174

in, holding their bowls of stew, a vade patty, and a fresh cup of milk, Heenbanda stands up at the head of them all and clears his throat, sounding authoritative but actually stifling a sob.

"Okay. Okay, everyone. I have something to say." The family members grow quiet, ready for the big announcement.

"As you know, our precious son, Neil Bandara, will be ordained as a Buddhist monk tomorrow. We are happy that all of you are celebrating with us." Heenbanda looks at Neil, sitting between Lalitha and Manel. "Little son, you have our permission to proceed with your ordination. You also have our permission to stay at home."

Neil doesn't hear anything past "You have our permission to proceed." He is so happy that he forgets all about the irritating mosquitos descending on him in the dusk. His dream is really coming true. He claps his hands together involuntarily and takes a big breath, not even realizing that he was holding his breath waiting for this permission from his father.

"Thank you my beloved father! I want to be a monk! I will be ordained tomorrow"

Heenbanda sighs as he looks down, ready to drop a bomb on his little son's joy. His next words hurt Neil, almost crushing his dreams under their weight.

"Now, little son, you know, after tomorrow you cannot come back here. I will not allow you to put your mother and myself through this grief and then change your mind. If you go through the ordination, and then you try to come back here, I swear I will kill you and throw your little body right into the river!"

The family is silent, shocked at Heenbanda's tough words. Lalitha is despondent, crying softly as her mother tries to comfort her. Neil uses his practice and breathes. He has reassured his parents that he will still practice filial piety, and he knows his beautiful sister will marry and have children. He can see that they will all be happy, well,

175

and peaceful. Neil chooses to be silent and calm, monk-like in his serenity.

That night, he sleeps in his home for the last time, shifting uncomfortably in the single bed, wishing he were at the temple.

The next day the family is sad and happy at the same time. So many parts of life are like that, Neil thinks to himself as he walks to the temple with his family for the last time.   He is dressed in white, signifying his purity and his readiness for the blessing of the ordination.

As Lalitha walks along, she thinks of the Buddhist story of the woman who was forced to find serenity in the midst of grief.

The story starts when the woman is late in her pregnancy; due to deliver a new child in the coming days. Evil marauders come to her village and she, her husband and her child are forced to flee. As they walk through the woods to the safety of the next town, the woman feels herself overtaken by pain and tells her husband the baby is coming. They go off the path into a secluded area, and the woman begins to give birth. Her husband goes off in search of a medicinal plant to ease her pain. On his way back, he slips on a pile of wet leaves and falls on a sharp rock, cutting himself in the chest.

As he struggles to stand up, the woman screams in pain as her second son is born. Her four year old watches in silence. Desperate to see his new son, the husband manages to stand and walk back to his wife and family.

When he sees the beautiful baby he is filled with joy, but when he opens his mouth to speak, blood flows out, the wounds in his chest from the fall destroying his heart.

He dies, whispering his great love for his wife and sons. The woman is holding her new baby, while her son looks on in horror, running over to his father and shaking him, saying "Wake up daddy! Wake up!! Mommy? Is daddy going to wake up?"

The woman begins to cry, shaking with the shock of this terrible event. She is a single mother of two children now, and she knows she must gather her wits about her and get them to safety. Numb from shock, she uses a sharp rock to cut the cord and stands us as she begins to nurse her newborn baby. She is not even aware of her nakedness, with only a flimsy scarf over her chest for comfort. She grabs hold of her four-year-old son's hand, and begins to walk in the direction of the river, where they might cross into the next town. Soon the young boy grows tired of walking, and the poor woman must hoist him up into her arms, doing her best to carry the baby and him, hugging both of her arms around them as she awkwardly moves forward. She is already in pain and weakened by the birth and her mind starts to play tricks on her, convincing her that all hope is lost, that she cannot survive. When they come to a stream, she discovers that the late spring monsoons have created a raging river, as high as the woman's waist. She is exhausted and she rests for a moment on the banks, wondering how to cross with her children.

Because she has lost her mindfulness, she does not think to stay where they are and rest, or go back to her village, which even with the marauders might be safer than the raging water in front of her. She decides to leave the 4 year old on the bank of the river to wait while she carries the baby across to the other side. She tells her 4 year old not to move a muscle until she is ready for him to cross.

"I will tell you when it is time. Wait for me. Do not move. We will go together. I will come back for you!"

The boy sits obediently while the woman trudges across the river with her baby exhausting herself even more, not even noticing when her scarf is pulled off of her by the water, floating out of reach, like her last hope. She places the baby high up on the bank and turns to get her other son. In the middle of the river, she sees an eagle circle overhead, and she becomes fearful for her baby's life.

She stops in the middle of the river and turns around only to see the eagle swoop down and grab her baby. She can hear cries of pain as the infant is carried roughly up into the air by the eagle. The woman begins to shout at the eagle, waving her arms and yelling, "Come back! Come back!"

Her son, not hearing clearly over the rush of water between himself and his mother, thinks she is saying "Come in! Come in!"

The little boy jumps in the water. The strong current, rapidly carries him downstream. He flails his arms and cries out. Mommy! Help me! The woman turns back, only to see her older son drowning as he is carried away. She cannot save him.

At this point, the woman's mind snaps, and she becomes deranged, running out of the water naked, crying helplessly, then screaming with rage and laughing with insanity. A monk sees her and practices loving kindness, standing in front of the woman and grabbing her shoulders, stopping her from moving.

"You must find your mind! Find your mind!"

The woman pushes him away, knocking the monk off his feet, and runs even faster. On a crooked path, she comes to the temple door and bursts into a meditation practice, not even caring that she is naked and bloody and crazed with grief.

The Buddha smiles at her, unperturbed. He speaks quietly. "Woman, what has happened? You must find your mind."

"Lord, oh lord! I cannot!" She breaks down sobbing, unable to speak.

The Buddha directs two of his disciples to cover her with their robes. "But my lord, our robes are sacred. They are important for our practice."

"Clothe her," says the Buddha, "That is using your robes for practice. Clothe her."

The monks obey their teacher and the woman calms down a little,

178

still sobbing and yelling that she has lost her only hope at peace and happiness. Her family is gone.

Again, the Buddha remains sitting and serene. He knows that even her justified grief is in her mind. He tells her to find her mind. He tells her that she is welcome here, that she can practice with him and his disciples, that she can heal her mind. Eventually the woman calms down and hears the wise words of the Buddha. She begins to use the practice as a way to ease her mind.

Many months later, she has healed her wounded mind. Although she is grieving, she knows that could not have helped her husband or her children that day in the woods. She is able to see that the kamma of others is not hers to control and then, she is able to take the important first step in the middle path of Buddhism, that of forgiving and loving herself.

The woman stays in the temple and eventually ordains as a Buddhist nun. Respected as a wise woman, she is able to use her experiences to help others who have been through terrible life experiences to heal their minds. She is fulfilled as a mother to her sangha, and lives with great happiness in her old age, earning merits as a wise teacher and faithful practitioner.

In the Buddhist philosophy, merits are earned through acts of loving-kindness; they are not "points" that total up into a reward of some kind. Rather, merits are positive forces towards our enlightenment. As we participate in meritorious acts, we grow closer to the truth about life. When we see the truth, we have reached nirvana, or Buddha hood. This can take many lifetimes to achieve.

Lalitha takes comfort in this story, knowing that she will find peace with her beloved son's choice. It will take time and patience, though, and for today, she is letting herself grieve. Softly crying as they walk, she hangs onto her little son's hand, not letting go, even for a minute, to wipe away her tears. When they come to the busy road crossing, Neil tries to let go and Lalitha refuses, gripping his little hand tightly and pulling him close. Soon, her son will have a new name. She will not be allowed to touch him, and she is taking advantage of these last minutes with her only son, her precious, gorgeous, shiny-haired, stubborn gift of a son.

As they cross the intersection, the family stays close together. Manel holds her father's hand as she keeps a protective hold on her little brother's elbow. Neil feels the family sadness. He tears up as they walk the beautiful jungle path to his new home, the Subodharama temple.

A little girl is running down the path, excited to see her cousins coming to temple. Her long dark hair flies out behind her and the little monk can see the silhouette of her young body outlined by her thin white garment, chosen for her brother's ordination ceremony. "She is beautiful!" thinks Neil. He shrugs his shoulders and sighs; He will never marry or touch a woman.

"Bhante, why can't a monk touch a woman? It seems so discriminatory the way that women are treated, unable to interact with monks like men.

"My friend, the Buddha did not have any rules to begin with, you know. His followers got into a little trouble, taking advantage of the way the women admired their practice. One monk had some trouble, an affair with a married woman, and the Buddha saw that this harmed the woman. He decided to make a rule. Monks should not touch a woman. That way, women are safe around monks. They can be at their most vulnerable when someone dies or a baby is born or their child is ill—and a monk can help them, never taking advantage. You see? The rule is about protecting women, not discriminating against them. We practice loving kindness, and we have to be careful not to take a chance that we will hurt people. This is also why we like to have at least four monks together when we chant at people's homes for a house blessing or when someone is dying. This way, people can be safe, and we have the support of our fellow monks in honoring our renunciations.

"And if the woman is related to the monk, like my mother, hugging

can hurt us, reminding us of what we lost, I think. She and I are better off remembering that I am no longer in this family. I am a monk, following the simple path, where I love everyone as much as I love my mother."

Finally the family arrives at the door to the temple. The visiting monks warmly greet them, directing the family to meditation cushions especially reserved for them. Neil is guided to a spot very near the front of the temple, in front of the elevated platform where the monks sit, facing the sangha, in front of a large Buddha statue, as they lead meditation and chanting and give the dhamma talks.

Bhante Dhammawasa smiles down at Neil. He is happy to see the young boy and amused by his shiny hair and the fact that the little monk is so concerned about shaving his head.

Heenbanda sits cross-legged with his back ramrod straight. He seems angry and uptight, but he is feeling pride and sorrow and love. His mind is mixed up. The monks cut a lock of hair off Neil's head, and ask him to hold it in his hands and meditate. Heenbanda's feelings of loss flood through him and he lets out a sob, gulping it back quickly, not wanting to show his emotions.

The temple is beautiful, dressed up in ordination glory. The entire community wears white out of respect for the purity of mind, heart, and soul demonstrated by the Buddha.

The senior monks sit in front of Neil, watching him and meditating with him. Holding his lock of hair carefully in his cupped hands, Neil breathes and thinks about his family sitting behind him. He feels proud of himself, and then realizes that pride is ego. He lets go of that thought, and for the first time, he experiences a quiet mind, a mind that is only focused on the present moment. He feels the cool air pass over his upper lip as he breathes in through his nose, and the warm air passing as he breathes out, and smiles, feeling the clarity that comes with the practice of meditation.

Bhante Dhammawasa smiles down on his young student, I happy to see him at peace. In Buddhist philosophy, there is no such phenomenon as permanence, and Neil's mind quickly starts to think again, this time about his hair. He shakes his head a little, feeling his soft hair brushing on his forehead. He wonders again what it will be like to lose his hair.

Behind him, his sister Manel is sitting between her parents, practicing meditation with the rest of the temple. She is thinking about her brother and the last time they played together. She wishes she had not pushed him off the branch so much when he wanted to keep swinging. She thinks that if her little brother would change his mind, she would let him swing all he wanted.

Her parents are so sad, and Manel feels like she is partly the reason that her brother is joining the temple. If they didn't fight so much, maybe he would not have been crying outside that day when Mrs. Attharagama came by and asked him to go to Sunday school. "Darn you, Mrs. Attharagama! How dare you steal my brother!" she thinks, and then she realizes she is in the middle of a metta sutra (loving kindness meditation). So she corrects herself, mindfully wishing Mrs. Attharagama happy, peaceful, and well. Manel likes to think about everyone in the world meditating, wishing her the same. Her mother reminds her often when she is lonely and missing her little brother that he is sending her loving kindness through his meditation all the time. This comforts Neil's big sister.

After Neil meditates with his lock of hair, three monks lead him to the back of the temple where they shave his head. The young boy is fighting back tears while the monks gently chide him. "See how light you feel? C'mon now, cheer up, you will love your bald head!"

Neil reaches up and feels his head. The newly exposed skin feels raw and soft. Shocked at the way his head feels, he feels tightness grip his chest. He has a hard time swallowing. Neil doesn't know this, but he is grieving.

The monks lead Neil back up to the front of the temple. When Lalitha sees him, she gasps involuntarily, leaning over on her cushion. Manel puts her small arm protectively over her mother. Heenbanda stoically stares ahead, looking cold, afraid to move and trigger his grief.

Now Neil receives his maroon robes. In the early days of Buddhism, the monks, having taken a vow of poverty, used discarded clothes and clothes from burial grounds to make their robes. They would wash the robes in a clean river, and then they would boil the robe with leaves, roots and spices, usually turning the material some shade of orange.

The maroon color reflects this tradition of the simple life chosen by monks.

Neil bows to Bhante Dhammawasa and holds his hands out, palms up, elbows bent at his sides. Bhante Dhammawasa carefully drapes the folded robes over Neil's forearms. Heenbanda coughs, fighting with his emotions.

Lalitha watches her son, so small in his white clothes, holding his robe just so, and she sees that her son is doing exactly what he was meant to do. She is still crying, but she can already feel the edges of joy. Her little son is fulfilling his destiny.

Neil requests his ordination as prescribed by the Buddhist traditions.

He offers Bhante Dhammawasa the robes, saying, "Venerable sir, I respectfully ask that you take this set of robes in my hand and out of compassion ordain me as a novice so that I may be free of the cycle of existence."

Then Neil bows again requesting that the senior monk hand the robes back to him. "Venerable sir, I respectfully ask you to give me the set of robes in your hand and out of compassion ordain me as a novice in order that I may be free from the cycle of existence."

Finally holding his robes, the little monk makes the biggest request of all.

"Venerable Sir, I respectfully ask you to ordain me as a novice in order that I may be free of the cycle of existence and attain Nibbana."

Heenbanda and Lalitha take a breath at the same time, neither of them realizing that they were holding their breath.

Now, Neil chants, with a high, clear voice:

"Buddha saranam gacchami (I take refuge in the Buddha).
Dhamman Saranam gacchami (I take refuge in the Dhamma).
Sangham Saranam gacchami (I take refuge in the Sangha).

Neil sings this chant three times, moving many people to tears with the beauty of his voice. Bhante Muditha, sitting next to Bhante Dhammawasa, thinks to himself that this little monk is something special. He looks down at Neil with his newly shaved head, so vulnerable before the community. "I will care for this young monk," Bhante Muditha thinks to himself. "I will help guide him on the right path. I will be there for him." He looks up at the little monk's family, catching Heenbanda's eye and nodding slightly, assures him that his beloved son's care is foremost in his mind. Heenbanda is reassured by this glance, and he sits back slightly, relaxing a little.

Now Neil makes his promises to live a pure and holy life. He recites the ten precepts, ways of living proscribed by the Buddha so long ago.

He promises to abstain from harming or taking life, stealing, sexual contact, lying, using intoxicants, taking food after midday, engaging in dancing, singing, music or any kind of entertainment, the use of garlands, perfumes, unguents, and adornments (jewelry and make up), using luxurious seats, and accepting and holding money.

When the little monk is finished, he asks Bhante Dhammawasa to be his Preceptor (teacher of the precepts) and the older monk clears his throat as he grants the little monk his new Buddhist name:

"Welcome to the monastery, Bhante Sujatha (Sujatha means well-born)."

And so it is done. Neil Bandara is now Bhante Sujatha, an ordained monk.

The little monk sits on the platform with the senior monks, looking out at the temple community.

His parents and his sister walk up to him and bow to the ground three times as they do with any Buddhist monk. Bhante Sujatha smiles kindly, feeling the shift to being a monk settle into him.

When the ceremony is over, Bhante Sujatha stands in front of the temple by the mango tree, watching his family leave. His mother turns at the bottom of the hill and looks up at her little son one last time. Bhante Sujatha smiles at her with trembling lips. He puts his hand on the tree for support and stands up on his toes, watching his mother for as long as he can. Bhante Dhammawasa comes up besides him and places a reassuring hand on his shoulder assures him that it will be alright. The little monk breathes in deeply and smiles through his tears.

Chapter Twenty-One

Life at the Temple

By the time the little monk is twelve, two more young monks have joined the Subodharama Temple. They are expected to don their robes and fold their sleeping mat every day at 4:30am. After meditating and chanting, it is time to get ready to collect alms for the morning meal. The younger monks are forever forgetting about holding their robes together with their elbows, reaching for a tree branch or raising their arms in happiness and excitement, tripping on their way down the path walking for alms.

The river is their favorite place to play. After a year at the temple, the little monk is already demonstrating his leadership skills and his cleverness by getting him and his brother little monks to the river as often as possible

The little monk loves to clean. He is happy to do the dishes, and unlike his brother monks, he always volunteers to clean the bathrooms, a task particularly unpleasant in the humid climate of Sri Lanka. The bathrooms at the temple were always wet. They were primitive according to our western standards, and teenage boys and men were constantly in and out, making a mess no matter how clean their habits. And most young monks were just like children anywhere, careless and sloppy when it came to bathroom time.

The little monk was passionate about cleaning. He liked the routine of it. It calmed his mind. He loved the smell of the coconut hair and the soap. Lalitha would often let her little son help when she swept or dusted the shelf for the Buddha. The little monk liked to do this with his mom, because she always breathed or hummed softly while they worked. He loved the sound of her breath and felt so happy when she thanked him after they cleaned. This feeling of service with someone he loved was brought up again as the little monk scrubbed with scrunched up coconut hair and dusted with old rags.

One day, as he was scrubbing dishes, the water shut off in the middle of rinsing the big bowl used for the alms. All the alms were poured into this bowl when the monks returned from their morning collections. Monks were not allowed to pick and choose among the alms. Their practice was meant to enhance humility and gratitude.

"So, would you eat whatever you got? I mean, wasn't some food kind of nasty?"

Bhante San laughs at me.

"Nasty? I don't know. I guess I would say yes, sometimes there was stuff we didn't want to eat, if that's what you mean, and sometimes we would get sick from something bad in the alms. Oh my, that was really bad, when we would all get sick at the same time. Sometimes I wonder how Bhante Sujatha and the other teachers did it. How could they clean up after so many teenage boys, you know?

"Anyway, let me tell you a story that the Buddha told to teach us that we could not be picky about what we ate, at all.

"One time, a monk was collecting alms, and a man sick with leprosy came to his door, wanting to contribute. The monk held out his bowl, hoping the man would change his mind about giving food when he was so obviously sick. He didn't. In fact, the man went to his cook fire and stirred the rice dish so vigorously that his finger fell off into the bowl. He came back to the monk and dished the mixture into his alms bowl. The monk watched as the bloody finger landed in his alms bowl. He wanted to throw it out, but he knew that his teacher would disapprove.

"When his rounds were finished and he was back in the temple, he asked his teacher if they could please leave his alms out of the bowl.

187

The teacher said no. 'The Buddha taught that we must take what we are given. We use this practice to lessen the power of our ego.' The young monk was sad to see his disgusting alms mixed in with all the good food. The teacher left the finger in the middle of the bowl, so the students did not have to eat it but they could see it. This helped them learn that they were to eat whatever was provided with no personal preference. In service they had to be willing to go as far as being sick to demonstrate compassion to the giver. They were taught to allow the contributor to earn his merits however he saw fit. None of the monks grew sick and all of them learned the valuable lesson of humility."

I remember this story in Sri Lanka. We were staying in a hotel in the mountains, overlooking the magnificent tea plantations. We sat down to breakfast at a table in the hotel lobby, not really a restaurant, but a place where they served a limited menu to guests. I notice a large plate of rice and curry at the table next to us, and I tell the waiter I would like that for breakfast.

My traveling companions ordered toast and eggs, and they were served while I waited for my curry. I did not complain. I was traveling with a chief monk, and so I was careful about my manners. In the Buddhist philosophy, it is best to stay silent and gracious. Unless real harm is happening, Buddhist do not complain.

Finally, the waiter asks the people at the table next to me if they are done. As they nod their assent, the waiter picks up the half eaten food and carries it over to me.

"Sorry," he says. "I was waiting for them to be finished."

I am silent as I take a portion off the tray and eat. I had no idea that I was waiting for leftovers. On the plane ride back, I start to think about that incident and how remarkably wasteful I am. It almost seems like we have an allergy to sharing most things with each other.

Bhante Sujatha went to the tank where the water was collected and saw it was very low. He ran into the dhamma hall where Bhante Dhammawasa was instructing a young monk in the proper way to form the collar of his robe. The younger monk was hidden from sight, reaching up as high as he could, encircled by his robe and trying to roll the pieces together like the senior monk showed him.

"Bhante, I don't know! I am having such a hard time!"

The younger monk's voice was high pitched, and Bhante Sujatha smiled, remembering his own struggles. He decides to practice loving kindness, clearing his throat before he speaks.

"Bhante Dhammawasa, we are out of water! And I am not even done cleaning the dishes! Can this little monk help me get more water from the river?"

Inside his robe, the little boy raises his eyebrows in excitement, thrilled to be getting a break from the impossible task of folding his robes in the formal way.

Bhante Dhammawasa, being a gentle teacher, sighs and acquiesces.

"Okay, my good student, yes, you may take this young monk and go to the river for water. Please be mindful that you are monks or monks in training. Conduct yourselves accordingly."

The little monk clears his throat. "Um, then, could I get my other brother monk to come as well? I will need help carrying the heavy water urns up the hill, you know."

Frowning, wondering if he is missing something, Bhante Dhammawasa agrees to let the little monk bring the other two young monks in training to the river.

Bhante Sujatha can already feel the cool water on his legs as he watches the younger monk twirl out of his formal robe folding and throw the robes over one shoulder casually, sighing with the

189

increased comfort.

He and the little monk walk as slowly as possible to the door of the Dharma Hall. Once they are outside and out of sight of the senior monk they break into a run, excited to tell the other young monk that they are going to the river.

The three of them each take an urn for water and walk down the path to the river. The littlest monk trips twice in his robes, and Bhante Sujatha helps him, showing him how to shorten the length by making the folds over his shoulder bigger.

Even on the shaded path the heat is oppressive. The young monks are wet with sweat, swatting mosquitoes away with their free hands. One monk swings his urn at a whole bunch of them buzzing together and driving him crazy.

When they get to the sandy bank of the Mahaweli River, Bhante Sujatha smiles and says, "Hey, let's swim a little before we go back, okay?"

The other two monks instantly agree, removing their robes faster than the little monk can tell them to be careful, jumping into the river and splashing each other. Bhante Sujatha joins them, feeling the cool water surround him with relief.

They play a game with each other, circling around and around until the water forms a whirlpool between them.

"Hey, you crazy monks! What are you doing down here?"

The little monk stops running so fast that the younger monks bump into him, laughing as they splash back into the water with arms splayed, floating on their backs and blowing river water out of their mouths.

Heenbanda says it again. "Hey, you crazy monks! You better settle down! What are you doing?"

The Subodharama temple and Bhante Sujatha's parents use the same river of course. The little monk is happy to hear his father's voice, even if it is to reprimand him and his brother monks.

"Hello!" says the little monk.

Heenbanda tilts his head a little and smiles before he turns around to make sure the stubborn cow is out of the water. He waves to the young monks as he climbs out of the water after the cows, following them back up the hill.

The little monk smiles as he watches Heenbanda, happy to see his father productive and well. He watches Heenbanda until he disappears from his sight and wonders if his mom is in the house with his sister.

The monks play with each other in the water for a few more minutes. The little monk, always thinking about the best way to accomplish a goal, tells his friends that they must get out and get the water or Bhante Dhammawasa will catch them. The little monk wants to be able to come to this river where there is relief from the heat and the chance to see his family all the time.

The monks walk together to the well and fill their urns with water, hoisting the urn up onto their shoulders and quickly resorting to holding them awkwardly pressed in front of them between their arms as they make their way back to the temple.

Soon the little monk is telling his teacher that the tank needs filling even when it there is enough water for a few more days. Bhante Dhammawasa is not fooled. He is compassionate to the young monks and goes along with their little game. He knows they are young and need to have some expression of their boyhood. Jumping and playing in the river will not harm them. The wise teacher knows he must let teenage boys blow off steam once in a while. Often he chooses to let small misbehaviors go, allowing the young monks to learn compassion.

191

"You know, Mary, I was really little and sometimes I would want to carry all the dishes at once, you know, not make so many trips from the sink to the cabinets. But I was not that strong, and I would always drop a dish or two and they would break on the floor. I didn't want to be caught, you know? "

Bhante Sujatha laughs so hard that he wipes a tear from his eye.

"So I would take the broken pieces and throw them out the door down into the jungle!

"Oh, my, I haven't thought of this in years! It is so funny to me now. I mean, we didn't have too many dishes so, of course, the senior monks and the lay people knew, but they never punished me for it. Everyone at the Subodharama temple was very compassionate."

I am driving the little monk to a workshop he is leading and using the time in the car to interview him. I ask him if he wants to take a break, knowing he needs his rest.

"No, no, you know, this is really helping me? I like it. I really do. I like reviewing my life; it is, I don't know, it is really something, you know?"

I think about Thoreau writing that an unexamined life is not worth living, and I think I know what he means now. Examining your life or any individual life is a miraculous and transformative process.

Bhante Sujatha is a good student. When he is 13, Bhante Dhammawasa realizes that he cannot provide this young monk with the proper education, and he asks Bhante Muditha to take the little monk to his school in Kandy where there are about 75 student monks. Bhante Muditha, remembering the little monk's ordination, readily agrees. He is eager to teach this special monk, knowing that he has such good kamma.

On a hot day in July—the day after the celebration of the Sarnath, the first Teachings of the Buddha—the little monk awakens in a reflective mood. It's dark in the sleeping room, and he thinks of the times with his father when he would be up too early and his father would gently lead him back to bed.

As he stretches and yawns, absentmindedly rubbing his bald head, he sits for a moment, thinking about the celebration yesterday and remembering the Buddha's teaching in Deer Park, celebrated on the full moon day in July.

Here the Buddha, after attaining enlightenment, sits with 5 former friends who mock him at first for his obvious comfort. The five others are thin from their asceticism, and they chide the Buddha for his habits—reminding him of the vows he took to remain hungry and poor.

On this day the Buddha changes the lives of all of his disciples by telling the five monks, "*Austerities only confuse the mind. In the exhaustion and mental stupor to which they lead, one can no longer understand the ordinary things of life and still less the truth that lies beyond the senses. I have given up extremes of either luxury or asceticism. I have discovered the Middle Way.*"

The little monk smiles to himself, admiring the simplicity of the middle path proscribed by the Buddha. He thinks to himself that he might be fasting or silent for years as a monk were it not for the gentle teachings of the Buddha, who taught people not to debate or be right, but to help human beings see the path that could lead to the end of their suffering

The Buddha went on to explain the Four Noble Truths to his friends who were now his first disciples. These were simple and easy for the little monk to remember. He knew them as a child in Singhal, the language of Peradiniya, Sril Lanka and now he knew them in Pali and Sanskrit. The little monk learned these different languages, which helped him quickly advance in his studies.

The Four Noble Truths are as follows:

1. There is suffering

2. Suffering has a cause

3. The cause is removable

4. There are ways to remove the causes.

The ways to remove the causes, the Buddha explained to the five disciples, were in a simple Eight Fold path: Right speech, Right action, Right livelihood, Right effort, Right mindfulness, Right concentration, Right attitude and Right view.

The little monk, sitting quietly in the predawn darkness, considers this Eight-fold path. He knows that he will be leaving the Subodharama Temple at the end of the summer to attend the monk school run by Bhante Muditha. Bhante Sujatha rubs his ear as he remembers the painful ear pulls that Bhante Muditha uses to teach lessons. The little monk is enjoying his freedom at the Subodharama Temple, and he is nervous when he thinks about all the mistakes he makes. Bhante Muditha will not be a gentle teacher.

"I wish for myself and Bhante Muditha to be happy, peaceful, and well," he whispers in the dark, with his hands folded in a prayer position.

He will meditate this morning on the Four Noble Truths and promise to himself that he will follow all the precepts. He will practice cleaning the dishes more thoroughly. He looks down at his little hands and commands them silently to stop dropping dishes already!

Bhante Sujatha is leading an introduction to meditation at the Blue Lotus Temple. A student asks him what to do if he is uncomfortable during meditation.

"You know, I can hardly sit cross-legged or straight in a chair for more than a few minutes! Then I start to think about my discomfort, and I lose my mindfulness."

The little monk laughs gently and smiles, nodding his head. "Oh yes, my friend, I think we all go through that."

A ripple of familiar laughter goes through the temple audience. "I learned as a young boy at the temple that you can actually talk with your body. If your knees hurt, you can assure them that you will take good care of them if they can stay with you through your meditation. Of course, you can switch positions anytime during meditation, but it is good practice to notice your body and let it know that you appreciate your heart beating, your legs feeling pain, or the stiffness in your back. All of these so-called bad feelings are evidence that you are alive, you know? So you can adjust your position lovingly and mindfully, practicing loving kindness for yourself.

The little monk is forever letting a dish slip and drop on the floor when he is cleaning after lunch. Sometimes, a bird will sing right near the window, or the little monk will hear his brother monks laughing outside. Mostly the water in the sink reminds him of the gently flowing waters of the Mahaweli River. As a young boy, the little monk just wants to get the dishes put away and go outside, usually checking the water tank twice to see if they might be able to go to the river and take a quick swim. These thoughts make him want to hurry, and so he stacks the dishes a little too high and almost always drops them, breaking one or two and then muttering to himself while he cleans up the mess.

When Bhante Dhammawasa notices a dish missing or a less than thoroughly clean eating area, he gently admonishes the little monk, assigning him extra reading and studying on the precept that might address his infraction. Under Bhante Dhammawasa's tutelage the little monk is becoming a gentle and wise young boy. The wise teacher hopes that the little monk will not become too tough when he is taught by Bhante Muditha.

After practice and chanting, it is time to collect alms. The little monk walks for alms alone. For the first two days, the novice monk went with him, helping him to memorize the route. Walking behind the novice monk, Bhante Sujatha would always get extra attention. His small size and big smile inspired people.

Monks do not knock on doors or ask for alms. They walk slowly past houses, and if people want to give them food they come outside and wait for the monk. The novice monk would stop and wait with his bowl as proscribed by the Buddhist teachings. The little monk would stand behind him, a little shy in his first days of collecting alms. The novice monk would step over to the side once the alms were deposited into his bowl, and the little monk would come into view, holding his bowl underneath his robe, not remembering to hold it out.

"Oh! Oh! What an adorable little monk! Oh, sweetheart, here, you are so tiny—here is some more food. Eat it so you can grow, okay?"

Soon the little monk's bowl would be overflowing, and instead of not contributing to his alms, people give him bags to hold the extra food.

Lalitha can see him sometimes struggling under the weight of the bags, and it breaks her heart.

"I cried when I saw my little boy, almost falling over from carrying so much food. I was so proud of him and so sad to see him struggle. My Chuti Putha was a popular little monk."

The little monk began to collect alms on his own after only two days. He is silent as he walks slowly, becoming accustomed to the way the robe is held tightly by his side with his right arm. Carrying an umbrella one day, he is struck by the thought that his dream has really come true. He remembers the day with Heenbanda, using a stick as an umbrella and pretending to be a monk. He smiles to himself, thinking that the life of a monk is better and harder than he could have ever imagined. It is his favorite activity to collect alms. He loves the walking meditation and seeing the people. Bhante

Sujatha loves being a monk.

Bhante Gunaratana ("Bhante G") is giving the dhamma talk at the temple. He has written two best selling books including the famous primer on meditation, Mindfulness in Plain English. He demonstrates walking meditation for us.

He stands up from his cushion slowly. He is eighty-six years old. He stands still, with his hands gently at his sides. Slowly resting his palms together near his thighs, he gently lifts a foot, heel first and places it mindfully in front of him. His movements are almost imperceptible. He stops after walking about a foot.

Stand for a full minute at least, and breathe mindfully, then turn. Your objective is to attain alertness, and to build an unblocked awareness of your movements. When thoughts come to you, let them pass as usual. The insights you gain from this unblocked awareness can be applied to your notion filled life in powerful ways.

I thought walking meditation was simply being silent while I walked. This is challenging, especially with a friend, but this kind of walking meditation is totally different. I find it more difficult than sitting meditation, which surprises me. I am learning that slowness is harder for me than stillness, and that mind cultivation is not the same as "zoning out."

Once the alms are collected and distributed, the little monk sits in the dhamma hall with his brother monks and eats mindfully. From a Buddhist perspective, eating represents an interaction with the universe. It is a task to be done slowly and silently, mindfully appreciating each bite for the nourishment it represents. It is very important never to be greedy with food. Monks are taught to chant, remembering that food is a gift that represents the hard work of all beings.

The little monk chants as he sits in front of his bowl. "*Wisely reflecting, I use this food not for fun, not for pleasure, not for fattening, not for beautification, but only for the maintenance and*

197

nourishment of this body, for keeping it healthy, for helping with the Spiritual Life; Thinking thus, I will allay hunger without overeating, so that I may continue to live blamelessly and at ease."

I can't get enough of the food in Sri Lanka. Most of the places we go are either buffet style restaurants, or private residences, with family style settings of large plates and bowls of food to share. I load up, especially at the buffets, and I often leave leftovers.

When we return to the states, we ask Bhante if he has any feedback for us on ways we could be better visitors to his home country. He admonishes us gently, telling us that buffets and family style settings in Sri Lanka are created so that people don't take more than they need. In other words, people are expected to consume less at a buffet than at a traditional sit-down meal.

" It is different in America, isn't it?" Bhante Sujatha laughs as he says this, but I still wince a little when I think about my eating habits in his country.

Now I pray before every meal, thanking all the people and beings involved in the growth, preparation and delivery of my food. This has been very helpful to me. No matter what I am about to eat, there is always someone to thank and something to appreciate.

Bhante Sujatha looks down at his bowl and sighs as quietly as he can. Bhante Dhammawasa sits at the head of the group of young monks watching them while they eat. The food is good today; especially the warm lentil stew prepared by one of the little monk's favorite village women.

This village woman met the little monk when he was first staying at the temple before he was ordained. Those days he climbed the mango tree all he wanted; a little boy in old shorts and worn sandals, relaxing on a branch, tearing into a juicy mango and letting the juice drip down off his hand as he squeezed the fruit. The woman was walking to the temple one day when some juice fell onto her head, which was carefully adorned with flowers for her temple visit.

Hearing a young boy's muffled laughter, the woman turned around and looked up; craning her head this way and that, shading her eyes with her hand, she tried to see what in the world was in the mango tree.

She spied a worn sandal hanging down off a tiny foot, swinging back and forth. Following the foot up to the leg with her eyes, the woman walks closer to the tree and looks straight up where she sees the shirtless little boy, holding his hand over his mouth to stifle his laughter, carelessly squeezing a mango with his other hand.

"Little boy! You get down from there! It is not safe in the tree! And the juice has spoiled my hair! Get down!"

The little monk shouts right back at her. "No! I am becoming a monk! I can sit here all I want! Bhante Dhammawasa said so! You just go on now!"

The woman furiously purses her lips and shakes her head, turning swiftly on her heel and walking swiftly to the temple where she looks for the senior monk to tell him about this disrespectful young man.

Laying back into the crook of the branch the little monk grins, satisfied that he can enjoy his mango in peace. Just when he is about to take another delicious bite, he hears the booming voice of Bhante Muditha who is visiting that day. Once again, the little monk experiences the famous and painful ear pull.

Now, when the little monk goes for alms, this woman laughs with him, remembering his little foot swinging in the tree.

"Oh little monk, I will get you something special today!" she said this morning as the little monk patiently stood at her door. The smell of something delicious wafts out to the little monk, and he takes a big sniff, stopping himself as he remembered the teaching that food could be enjoyed mindfully, but to never be greedy with food. Taking a big long smell seemed sensual and greedy to the little monk. Still, he looked forward to this food. Using a ladle, the woman didn't

199

notice that the stew was too hot for the alms bowl.

"Ow!" cried the little monk as he struggled to keep from dropping the bowl as it burned his hands.

"Oh my! I am so sorry! Here, here! Let me give you a towel!"

The towel was wet and slippery from soap. Now the little monk shifted the bowl crazily in his hands trying again to keep from dropping it. The women starts to laugh and soon Bhante Sujatha joins in. They smile at each other as the little monk hands her back the soapy towel, saying, "Now you are even with me for the mango juice!"

"I dreamed about that woman one night, Mary," says Bhante. I hadn't thought about her in years, and I dreamed about the time I was in the mango tree. The next morning, my mother called me to tell me the woman died. I think maybe she was thinking about me before she died. We had some kind of karmic connection, you know? I really loved her."

The little monk wants to tell a story as he eats. He wants to relax and walk around a little. He misses talking with his family. Obeying the rule to be silent, he releases his pent up energy by playfully poking the young monk sitting beside him in the ribs, making the monk smile a little and poke him back.

"Hey!" says Bhante Dhammawasa. "Hey you! Stop that!"

Both of the little monks hold in their laughter, trying as hard as they can to stare down at their food and eat slowly and mindfully. By the third bite both of the young boys spit food out as they burst into laughter.

"What in the world? You two, separate! NOW!"

Bhante Sujatha stands up and moves down to the other end of the line of monks, walking as slowly as he can. Of course, once a

200

young boy starts to laugh it spreads and soon all of them are giggling, holding their bowls, shoulders shaking.

Bhante Dhammawasa can't help but smile. The sound of the laughter is like music in the quiet hall. In his wisdom as a senior monk, he knows that joy is fleeting, and so he lets the boys have a minute or two of fun before he stands up and corrects them.

"Please! We must be mindful! This food is brought to us as a result of hard work. We cannot disregard those efforts by eating without awareness. Let's all take a breath and be silent as we eat!"

Bhante Sujatha senses he must set an example and goes back to mindful eating, staring into his bowl, eating slowly and carefully, doing his best to be a good little monk. The other young monks follow his lead, and Bhante Dhammawasa thinks to himself that the little monk will be a great leader one day.

Lunch at the temple is brought in and prepared by lay people from the village. Again the monks eat together mindfully and silently. The little monk eats this meal as slowly as he can, knowing he will not eat again until breakfast the next morning.

The little monk knows that his concentration should be better when he follows the Buddha's teaching about not eating after noon. But for him, hunger has always been a distraction. His vision blurs and his head hurts as the day wears on. Usually the sweet night tea helps, and he can study his Pali and Sanskrit with a clear head.

"Bhante," I ask, "Do you think your illness might have been caused or at least exacerbated by that way of eating? It just doesn't seem very healthy to me." Bhante Sujatha looks down and smiles. "No, no, I don't think so." He looks up, making sure I get this. "No, I was hungry sometimes, that's all."

I realize that Bhante Sujatha accepts his illness as his kamma. The reason for it does not matte

201

Chapter Twenty-Two

The Gift

The little monk adapts well to temple life. He likes to study and he sits in his sleeping area at night, studying his Pali and Sanskrit, leaning over and writing on paper on top of a book in his lap or laying down and writing on the floor. As the Buddha said, we cannot stop our desires, and soon the little monk imagines a table with a chair for his studies. He pictures himself sitting comfortably, studying for hours while he occasionally sips a cup of tea, sitting near a teapot on the desk in just the right place.

Down by the river one morning, he talks with Heenbanda who has sold the family dairy cows and is hard at work building a workshop on the land he has cleared near the river where the little monk's special resting place sat so long ago. Heenbanda is in the river, rinsing the tools he is using to plaster the walls of the workshop.

Sunshine is sprinkling down on the river through the trees, highlighting drops of water on the little monk's head as he makes his way over by his father, trailing his hands in the cool water as he walks. He laughs a little to himself, remembering that stubborn cow and his swims in the river with the huge animals.

Heenbanda watches his son, feeling so happy that he and Lalitha allowed him to become a monk. Bhante Sujatha moves through the water with the grace of a diligent practitioner now, and Heenbanda is moved by his presence. As the little monk approaches, Heenbanda bows as deeply as possible three times, paying him great respect.

The little monk smiles at his father and tells him about his musings last night. "I would just love a table and a chair, father. Perhaps my uncle could build me one. It is tiring to sit on the floor and study, and I think I could learn more if I had a comfortable place to sit and read and write."

Heenbanda readily agrees to ask his brother. He is so happy to be able to help his son that he forgets that Bhante Dhammawasa is now the little monk's father, and that this request should be made of him. The little monk and his father part ways, bowing to each other in the water as they leave. Heenbanda wants to hug his son of course, but he knows that his little boy wears the robes of the Buddha now, and touching him would be disrespectful to the great Siddhartha.

Bhante's uncle is very happy to build a table, and within a few weeks, he happily goes with Heenbanda to deliver his present to the little monk, who jumps up and down and claps in happiness, reminding Heenbanda and his brother of the little boy they loved.

In his enthusiasm, burdened by desire, the little monk forgets his teachings and runs to get Bhante Dhammawasa who is in the kitchen, counting the dishes for a big temple celebration the next day. He and Mrs. Attharagama are shaking their heads and smiling as they joke about the little monk's habit of throwing the broken pieces into the jungle.

"Bhante! Bhante! I am so excited! You will be so pleased when you see what my uncle has made for me! I will be able to study harder and learn more. Oh, come, and Mrs. Attharagama, you should come too!"

Bhante Dhammawasa takes a breath, accepting his role as the little monk's only teacher and father. He tells Mrs. Attharagama to keep working in the kitchen and follows the little monk to the front of the temple where Bhante Sujatha, his father and his uncle stand together, smiling, in front of a beautiful little table and chair, exactly the right size for the little monk. There is even a special indentation on the top for his teapot and cup.

Heenbanda and his brother bow to the ground three times as Bhante Dhammawasa approaches and thanks them for their respect.

"Of course, you know we cannot accept this table."

The little monk looks up at his beloved teacher, surprise and hurt showing on his face. He looks to his father, silently pleading with him to defend his beloved son.

Heenbanda frowns, looking at his son, knowing he must support Bhante Dhammawasa in his efforts to train the little monk in following the precepts.

"My son, did you ask permission for this table?"

Bhante Sujatha's smile fades, realizing his mistake. He looks down at the ground, tears welling up in his eyes. He is silent, not wanting to let the men know he is on the verge of crying.

 Heenbanda is a good man and has great respect for Bhante Dhammawasa. Even though he was heartbroken when his son left his home to become a monk, he knows that interfering with kamma and the wise choices of a senior monk will not afford him happiness in this life or the next.

"I think you need to apologize to my brother who worked so hard on this table and chair for you. If he had known that you did not receive permission from your teacher, he could have worked on his own project in that time. Now he has come all this way to offer you the fruits of his labor and you cannot accept his gift."

Bhante Sujatha sighs, caught between being a furious, hurt little boy and a monk in training.

He turns to Bhante Dhammawasa.

"Can I accept this table, with your permission? My uncle has worked so hard, and he has carried the table and the chair all this way with my father. I will use it to learn more so I can become a wise monk. Please, my wise teacher, grant me this wish, so that my father and my uncle will not be hurt."

Bhante Dhammawasa folds his hands in the prayer position and quiets his mind for a moment. He clasps his fingers together and holds them at his waist, comfortable with his choice.

"No, of course not. You cannot learn this lesson if I allow you to have this table, which you requested without my permission. In order to teach you to become a monk, I must have respect as your father in this regard. This is an opportunity for you to learn the consequences of careless behavior and attachment. No, I will not allow you to have a table to study at this temple. You will sit on the floor while you are here, and you will learn the materials you are given. The inconvenience and pain of sitting on the floor will remind you of the importance of right speech, right action, right attitude and right view. Your violation is a gift that will teach you the precepts well."

Bhante Dhammawasa looks over at Heenbanda and his brother.

"You have also disregarded the precepts in your actions. Bhante Sujatha is still a young boy, only 12 years old. As his father before me, you knew to ask permission to bring this gift to the temple. Now your brother will suffer, carrying his beautiful work back home where it will not be useful to his family. This is a gift for you as well, a lesson that can remind you about right view and right actions. Thank you for this useful lesson for my student and his family."

The little monk is so sad that he cannot sit in the comfortable chair and study on the sturdy table, and he feels the pain of desire and ignorance, the cause of all suffering according to the great Buddha.

Desire, defined as a craving for pleasure, material goods and immortality, can never be satisfied. Then, without cultivating our minds through the practice of study and meditation, we are left ignorant, unable to grasp the nature of things. We cannot see the world as it really is.

This desire and ignorance lead to greed, envy, hatred and anger, which cannot be expressed mindfully.

The little monk tears up with his sadness and takes the hand of his teacher offered to him with compassion. Bhante Dhammawasa squats down in front of the little monk, looking into his eyes.

"My precious student, this lesson will be so valuable. It has been an opportunity to demonstrate my compassion and wisdom as your teacher. I am grateful for this event. The table is an object, nothing more. You do not need it and your attachment to it will distract you from practicing mindfulness, which would take you away from your good kamma. I agreed to help you end the cycle of your existence in your ordination, do you remember? I want to walk the path to enlightenment and nirvana with you. This event is helping us move towards that light."

Heenbanda is humbled by the wise teacher's words. He will carry the table and chair for his generous brother and somehow compensate him for his efforts.

As they leave the temple, Heenbanda and the little monk are forever changed by this lesson. Heenbanda's respect for the little monk's teacher is so great that he will never think of failing to ask permission or paying his respect to this great man.

"You know, Mary, my parents are happy with my success. I like to help them, and I took them all over India on a great trip. We travel comfortably and see all the sights. At the end of the trip, my mother thanks me, and I like that. But my father, he never thanks me, even once. He says to me, I am so grateful to your teacher. Please let him know that.

"When my parents come to the Blue Lotus Temple to celebrate Visakha Day, my father stands up and acknowledges my teacher,

not me."

"How do you feel about this?" I ask.

"I don't know. I feel good, I guess. I do. I feel good."

When I interview Bhante Dhammawasa by Skype, he doesn't remember the incident with the table. He tells me it is his character to forget things. He smiles as he shares this with me, saying, "It is not important to remember so much. It can lead to attachment. It is good to forget."

It is good to forget. All of this, I can see, enhances humility in these monks, the happiest people I have ever met. I wonder with all of our pictures and possessions and diplomas and other markers of our lives and our children's lives, are we just making egos bigger and harder to control?

Do any of us remember to forget once in awhile? To let go of our attachments, even to our achievements and our good fortune and our hard word? We are taught to learn from our past and remember our mistakes and our victories. What if we deliberately forgot? Maybe forgetting is useful sometimes. It is a big experience for me to consider ways of being that enhance mindfulness, humility and loving kindness, rather than material success or personal satisfaction. Bhante Dhammawasa tells me that forgetting helps to create a beginners mind. In order to see the present moment as it really is, we must let go of the moment before this one.

Chapter Twenty-Three

Justice

An unfamiliar slapping sound wakes the fourteen-year-old little monk, who is sleeping fitfully in his new residence. He has been sent from the comfortable and familiar Subodharama temple to this school under construction, headed up by Bhante Muditha. The slapping sound is being made as a robe flaps open and closed on the hole in the wall that will one day be a window. The little monk swats at a mosquito buzzing around his face, already feeling the day's heat seeping into his pores. His index finger is wet as it brushes against his sweaty cheek while he fends off the persistent mosquito.

Sitting up in the dim moonlight, the little monk sighs. He unconsciously tugs at his ear as he thinks about Bhante Muditha and this school in Kandy. He is a young man now and ready for this rigorous training. Bhante Dhammawasa also felt that his young student would benefit from the company of other monks. Forty-nine other monks are sleeping in the dhamma hall with the little monk, and he feels crowded this morning.

The little monk mindfully stops swatting at the mosquito, being careful not to harm another being. After a few furious attempts at diving into the little monk's ear, the mosquito gives up and flies away at the same time the air stills outside and the robe stops flapping. Breathing in the silence, the little monk smiles—he is happy to have his training with him in this new experience.

"I know we all say practice when we refer to meditation, and of course, it is important to practice meditation. But I would like all of you to listen to this story."

208

It is Saturday morning in Illinois, and I am happy to be sitting on a chair in the Blue Lotus Temple, listening to Bhante Sujatha give the dharma talk. He has just returned from a month long trip to Sri Lanka, and the entire community seems relieved to have him back. I am learning that this feeling indicates an attachment, and I doing my best to be mindful about my joy at seeing him again.

Bhante Sujatha starts the dharma talk.

A man is on his way to his loving kindness meditation practice at his temple. On the way there, he walks by several tents in a poor community where people do not have enough money for homes. A man cries out for help as the practitioner passes his tent.

'"Help me! Help me! I must have water!'

The man, who will be late for his meditation if he stops, replies, 'I am so sorry, my friend, but I am on my way to my loving kindness meditation. I will get you some water on the way back.'

'Oh no!' the thirsty man cries out. 'Please don't leave me! I am dying and I am so thirsty! Please!'

The practitioner, already near the door of the temple, doesn't even hear these last words. At the end of his meditation he asks the monk for a container of water for a thirsty man he passed. The monk quickly provides water to the man and admonishes him for missing the chance to practice loving kindness on the way to the temple. The practitioner tells the monk that he did not want to be late for the meditation and that he is committed to practicing loving kindness.

"My friend,' says the monk, 'you are not practicing loving kindness in this meditation. You are training yourself to practice loving kindness. By passing the thirsty man's tent without stopping, you demonstrated attachment to this meditation practice. I forbid you to come here until you practice loving kindness every day for 90 days.'

The man thanks the monk for his wise lesson and leaves the temple. He stops at the tent of the thirsty man, and calls out. 'I am here now! I have water for you!'

Hearing only silence he opens the flap, peers into the tent, and finds the man dead.

The practitioner has learned the true meaning of practice. He commits to using his meditation to train his mind to practice loving kindness whenever he can."

Sitting in the silence, wishing himself and Bhante Muditha to be happy, well, and peaceful, the little monk grows sleepy. As he thinks about the wise way that Bhante Dhammawasa taught him to practice loving kindness meditation on difficult people, he lies back down on his sleeping mat and falls fast asleep.

When the little monk arrived at the school yesterday, Bhante Dhammawasa reassured Bhante Muditha that the little monk was always up on time, and it would be good training for him to be assigned the task of waking his brother monks for practice the next morning.

Sunlight is flooding the room when Bhante Muditha enters, shocked when he sees the little monk snoring on his sleeping mat.

"Ow!" shouts the little monk as Bhante Muditha grabs his ear, pulling it until Bhante Sujatha stands up all the way.

"Meet me in the practice room when you are dressed!" he shouts as he walks purposefully out of the room, leaving the little monk standing alone in the room with all of his brother monks who have now missed their morning practice.

The shout and the sunlight cause the other monks to awaken, and they start to talk to each other, saying that Bhante Sujatha let them down and now they will be in trouble. One monk says he did not want to miss practice today and that he might disrobe in his embarrassment.

"I don't want to be in trouble anymore," he says, as he sighs, frowning while he rubs his ear.

Hearing this, Bhante Sujatha feels sorry. He wants to help this monk to stay at the school. If he disrobes, it will represent bad kamma for both of them.

The little monk says he is sorry that he overslept and tells them to dress quickly. A few students grab their garments off the open window, letting the heat and the insects flood into the room. The students shake the morning dew and clinging insects off of their robes before donning this symbol of the Buddha. It would seem that this practice might be disrespectful to the robes, but the Buddha would agree that using their robes as nighttime windows so that their brother monks can sleep peacefully is a meritorious act.

As the monks dress and talk the little monk pays special attention to the young monk who talked about disrobing, concerned that his action of over sleeping might have turned the boy away from the monkhood.

In this school there is a principal who works under Bhante Muditha making sure the school is run properly and that the students are learning the lessons they will need to graduate. This is a middle school, and after this training many of the monks will go to colleges in the area. Education is a top priority for monks in training.

When the students arrive in the Dhamma Hall, the principal and Bhante Muditha are waiting there. The little monk stands near the student who was distraught over getting into trouble again.

Bhante Muditha, in his deepest voice, talks first.

"So, Bhante, do you have a reason for sleeping late and missing our practice this morning?"

The little monk cannot stay silent.

211

"I think you should leave him alone! We are all tired all the time! We don't eat enough here and our beds are uncomfortable! In my temple we had windows at least, and no one ever pulled my ear!"

The principal steps up besides Bhante Muditha. In his hand he has a swatting stick, a flexible wooden piece as long as his forearm, easy to whip down on a hand or a buttocks.

"Hold your hand out!"

The young monk folds his arms in defiance.

"No!"

Bhante Muditha grabs his ear, and the young monk cries out.

"Okay! Okay! I will hold my hand out!"

Snap! Swish! The stick snaps on the back of the student's hand, and he bites his lip to keep from crying.

Bhante Sujatha watches as the principal chides the student, telling him not to disrespect the senior monk again.

"If I see something unfair, I say something, you know? I don't care! I always have to say something!"

Bhante Sujatha tells me this after temple service one day when I ask him to clarify an event in the book.

"I think being quiet when you see an injustice is wrong! In fact, I think it is worse than the injustice. If you say nothing, you are a big part of the problem. We must speak. Buddha talked about right speech; sometimes we speak too much and sometimes we speak too little. When we see something wrong and we say nothing, we are really saying something. We are saying that injustice is acceptable. That is NOT right speech!"

212

The young monk hangs his head in despair, and Bhante Sujatha becomes concerned that he might disrobe. The student is a good practitioner, and Bhante Sujatha does not want him to go back into the cycle of existence by disrobing.

The little monk speaks up. "That was unfair! It is not his fault that he overslept! It is mine. He is having a hard time today! You can see that! Do you want a monk to disrobe?"

"Hold out your hands!" says the principal, red-faced with anger.

"I can hold out my hands all day, and you can hit them. Just leave the young monk alone!"

With that, Bhante Sujatha holds out his trembling hands and feels the sting as they are swatted with the stick. Although he has learned compassion and gentleness from Lalitha and Bhante Dhammawasa, Bhante Sujatha has a tough core, like his father. The little monk cannot stand to see someone treated badly. He knows that it was unfair to blame the other monk for his mistake, and he thinks that Bhante Muditha and the principal will be responsible if the student disrobes. His anger numbs him to pain. He does not even flinch, no matter how hard the principal slaps the stick against his hand and wrist. "I will not stand for this kind of unfairness. I will not," he thinks to himself as he looks peacefully at the principal. Showing emotions usually results in trouble, so the little monk doesn't say anything about his real thoughts. Heenbanda was a good teacher to his son, demonstrating compassion and control.

When the punishments are over, Bhante Muditha and the principal are kind and gentle again. Of course, being Buddhist monks, they do not practice resentment or carry grudges. They let go quickly, moving on to the next moment and the next, never carrying the past with them.

I am talking with Bhante San in the basement of the Blue Lotus Temple.

213

"San, when you make an error or do something wrong like eat after 11:30 or if someone offends you, do you practice forgiveness?"

"Forgiveness? No, there is nothing ever to forgive really. All of our actions affect our own kamma only. We do meet once a week and tell our brother monks if we did something, so that we can make up our merits. You know, if I ate after 11:30, maybe I would be responsible to clean the dishes for a week. We let go quickly. We don't stay angry or guilty."

There is a classic Buddhist tale that illustrates this concept well

Two monks are at the bank of a river, debating the meaning of the word enlightenment. As they stand there talking, a young woman comes up to them, distressed by the height of the river, afraid to cross it.

One of the monks offers to carry her, and she accepts. The monk picks her up, carries her in his arms across the river and sets her down when they reach the other side.

He and his brother monk walk together for a few miles and finally, the brother monk can't help himself from expressing his feelings.

"My friend, what were you thinking? How could you pick up a woman and carry her all the way across a river? You know that is against the rules! Why, we are not even allowed to touch a woman and you carry a woman in your arms?"

The monk who carried the woman is silent for a few minutes. He speaks calmly.

"My dear friend, I put the woman down many miles back. Why are you still carrying her?"

Bhante Sujatha devises a plan to let the principal know that he was unfair and should quit his job as the principal. After the monks leave for alms collection, and the principal and the senior monks take their daily walk to the Bodhi tree for conversation and meditation, the little monk sneaks into the principal's office. Using paper and a pen he finds in the desk, he fashions a sign that says, "You are not fit to sit here," and tapes it on the principal's chair.

When the principal finds the note, he calls the monks to assemble in the dhamma hall, asking who wrote the note. Bhante Sujatha does not say a word.

"So, you know, years later the principal monk is living at the temple in Australia, and I finally tell him.

"'Do you remember that note on your chair?'

"'Yes,' he says, 'Yes, I do! I still don't know who wrote that!'

"I tell him it was me and he says you are kidding me! No way! Oh, my friend, I should have known! You were always standing up for people. Oh this is so funny!

"And we laughed so hard, you know? We still laugh about it even now.

"You know, people think we are so serious—and we meditate and we are quiet—but we are mostly so happy. We laugh all the time. If you ever come to see us, you will almost always hear us laughing or see us smiling. We are so happy."

Chapter Twenty-Four

Adventures of a Young Monk

The little monk is feeling playful. He loves drama and plays. A television station has been started up the hill from the temple, and Bhante Sujatha really wants to see it.

He waits until Bhante Muditha and the principal are busy preparing themselves for a temple celebration and asks his brother monks a question.

"Would you like to go on an adventure?"

"An adventure?"

"Yes, an adventure! We can go listen to a television show! We can do it tonight! Wouldn't you like to hear a real show? "

With an infectious smile and a playful heart, the little monk attracts his brother monks to his crazy idea.

"Okay," they respond. "We will go with you! But what if we get caught?"

Bhante Sujatha smiles. "Oh, you see, we won't! Our teachers are busy tonight! We will be there and back before they are done! Let's go!"

The four young monks leave their sandals on the dhamma hall floor and take off up the hill, barefoot so they can move faster. They look like little ladies, holding their robes up as they run up the hill, Bhante Sujatha encouraging them, breathing hard as he barks commands.

"Come on everybody! Hurry or we will miss the show! You can do it! Come on!"

"You can do it, my friend, you can do it!" Bhante Sumana, the youngest monk at the Blue Lotus temple is offering encouragement to me, as I confess my fears about finishing this biography.

Bhante Sumana smiles at me. "Bhante Sujatha always reminds us of this. He says this to me when I am tired. 'You can do it! You can!'"

"Now I say it to you, Mary. You. Can. Do. It!" I hear Bhante Sumana's voice in my head every time I want to quit. I can do it! I tell myself, I can!

The monks have so much fun visiting the station. They are allowed to sit on a bench and listen to a western show about cowboys and Indians.

Sitting close to each other, swinging their feet back and forth and giggling, they whisper to each other behind cupped hands.

Sooner than they want the show is over, and Bhante Sujatha reminds his brother monks that they must hurry back, so that the senior monks don't find them gone. They skip back down the path to the temple, sharing their excitement with one another.

"Bang bang! What a gunfight!" says a young monk. They laugh and talk in the dark, skipping down the hill to the temple.

The little monk is feeling quite sure of himself, certain that no one will see them on this dark path. He skips along, telling a brother monk that he always wanted to be an actor if he didn't become a monk, when something hits him in the head.

"Ahhhh!!!!" he screams. "What was that?? I think a snake has bit my head?"

Bhante Muditha, hiding in the dark, cannot stifle his laughter. "Oh, my little monk! Oh, that was so funny."

The little monk turns and sees his teacher, white teeth gleaming on the dark path, holding a thick vine in one hand. Bhante Muditha wipes a tear from his eyes and stops laughing after a few minutes. He straightens up and looks sternly at the young monks, remembering that he is their teacher.

"Now! All of you! I will see you in the dharma hall!"

The young monks scramble together down the path, anxious to get to the temple and find out what punishment will be meted out for their crime. One of the monks, the youngest in the group, confesses his fear as he breathlessly follows Bhante Sujatha into the dhamma hall.

"I am going to hide! I cannot get in so much trouble. Goodbye!"

The little monk wants to tell his friend that he should stay with them, but by the time he is finished gathering his robes around him properly, the younger monk has disappeared.

"This was so funny. I see this little monk, a few hours later, sleeping curled up in a little ball in the dining hall. O my gosh, he was so cute!"

Bhante Muditha laughs heartily and I have a hard time imagining him being tough. He has been just wonderful during this interview.

All of the monks got hit with the stick on a regular basis. Their ears were painfully pulled. Now this seems abusive, but it was normal practice at monasteries. None of the senior monks ever carried their anger past the punishment.

The little monk's days are filled with meditation, chanting and studying. He loves collecting alms and visiting the people in the village when monks visit people and chant blessings or help them.

Bhante Sujatha stays at the school run by Bhante Muditha for 3 years, learning valuable lessons from his toughest teacher.

"I think I have found the middle path in teaching now. I got the practice of being tough from my father and Bhante Muditha. Bhante Dhammawasa taught me to be gentle. I think you need both, you know?"

Bhante Sujatha tells me this when I ask him about his gentle ways now as compared to his tough teachings then. I have talked with the monks at the Blue Lotus Temple about their past experiences. I know that they were afraid of Bhante Sujatha's punishments when they were young monks in Sri Lanka.

Chapter Twenty-Five

College at the Subodharama Temple

Over time, Bhante Dhammawasa becomes concerned about the monks under his tutelage. He knows they must go to college and become educated in the Buddhist teachings and the Pali language. He does not want to send these precious young men, raised under his gentle and wise hand, out into Colombo or another college where they might fall prey to outside influences and learn wrong ideas or even disrobe. The venerable teacher is particularly protective of Bhante Sujatha, the little monk who was the first student at his temple so long ago. Bhante Muditha and Bhante Dhammawasa agree that the little monk would be well served by an education at the Subodharama temple. They work together tirelessly while the little monk is at the school run by Bhante Muditha to obtain credentials to add secondary school and college to current recognition of the Subodharama temple as a primary school for monks.

Because of his wonderful teachers, Bhante Sujatha is the first student to register officially into the college for monks at the Subodharama Temple, also known as the International Bikkhu Training Center, now respected all over the world.

The interplay between Bhante Dhammawasa's gentle ways and Bhante Muditha's tough, yet loving style made for an extraordinary educational experience for any monk lucky enough to attend this training center.

Bhante Sujatha's higher, more permanent ordination occurs when he is 20 years old. By now his parents are comfortable with their son's life choice, and they are able to enjoy the beautiful ceremony, proud of their son's accomplishments as a young monk and teacher. The Subodharama temple now has about 50 monks being taught there.

Lalitha, reflecting on the little monk's path, is often grateful to Heenbanda for being strong enough to allow her son to walk down the path to his dreams. Manel has married and is expecting her second child at the time of Bhante Sujatha's higher ordination.

Heenbanda has never stopped working, and he has moved far from the days of living in the small mud house. Now the family owns a workshop on the same land that he cleared for Bhante Sujatha's special resting place near the Mahaweli River, and Manel works their part-time, helping her father sell the steel tools and other items he forges in the workshop. The dairy cows were sold a few years after the little monk left for the temple, and often Manel and her father sit together near the river and remember those magical times. Manel knows her sons will have a different path as the areas around her are deforested now and the small mud huts are gone, replaced by Western Style houses.

She is reassured by the Buddhist teachings, remembering as she watches the river flow by her, that life is comparable to that river. Her life and the life of her family and others is not a continuous flow, although it can appear that way. Life is actually a series of moment-by-moment choices, karmic actions that are beneficial or harmful. Each moment is separate from the one before and the one after and each moment offers a choice for better or worse kamma.

It is considered ignorance to think that an old woman, a young woman, a mother and a grandmother are the same person. Ignorant minds do not see the continual change and impermanence of all things

Chapter Twenty-Six

Students

It's dark in the Dhamma Hall. Bhante San holds a finger up to his lips, showing gleaming white teeth in the dark as he smiles. "Shhhh!" the young monk says to the smaller monk with him. They are both starving. San stumbles on a piece of pottery, undoubtedly broken off earlier that day when 22 year old Bhante Sujatha, his junior teacher, dropped a bowl as he quickly cleaned the kitchen before their afternoon meal. Bhante San's teacher was a cleaning fanatic. To the young monk it was unreasonable the way he forced them to make their beds perfectly and clean their rooms before practice in the morning. The monks shivered when they heard the little monk's sandals slap briskly against the floor as he made his way to their rooms every morning. The sound reminded San of gunshots. Like many young monks at that time, San had grown up in a time of terrorism. He was all too familiar with the sound of gunshots.

As his stomach rumbles painfully, San steps back from the broken pottery, quickly inspecting his foot for blood. Other than a small cut near his heel, he finds no cuts that might leave a bloody footprint, a tell tale sign of his crime.

Walking on his toes now to avoid leaving a bloody heel print on the floor, he guides his young accomplice to pick up the broken pottery and throw it out the kitchen door, flinging it far into the jungle down the hill.

The moment the pottery piece starts to fly down the hill, Bhante San feels fear added to the rumblings in his stomach as he considers whether Bhante Sujatha will notice that the pottery piece has been picked up and thrown away. Sometimes it seems the senior monks know so much that San and his brother monks in training feel tricked.

Sighing, San directs his young friend to the large alms bowl on the counter. Several of the monks were at Bhante Muditha's school today, leaving leftovers after breakfast. Bhante San tiptoes with his friend over to the bowl and peers inside. He remembers when this food repulsed him.

"That was before I was starved every day after lunch!" he thinks as he reaches his hand into the bowl, taking a big handful of food and stuffing it into his mouth. The younger monk watches him, and Bhante San picks up the heavy bowl and holds it lower than the counter so his friend can grab a scoop. They both grab two more large scoops, hungrily shoving the food into their mouths and smiling at each other, forgetting all about mindful eating.

Bhante San thinks that Bhante Sujatha is sleeping, but he is actually not in the temple or the sleeping area. The little monk has made his way up the hill again to his friend Upolu's hut. Upul is now teaching at the Subodharama School, and they now have 20 monks being educated there. Bhante Sujatha is known for his disciplined rigor about cleaning and chores at the temple.

Bhante Sujatha often snuck out of the temple after dark to see his good friend Upul. They would study the dhamma teachings together, often getting sidetracked, dissecting a word or a phrase that moved them. Tonight they had discussed enlightenment, and both had arrived at the conclusion that enlightenment was simple and impossible. Bhante Sujatha decided it meant just happiness.

He shrugged his shoulders and smiled, yawning as he said, "My friend, isn't is it just simple happiness, improved upon by wisdom and loving kindness? Is being happy the only real state of enlightenment?"

Upul smiled at this. "Yes, I think so, my friend. I do. Happiness is not so easy to attain though, especially with the constant suffering."

"Yes, suffering is constant. But don't you think that all life can be happiness when we know all life is suffering? Isn't that enlightenment, when we know we have a choice?"

Sometimes they talked all night, leaving the little monk asleep in Upul's hut, waking up near 4:30 am and running down the dark hill to the temple.

"It could be so dark, you know? But I know this path so well. I know it by heart. I can run down it in bare feet and never trip or anything. I know every rock and muddy part and plant and bump." Bhante Sujatha smiles, remembering.

"Have you ever known anything this well? I think being familiar with something is a wonderful experience, you know? I like that. Then, of course, like all people, the minute I am comfortable, I want to change. It's funny, this life, you know?"

I do know. I want a familiar life again. I seem to be on a new path every minute since I started writing this book. I am never comfortable.

The concept of annica is a fundamental difference between Buddhist philosophy and other eastern and western religions. There is not a fixed point of reference, an unchanging God or condition, in Buddhism. Annica describes impermanence and this nonstop change is an undeniable and inescapable fact of human existence. Nothing, no human or any life form, can escape Annica. All humans go through five processes, growing old, falling sick, dying, decay in things that are perishable and the passing away of that which is liable to pass.

Escape from these processes is described as nirvana, the ultimate state of being to which Buddhists aspire in their practices.

"Tomorrow we will re-study the 8th precept!"

Upul smiles at his young friend, so small in the darkened doorway. He shakes his head as he considers the astounding mental prowess of this small man, known as the little monk by so many. Upul often remarks that he has never seen a monk study harder than Bhante Sujatha. He wonders if it was his father or Bhante Muditha that gave him this ability to discipline himself so well. When other monks were joking around or distracting themselves instead of studying, Bhante Sujatha was having fun studying—diving deeper and deeper into the Buddhist concepts until he had the simplest interpretation, available to anyone in the world.

"Happy, well, and peaceful."

The little monk silently hurries his way down the dark hill back to the temple, arriving at the door to the kitchen just as Bhante San's young friend tosses a banana peel carelessly towards the door, laughing as he exclaims in a loud whisper, "San, my dear friend! Thank you! That was delicious! Thank you! Woo hooo!" They are both laughing, until the little monk's foot shows up in the doorway, followed by his robe, then a small hand holding the banana peel the younger monk just threw.

Bhante Sujatha steps into the kitchen, staring at San. Dropping the banana peel back on the floor, the little monk issues a stark command. "Whoever threw this banana peel, pick it up now."

The younger monk starts to take a step towards his teacher, relieved.

He leans over to pick up the yellow brown offender when the little monk tells him to stop.

"Not with your hands, my friend. Pick it up with your mouth."

Bhante San is so unhappy in this moment. He feels so bad for the younger monk who was just trying to relieve his hunger and have a little fun. San cannot understand the purpose of so much discipline and suffering. He is tired of so many rules.

The younger monk kneels before Bhante Sujatha and picks up the disgusting peel with his mouth, swallowing down his bile as he stands up with the banana peel in his mouth.

"You feel embarrassed and foolish? Of course you do, and that is the way you will feel when you leave a mess or disrespect the precepts and the rules of your monk community. You will feel like you do right now, do you understand?"

The younger monk, tears streaming down his cheeks, nods in agreement. Bhante Sujatha ignores his obvious discomfort and tells San and the younger monk that they are to clean the bathrooms together, every day, for the next month.

"You must learn the consequences of leaving a mess. You can learn to be mindful of the dirt you create. Cleaning bathrooms is a wonderful path to letting go of your ego, to smashing your ideas of yourself as somehow separate."

"Now, you may keep the banana peel in your mouth until morning time. I do not want you to forget this. San, you may hold out your palms please."

Bhante San knows what is coming. The stinging slap of the cane that the little monk carries, always buried in his robes, whipping it out whenever he sees the need for discipline. Bhante Sujatha takes a deep breath and raises his cane, bringing it down hard on Bhante San, feeling pain is his heart as he hits his student, accepting the pain he feels and the pain his student feels as a part of the path of learning to be a good monk.

Cleaning the bathrooms at the school was a bigger chore than cleaning a Western Bathroom. The monks used small bunches of coconut hair and wore plastic bags, which tore easily, on their hands in lieu of modern rubber gloves. Bars of soap, hard to maneuver,

226

were used to create lather. The soap was difficult to rinse off.

Bhante Sumana is giving the dhamma talk at the temple. He is just mastering English and his refreshing, kind and wide perspective is a welcome addition to the Saturday morning service at the temple.

"You know, when I first started meditation, I did not understand it at all. In fact, I got comfortable in my sitting posture, and I fell asleep. For three years," Bhante Sumana says emphasizing the three, "THREE years! I woke up at 4:30 and practiced for two hours in the morning and then two hours at night. We would do one hour and a half meditation and a half hour chanting, you see? So I was tired!"

The sangha laughs, many shaking their heads in appreciation of this monk and his authentic sharing. There are many newcomers today, and this is the first time they have ever heard a monk speak.

"Well, you know, I saw people as separate, you know? In Sri Lanka, there are lower and higher castes. I come from a higher caste, and so I see people as separate, different. You know, lower castes, they sit on the floor in people's houses, they are not allowed on chairs and sometimes they must stay outside. People talk about me. They say, 'that guy, he's no good. He's not so nice. He talks down to the people; he won't help lower caste people.' One day, I really want to change, you know, so I talk with my teacher.

"He is confused, of course. He cannot understand how I can practice 3 hours every day for years and still feel separate, still have so much judgment. I break down and tell him the truth that I am sleeping or thinking all the time, that I am the worst meditator ever."

We all laugh, enraptured by this charming tale. I am especially happy as I know that this story will fit into the biography, helping to fulfill the mission assigned to this book by Bhante Sujatha, to fill people with joy

"So, my teacher, he smiles at me and says he knows exactly what I should do. He tells me, you must clean the toilets, every day for

227

three months, morning and night, after practice.

"Oh, these toilets!" says Bhante Sumana, causing someone to guffaw loudly, "they are terrible! Remember, we have over 75 monks, young and old boys sharing 6 bathrooms. They are underground. They are not like you have here, and we do not have gloves or liquid soap. We use the small bunches of coconut hair and scrub and scrub. Oh, the smell, it is so bad!"

"At first, I am so tired and unhappy, and I think to myself, what will I do? What should I do? I cannot stand this, you know?"

"But slowly, very slowly, I start to change. One day, I am teaching children in Sunday school, and I notice these three children are so quiet and shy, staying away from the group. I ask my friend, why are they separate and he tells me, they are lower caste, you see?"

"I feel my heart, and I know that this is not right. We are not separate or different. We are all human beings, all of us the same. In Sri Lanka we look at the lower and higher caste. Here you might look at black or white or young or old, but you see I start to be a nicer person. I see that loving-kindness is the only way, you know? I am so happy then, I become better at meditation and after three months of cleaning the bathrooms, I am changed. I become a better person."

The temple is silent. I am thinking about the way that monks seek to diminish rather than elevate their ego. I think of Bhante Sujatha saying over and over again, "No ego, no ego, no ego," when we talk about the book or someone pays him another compliment.

Bhante Sujatha tells the younger monk that he can take the banana peel out of his mouth and receive the slapping of the cane on his palms instead. He may choose his punishment. The younger monk spits out the banana peel, relieved, wiping his mouth with the back of his hand and resisting the urge to spit out the awful taste.

The little monk slaps his outstretched hand, working hard not to wince in sympathy when his student cries out softly.

After the punishments are done, Bhante Sujatha reminds both of them that tomorrow is their acknowledgement meeting before they go to the retreat center, so Bhante San and his friend should talk about sneaking food and making a mess.

These meetings are held weekly in the temple. The teachers and the students meet in a group and talk about the week, specifically detailing their transgressions. No one is exempt from truth telling and the consequences of any misbehavior.

The most senior monk will sometimes confess that he has eaten after noon or missed a chance to practice loving kindness. Usually the consequence is cleaning the bathrooms or the kitchens.

So Bhante Dhammawasa himself might be found scrubbing the bathrooms for a week for his own transgression. Although cleaning the bathrooms was awful for the senses, it is a common punishment or karmic task, which is considered somewhat of a gift for its great humbling effect.

Bhante San tells me he is grateful for the lessons from Bhante Sujatha. "So, you know, Mary, I don't mind so much now, you know? I am humble and clean. I am proud of the way my room looks, and I never have problems that come with leaving a mess, you know?"

229

Chapter Twenty-Seven

Retreat

The monks at the Subodharama temple wake up excited when it is a retreat day. They get out of bed quickly, joking with each other about the day and betting on two breaks for walking meditation. Walking meditation is an assignment often given to Buddhist practitioners, giving them the chance to be present to loving kindness in others or the impact of being silent while walking.

There are different methods for walking meditation. A practitioner can pay attention to the soles of his feet as he walks, noticing the ball of his foot hitting the ground and the sensation of his heel as it bounces up in the step forward. This is a great way for beginners to practice mindfulness as they meditate, allowing them a brief respite from the nonstop thinking that goes on in most of our brains while they focus on their feet.

Monks practice walking meditation as they collect alms in the morning, when they walk silently, mindfully, and slowly. The first time I try this form of meditation, I forget about my feet every other step, reminding myself to focus again and again, worrying about my lack of focus, noticing the weather, surprised at how quickly I forget my mind as I walk, making me painfully aware of my humbleness in the practice.

For the students at the Subodharama temple, walking meditation at the retreat center means the chance to run and play. The teacher monks stay in the center's meditation space while the younger monks are instructed to go on a walking meditation. The wise teachers know that the youngsters are doing the same thing they did in their youth, walking mindfully to the foot of the path up the mountain outside the center and then running and laughing all the way to the top where they play like young boys anywhere.

San and his friend quickly clean the bathrooms, laughing as they vigorously rub the coconut hair in the soap and scrub. "Faster, faster!" they say to each other. "Faster!"

After a quick breakfast, eaten silently and mindfully with no incidents, the monks clean the kitchen together and happily walk outside, skipping with enthusiasm to the waiting temple vans.

It is hot already, and San is grateful for the occasional breeze cooling his legs underneath the robes. He notices a monk that has awkwardly folded his robes the wrong way, and he stops him, tapping him gently on the shoulder. His brother monk turns to him, curious as to why San has stopped him.

"Hey, you folded your robe the wrong way. Here, let me show you the right way." Bhante San expertly helps the monk fold his robe correctly for the trip to the retreat center, led by a dear friend of Bhante Sujatha, Godwin Samarartna.

Godwin, famous for his lifelong devotion to the dhamma, attended the Subodharama Temple and enjoyed especially the teachings of Bhante Sujatha who was so enthusiastic about the dhamma and the Buddha. The little monk would often be seen arguing with a fellow monk about his interpretation of a teaching, usually in disagreement about even the smallest implication of judgment or separation. Bhante Sujatha and Bhante Dhammawasa made a habit of bringing the monks to the Nilambe retreat center in Kandy once every few months.

For his part, Godwin kept these times sacrosanct, not allowing lay people on the days the monks were in attendance. He felt that the pure presence of these monks enhanced the sacredness of his center.

Piled into the van together, hot breezes blowing through the open windows, the monks practice mindful silence, leaning forward across one another to look out the window at the passing scenery. The van ride is filled with twists and turns, often running into large bumps and kicking up so much dust that the monks cough as the dirt swirled around in the van.

The van passed through the jungle territory surrounding the temple and through the breathtaking landscape of Peradiniya University, part of the same territory that is now occupied by the revered botanic gardens in Kandy. As the van traveled higher, the tea tree plantations spread out on either side of the road as far as the eye could see.

Short green trees cover the ground for miles, looking so orderly compared to the jungles in the lowland. As the monks ride along, they can feel the cooler weather at the level of the tree plantations. Many of them would sink back in their seats, sighing with relief as the cool air of the hilly upper mountains hit their sweat-soaked, road dust dirty skin.

Pulling into the retreat center space, the van stopped in a dirt lot in front of a smooth rock outcropping, facing away from the doors of the retreat center. The saffron colored robes fluttered in the breeze as the student monks ran up the smooth cliff like rock in bare feet, slipping a little and helping each other reach the top, where they could look out at the tea tree plantations spreading for miles.

The teacher monks would wait for their students underneath the bountiful guava tree in front of the retreat center, occasionally grabbing a piece of fruit to enjoy while their students played for a few minutes.

Godwin always enjoyed these visits, welcoming the monks by graciously offering his space, cleaned and prepared especially for them.

There was no electricity at this simple retreat center. The floor was concrete, and the student monks would sit on the floor on their brought along meditation cushions in front of the senior monks and the teachers, who sat on a plain, raised platform around a modest statue of the Buddha. It could be considered a gloomy space, but the chanting and meditation that occurred there provided the light of so many people seeking and finding enlightenment as they practiced.

The monks chanted and meditated for a few hours, sitting straight and still in cross-legged seated positions. Before lunchtime the teachers smiled at each other as they instructed the young monks to embark on a walking meditation up to the top of the hill behind the retreat center.

"This is my favorite part, all of our favorite part," says Bhante San, smiling at me in the basement of the Blue Lotus Temple.

"We would not meditate at all." Bhante San has the playful grin of an imp as he describes the young monks running and pushing each other, throwing stones out into the vast landscape at the top of the mountain, yelling and having fun.

"Did Bhante Sujatha or Bhante Dhammawasa ever come up to the mountaintop and tell you to stop goofing around?"

"No," says Bhante San, shaking his head, smiling compassionately at me, "No, you see, we are Buddhist monks, you know, but we are young children, just like any children anywhere. Our teachers, they know this. They are compassionate people, you know. They are Buddhist; they know we need to use some of our energy. When we return, we slow down as the retreat center comes into view, mindfully stopping our laughter and looking serious as we come back."

The picture of these young monks bouncing along in the van, chanting and meditating in the simple and beautiful space of the lay retreat center, then playing at the top of the hill, is enthralling to me. I swear I can hear their laughter as Bhante San shares with me.

The young monks hike up their robes and start running the moment they are out of sight of their teachers at the retreat center. "Whoop! Whoop!" they holler, skidding to a stop at the top of the hill, resting for a moment while taking in the view of the tree plantations and the distant mountains and villages of Sri Lanka.

"I am the king of this hill!" shouts a young monk, playfully challenging any opponents to a fight for the kingship. Soon enough, a few monks gather around the self-proclaimed king, pushing him and knocking him back down, while one at a time they take turns flexing their muscles and puffing out their chests, looking royal and haughty as they issue joke commands.

"You! You walk all the way down and back up the hill! You clean the bathrooms every day for ten years; you bow down one hundred times and kiss my feet!" Laughter peels out over the mountain, embracing the young monks with joy and release as they push and shove their ways to being the king for a moment. An observer would notice, maybe for the first time that day, that these are children, universally engaged in the joy of the present moment like any child, anywhere.

The monks are tired and happy as they lean against each other in the van on the way home, some sleeping with their heads on their seatmate's shoulder, bouncing lightly as they rest. Godwin bows to them as they leave—giving them fresh guava and telling them he is looking forward to their next visit.

Bhante Sujatha is thoughtful on this trip back to the Subodharama temple. He is mindful of his restlessness, the familiar feeling that it is time to expand his practice and spread the message of loving kindness and meditation around the world. Sometimes he thinks about the billions of minds, polluting the world with their impure and angry thoughts, and the power of changing those minds with the practice of meditation.

A mindful world is the solution to all the problems, he thinks. There cannot be violence or resentment; families cannot be split apart by something as meaningless as money or a personality difference in a world ruled by mindfulness.

Chapter Twenty-Eight

Sumana

Back at the temple, the little monk is greeted by Bhante Sumana, the newest young monk to join the Subodharama school.

Bhante Sumana became a monk in a most unusual way. When he was 8 years old he met a monk crossing a road to board a bus. The monk was carrying a package, and Bhante Sumana, being raised in a Buddhist country, naturally offered to help the monk by carrying his package across the road for him. The monk accepted the youngster's offer and asked him if he would like to become a monk, impressed with Sumana's kindness.

Bhante Sumana was a little boy who loved to joke and tell lies and he believed that telling this monk yes would have no consequences for him. It was unlikely that he would ever see the monk again, living in a tiny mud house in a small village.

A few years later, sitting inside his house, Sumana is startled when he hears the voice of the monk from so long ago. He was just rolling his eyes as he listened to his brother complain to his mother about his harmless prank. Sumana jumped out of the woods in the dark as his brother came back from helping his father fix a gate, pretending to be a giant cobra, hissing and scaring his brother so much he ran like a wild person all the way home, sobbing and yelling.

"Yes, I am your husband's cousin," he is saying to Sumana's mother, "and your son told me he wanted to become a monk. I have come to invite him to the temple to keep his promise."

Bhante Sumana blinks his eyes in the sunlight as he comes out of the small house, pinching his own arm to wake himself from this bad dream. He smiles as he approaches the monk and his mother and brother, saying "Mother! Of course he is joking! He is not my father's cousin! He is not taking me to be a monk!"

As his mother and the monk turn to look at him—the monk with an intent gleam in his eye and his mother with tears streaming down her cheeks—the young boy realizes that this is serious.

He furrows his brow and backs up a step, putting his hands on his hips. "Mom! No! NO! Do not make me go! Of course, you will not make me go! I was joking! I was kidding, you know I always kid!"

Bhante Sumana's brother looks at him, squinting his eyes in a sneer, "See, I told you! You have to stop teasing so much, being so mean. See?"

Bhante Sumana's father returns from his work in the village and bows to the monk standing outside his modest mud home talking with his wife and sons.

"Why, hello, and how are you, cousin?"

Bhante Sumana swallows. This monk is really his father's cousin. "Father! Please! This crazy monk has come to take me away from you! All for a joke when I was little! Please tell him no!"

Bhante Sumana's father ignores his young son's cries, paying respect to the monk. "I am so sorry for my son's outburst. What is this, are you here to take him to the temple to become a monk?"

"Yes," says the monk. "Yes, he carried my bag for me when he was younger, and I asked him if he would like to be a monk. He said he would like that. He promised me if I came, he would become a monk."

Sumana stands in front of his father, young and vulnerable. His

237

mother closes her eyes and pleads silently with her husband, "Please," she thinks silently, careful not to disrespect her husband or the monk, especially in front of her sons, "Please do not say yes to this monk. Please keep our precious little boy at home. Please!"

"Well, then, my son, you must go to the temple. You must go now. You promised this kindly monk? It doesn't matter if you are joking; you have to honor that promise now. Go, get ready, you must go."

Sumana's brother stops sneering, looking at his father in disbelief, then at his mother, who is doing her best to stand straight while she lets out an involuntary sob.

Bhante Sumana realizes that his joking and lying have caught up with him. He sees that his actions, his kamma, have led him here, forced to separate from the family he loves. Sumana and his family are especially close. They had to rely on each other when their village experienced terrorism. Once Sumana woke up and found members of the village dead all around him.

Families who experience trauma like this rely on each other more than most, as they can only survive as a solid unit. Sumana tries one more time to reason with his mother and father His mother can't bear it and looks to her husband to make the final rule.

"Well," says Sumana's father, "say goodbye to your mother and brother! You are going!"

Sumana runs to his mother, hugging her around the hips, crying into her side, snot and tears running down his face. Now the little boy is panicked, clinging to his mother for comfort. His mother is a good Sri Lankan wife, earning great respect for her obedience and love for her husband. Independence is not seen as an admirable trait in women whose roles were clearly defined in Sri Lankan Buddhist culture.

She pushes Sumana away, feeling her chest tighten as she does so, hoping he will leave soon so she can break down out of his sight.

238

"You will be all right! You must listen to your father! Now go, go! You will be okay!"

Sumana cannot believe his mother is letting him go, but he knows now he is going. He hugs his brother, tearfully telling him he is sorry for his teasing, promising to be nicer if he can come back home.

His brother hugs him back, telling him he must be strong.

Much too soon the monk leads Sumana away from the only home he has ever known, the 11 year old boy trailing behind the monk, glancing back to see that his whole family has disappeared into the mud house. He feels abandoned, not knowing that his mother is on the ground in the hut now sobbing while her husband and son try to reassure her that her precious son will be safe.

The date is fixed forever in Sumana's mind. February 10, 1995. After a sleepless night, filled mostly with tears and regrets about his behavior as he tossed and turned, his father's cousin offers him a way out.

"If you study these books and memorize them in three weeks, I will let you go home."

Sumana is a smart young boy, raised in poverty by intellectual parents. He takes on the task of learning the Buddhist precepts and principles that monks usually take two years to learn before their first ordination. He studies diligently, waking up every day before 4:30, opening the book and memorizing in the early dawn, studying under the Bodhi tree after morning practice, essentially studying at least 12 hours every day. Sumana is powerfully motivated by his desire to reunite with his beloved family.

After three weeks, Sumana tells his teacher that he has memorized all three books, proving it by reciting several passages enthusiastically. The teacher smiles right back at him, happy that he was right. Bhante Sumana is as smart and kind as his father. The little boy doesn't realize this, but he has just proved to his teacher

239

that he is well equipped for ordination. Before Bhante Sumana realizes what is happening, his family is planning the party for his ordination. One month after his arrival at the temple, on March 6, 1995, he is ordained as a monk.

It takes him years to establish good practice habits, celebrating quietly the first day he stays awake during an entire 90 minute meditation, sharing his joy when he has long stretches of a quiet mind, with his new teachers at the Subodharama temple when he arrives there under the tutelage of a wise young teacher, Bhante Sujatha.

Chapter Twenty-Nine

Australia

Bhante Sujatha enjoys his life at the Subodharama Temple, but he often thinks about his wish, his mission in this life. He hopes for a chance to bring the message of loving kindness and meditation to the world.

When he is 25, he jumps at the chance to go to the temple in Australia. The monks need support and everyone knows that Bhante Sujatha's natural charisma will be an asset in any temple trying to grow.

As the little monk walks up to the living quarters in Australia, he is surprised to see a dilapidated house. Of course he has lived without comfortable furniture and spaces. His standards are not Western middle upper class standards, but by the time he went to Australia he had become a little particular about cleanliness and safety. This house did not seem comfortable or safe. The moment Bhante Sujatha enters the house, he wants to get out and see Australia. He tells the monks there that he wants to take a bus into the city of Brisbane, located about a half hour bus ride from the house.

The Australian monks do not share the vision of doing whatever it takes to teach Westerners how to be happy. They are good practitioners, happy to be leading meditation and creating a temple for people that practice Buddhism. Unlike Christianity, Buddhism is not an evangelical practice. Most Buddhists will tell you that Buddhism is not a religion at all, but a philosophy or a way of life, a method of practice that can greatly enhance happiness and improve kamma in this life. For this reason many Buddhists are reluctant to share their philosophy with Western people who might not understand it. Like the snake in the Buddhist cobra story at the beginning of this book, some monks believe that being around non-Buddhists, who might disrespect the monk, the robe or the Buddha without knowing it, is actually harmful to these people.

Bhante Sujatha's view could not be more opposite. He enjoys demonstrating and teaching the practice of meditation, the study of the dhamma and the Buddha's life, and most importantly, loving-kindness. He insists that he will take the bus to Brisbane to see Australia and that he is ready and willing to deal with the ways that Westerners might treat him. "I will be fine!" he says as he ignores their entreaties to wait until he is familiar with the Australian culture before he takes the bus into Brisbane.

"There is not so much time you know? I have to do this now. I might be sick and at any time, I could die, you know? I mean we have to hurry up! Life is short. So since I have been gifted with charisma and the kamma of being able to relate to Westerners and caring about them, I must get out there and say hello to them! How will they find out about meditation and loving kindness as a practice if I don't? Of course I know I am not the only one, but I am one of the ones to do this, and so I just think, I must do this now, not later, NOW."

The little monk, mindful of his wish to influence the Western World, tells his brother monks that he is going on the bus ride to the city and that they should not worry. As he waits for the bus in a small crowd of people, he sways a little, shifting his weight from one foot to the other, a little uncomfortable as he realizes that people are paying no attention to him other than a passing stare here and there, curious about this little man in the saffron robes. His mind is filled with thoughts about what a bad idea this is, and that he should just go back to the monks' house where they know to respect his training and his dedication to a holy life. Because the little monk practices meditation he can let these thoughts just go by and patiently observe himself struggling with being an anonymous part of a crowd who is not moved or inspired by his robes.

242

It feels like a long time to be standing there with all the English being spoken. Bhante Sujatha only understands a few words, and even the smells and the sounds are unfamiliar. Not understanding a word—smelling the unfamiliar smells, hearing the unfamiliar sounds and seeing the dusty road filled with vehicles before the bus comes. Again, the little monk is able to observe his impatience and just stay with the feeling until it passes.

John Bardi, the professor of philosophy at Penn State University, is sharing his experiences with Bhante Sujatha with me over the phone. This conversation with him is one of the most inspiring experiences of my life.

"You know, Mary, the spiritual path is hard; it takes more than most people have to give. Staying in the relationship or staying with the way you really feel, being with yourself until it passes, is hard. It's easier to go outside of yourself and seek relief from the way you feel. And you know this doesn't have to be extreme. We're not talking just about numbing out in front of a TV or overeating or indulging in some unhealthy distraction but even reading an interesting book or having an intellectual argument, painting a great painting. These are all distractions, and we only realize this when we sit with ourselves, practicing meditation, committed to experiencing just being here now—alive, just here.

"You will feel the pain of your life and that is steep price to pay for any enlightenment. Somehow, Bhante Sujatha invites Westerners, overindulged in every way, somehow he invites them to take on this tough spiritual way of life and they agree readily, happily; they take it on. He has really stripped the culture out of the Buddhist loving kindness message and offered up a pure, beautiful, life-changing opportunity for practice. It's amazing when you stop and think about it: how he has brought not so much the east to the west, but Buddhism to the West. "

As the bus screeches to a stop, the little monk reminds himself of an important Buddhist teaching. "Empty empty. Happy happy." No expectations, no suffering.

For the first time as a Buddhist monk, Bhante Sujatha experiences the humility of being ordinary in a public crowd. He is awkward as he puts his change, counted out to him by his brother monk the night before, into the machine as he enters the bus. The language spoken around him is heavily accented English, a language the little monk has never studied.

Bhante Sujatha does know three languages fluently: Pali, Sanskrit and Singhal, all difficult to master. He wishes that he had added English to his studies and tries his best to focus on the expressions and movements around him, trusting that he will know when to get off in the city and explore. His regret about English is another opportunity to practice mindfulness. Of course he does not know English. Pali and Sanskrit were important in his Buddhist studies. Bhante Sujatha can reassure himself in difficult situations because he practices loving kindness towards himself, starting every meditation by wishing himself well

"May I be well. May I be peaceful. May I be happy."

He is glad for the opportunity to be a humble beginner in the English language, with all of his studies meaningless in this circumstance. He tells himself, "No ego. No ego." He knows that absolute humility is an important part of the path to Nirvana.

The people sitting in the front seat do not get up, even when Bhante Sujatha clears his throat loudly trying to make them aware that he is a Buddhist monk. He feels his judgment creep in. The little monk is becoming aware of the culture's influence on his view of people and their way of life. In Australia, the little monk learns that Buddhism and the culture in which Buddhism is practiced are separate.

In Sri Lanka, people would immediately move out of the way and make room for a monk in the front seat. Many times they would stand on the bus, leaving the front seat empty just in case a monk boarded.

Bhante Sujatha sighs loudly and grabs onto the vertical rail behind the driver, wondering why no one would earn merits by offering him a seat. He hears the warning of his compassionate teacher, Bhante Dhammawasa, telling him that Australia is not a Buddhist country and that it might be tough on the little monk.

Closing his eyes, focusing on his breath, reminding himself that he can use this situation to practice mindfulness and no ego, he almost falls when the bus comes to a sudden stop, but he stops himself by planting his front food hard on the sticky floor. He knows his mind is in the right place when he feels compassion for people who stand on buses.

He thinks of his mother, stopping in the middle of some crisis, closing her eyes or looking down and breathing, showing her young son the way to a peaceful, happy life through diligent practice. As he struggles to stand on the rocking and rolling bus, he smiles as he thinks of Heenbanda, Lalitha and Manel and all the lessons they taught him.

At that very moment, Manel is on a bus in Sri Lanka, stumbling up against a young girl with her little brother, smiling at the little boy as she uses his knee to stop her fall. Manel sends thoughts of loving kindness to her little brother in Australia.

When the bus arrives in Brisbane, a woman swings her bag carelessly over her shoulder, hitting the little monk behind her. She hardly glances back as she laughingly joins her friend. Bhante Sujatha wonders if she is laughing about him, and then chides himself for that thought, practicing the discipline of no ego.

All day as the little monk walks around the city, people brush up against his robes with no thought about the Buddha. At a noisy intersection someone pushes him rudely from behind, in a hurry to get to their friend on the other side of the road.

On the bus ride home Bhante Sujatha is more determined than ever to make a difference in the West. He notices that there are many cars on the roads. At the bus stop he sees a woman get out of the passenger side of her car to walk around the front and kiss her husband goodbye as she eases herself into the driver's seat.

"I must learn to drive in this culture. These people drive," he thinks to himself. When he gets back to the monks' living quarters, Bhante Sujatha announces that he is going to learn to drive and asks if there is anyone who will teach him.

"Oh no, my friend! You cannot drive! What will we do if you get in an accident? How can you risk a policeman giving you a ticket? What will happen to his kamma?"

This is another pivotal moment for the little monk.

"Well, if I want to teach these Westerners about loving kindness meditation, I have to be part of their culture. They are not a part of mine, you see? My Buddhism is about loving kindness and the end of suffering. And the only way I can teach this to them is if they listen to me, and the only way they will listen to me is if I adapt myself at least a little bit to their culture. I will seem separate and unapproachable if I do not drive. I want Westerners to know I am not judging them or their culture. I want them to feel my loving kindness. I want to feel their loving kindness. Please, help me find someone to teach me to drive."

The people at the monastery do not believe that the little monk should drive. This is one of Bhante Sujatha's first experiences in the West with people who seem attached to tradition. These are good people. Many Buddhists around the world honor the Eastern traditions of treating monks as separate and too important to engage in mundane tasks like driving. However, these traditions often separate practitioners from Westerners, many of whom cannot even imagine not being able to drive.

"You know, Mary, sometimes I just say what I think, even if people are mad or disappointed. I can't waste any time you know? I carry that wish around with me in my heart, and I must carry it out. I have to help the people, even if it means disrespecting some old rules

246

that do not serve our cause of spreading loving kindness. I am not here to be liked, or popular, or even to run temples. I am here to practice my path, the middle path, with my gift of being inspired by that wish."

In a few weeks, Bhante Sujatha meets someone who agrees to teach him to drive. He goes to a driving school and a community member in Australia, who benefits greatly from the teachings of Bhante Sujatha, provides her car for the little monk. He is then able to see Australia and teach the practice of meditation in different areas.

Eventually, the little monk and the others in the community succeed in replacing the old house with a bigger, newer home and a temple. After 4 years, it is time for the little monk to move on. He learned a valuable lesson in Australia—that the problems he is having with the way people treat him are his problems, not the country's problem.

"It is a cultural difference, you know? In Buddhist countries, we have a whole advanced Buddhist culture with so many accepted practices and rules. Great respect to monks and the Buddha, life-long connections with parents and family; so many things are expected in that culture. But here in the West, it is a different culture.

The Buddha did not create most of the rules. I started to think maybe there was a way to teach Buddhist practices in a Western Culture, which might not look anything, like Buddhist practices in a Buddhist culture.

John Bardi, a noble friend and a professor of philosophy at Penn State University, explains this to me.

"You know, many of the things that we think are so deep or spiritual about Japanese or Chinese or Sri Lankan Buddhism, are actually cultural. That's the magic of Bhante Sujatha. He manages to extract the Buddhism from the culture. It's quite remarkable really.

247

He brings this global Buddhism that can be practiced within any cultural background, to the world."

Bhante Sujatha explains.

"When people show their feet in the temple, or women wear a tank top, I have learned they don't mean disrespect. They have just been raised in a different culture. And so I have to ask myself, how can I teach them the middle path? And I have to be careful to separate the teachings from the culture."

In time, Bhante Sujatha learns that being a nobody in a culture means he is freer and that it can be wonderful to be anonymous. He learns that lonely means free, uncomfortable means we are growing, and disrespected really means humbled and enlightened.

Chapter Thirty

Wandering

After four years, the little monk decides that he has done all he can in Australia. Since his higher ordination at 20 he is not compelled to follow a teacher's advice, and he can travel when and where he pleases.

At 29 years old, the little monk is starting to become a little restless. He feels a little discouraged after his experiences in Australia, and he decides to go to Korea and visit a brother monk at his temple. It is the middle of a cold winter there, and Bhante Sujatha decides he wants to live somewhere warm. Hardly noticing as his mind starts to slip; he is becoming interested in things like staying in a warm climate and visiting with his brother monks.

Bhante Sujatha still practices diligent meditation and chanting every day, but even the most habitual practitioner can forget his mind. Practicing mindfulness is a moment-by-moment, breath-by-breath phenomenon. It is typical to remember and forget over and over. Bhante Sujatha teaches this gentle concept: you will never get it right, never clear your mind, and never be free of being human. And losing this hope is the magic. Students learn that the only moment we really have is now. As we focus on our breath, we become aware that our ordinary breath is enough to keep us present. If we are feeling angry or tired or confused, we can remember to breathe, over and over. Breathing allows us to remember the present moment. This is called being present, and it means that we let go of our thoughts and our reactions and just be here now. Many practitioners consider this good practice for dying. In the Buddhist traditions, dying is an unavoidable part of life and letting go of attachments, desires and thoughts is a way to practice this ultimate letting go.

Monks, usually in groups of four for support and accountability, are called to chant blessings when someone is dying. Bhante Sujatha remembers being at these bedsides as a young monk with no fear. Now, because he can see that death is a closer reality as he ages, he sometimes struggles with fear and sadness at these rituals.

In this example, we can see how attachment and desire cause suffering. When we are young, our lives seem endless and death is so far off in our minds that we don't even notice life as a temporary gift. It is like the air around us, or water around a fish, unnoticed or appreciated until there is less of it left. The Buddha saw this as attachment and a primary cause of suffering. Meditation is effective in relieving us of this fear of death by teaching us that we can let go of everything.

Bhante Sujatha welcomes the children from the Buddha kids program at the Blue Lotus Temple. When our dharma talk is finished, they walk up to the front of the temple with their volunteer teachers and sit in a half circle near the monks, facing us.

They are adorable, of course, and the teachers present the lesson for the day: a clear, plastic small bottle filled with a pretty blue gel-like substance and glitter. The young teacher speaks.

"When we are angry or upset, what can we do to help ourselves?"

Three of the kids, ranging in age between three and eight, raise their hands. The teacher calls on a young boy, probably about five years old.

"Well, we can shake the bottle and watch the glitter!"

"Yes, exactly," the teacher says with a smile and then calls on a little girl who is about eight. She stands up in excitement as she says, "Yes! When the glitter floats down we can watch it, and we breathe *in and we breathe out! By the time the glitter is in the bottom, we feel better!"*

The other child puts her hand down, and the teacher encourages her to speak. "Go ahead, sweetie."

"Well, if my brother makes me mad, then instead of yelling, I can go and shake my bottle. We don't have to fight so much.

As I watch this, I realize that meditation is such a powerfully good idea, and I feel shocked that we don't teach this in school to our children. Bhante Sujatha is probably right. If he can get to most of a generation of kids with this message, the world can change.

Bhante Muditha calls the little monk, curious about his progress in Australia. He is surprised when the little monk tells him that he has been in Japan, enjoying himself at the temple there.

"So you are not in Australia? What happened?"

"You know, I did all I could there, and I felt like it was good to leave and see the world."

"Yes, of course, so are you staying in Japan? Will you be living at the temple there?"

"No, I am just exploring a little."

Bhante's teacher is concerned. A wandering mind is an unhappy mind. Focusing on the right things can provide relief from negative thoughts or relentless ideas. Concerned that his favorite student is becoming restless and is in danger of wandering off path of monkhood, Bhante Muditha invites his beloved student to come to the temple he has started in America in Southfield, Michigan.

"My friend, I think you would benefit by coming here. We need your help and you can give good service here in the West."

251

Bhante Sujatha smiles into the phone, realizing that this is his chance to come to America and fulfill his mission to make a difference for Westerners.

"Alright, I will come. I will come right away."

"Well, good. Okay. Now, you realize you must travel back to Sri Lanka, where I can send you a sponsor letter. You can come here on a religious visa and we can work together in this temple."

Like most people, Bhante Sujatha's mind tells him he should hesitate. Good ideas are everywhere, all the time. Success, of course, lies in the execution of these ideas, which our untrained minds often prevent with thoughts about why we could never, or should never, do this or that.

"You know, I don't speak any English. I am a little nervous going to America."

"My friend, we have many Sri Lankan people here. The temple will feel like home to you," Bhante Muditha says. "You will really like it. I know it will be good for you to be here. I want to help you stay in the monkhood."

The wise teacher states his intentions on purpose to get Bhante Sujatha's attention. The little monk's mind turns from why he shouldn't go to America to the great big reason that he should. He must fulfill his destiny and honor his wish.

As always, once the little monk has made up his mind, he moves fast. Three days after that phone call, he is on a plane to Sri Lanka, his last stop before the exciting move to the land of the free, America.

Chapter Thirty-One

Goodbye to the Temple

Bhante Sujatha arrives the next day at the Subodharama temple in Sri Lanka, pleased to see young monks studying the suttas and chanting with each other, walking mindfully, and sitting in silence. Moved by the peaceful scene and inspired by the young monks, Bhante Sujatha again feels hesitant about leaving for America. He resolves the doubt in his mind by deciding he will be there for only a short while.

As he walks mindfully under the mango tree, a pit dropping on his shoulder startles him. He hears a giggle and looks up to see a little boy sitting in the tree in his old familiar spot. Instead of chiding the young boy, Bhante Sujatha looks up and smiles. The expression on the boy's face changes from worry to happiness and the little monk continues his mindful walk to the temple, feeling good about the happiness he has caused.

Bhante Dhammawasa is happy to see the little monk, complimenting him as he walks up. "You look wonderful my friend! I hear you are going to America!"

"Yes, yes, my teacher, I am." Happiness and fear flood through Bhante Sujatha's body, mixing into a deep joy.

"So, my beloved teacher, how can I serve for the next few days while I wait for my visa?"

This is it. I am here, walking with Bhante into the Subodharama Temple. We are meeting with Bhante Dhammawasa, his beloved teacher. As we pass through the doorway into the temple office, I see him, smiling at me. I bow before him and sit on the floor with the other Blue Lotus Temple Members who have made the trip to Sri Lanka. We are there to celebrate Bhante Sujatha's designation as the chief saganayaka of North America. So far, it's been the experience of a lifetime, with people lining up to bow to Bhante and offer him gifts everywhere. I am humbled by his obvious fame in this country.

As I sit down, Bhante Dhammawasa smiles at me and says, "You did a great job. I loved your book."

I actually pinch my wrist, making sure this experience is real. Bhante Dhammawasa offers tea and I think about Bhante Sujatha's definition of noble leadership. He explained it to me as we sat in the temple basement talking about his teachers in Sri Lanka.

"A great leader is a servant to the people, not their master. I scrub the floors, carry the chairs, and take out the garbage. Bhante Dhammawasa taught me to do this. When I start to do the work mindfully, and I smile as I work, my students and the people around me want to join me. That is how I lead. I don't ask anyone to do anything unless I will do it. And I smile as I work. I want people to see that I am enjoying service. They enjoy it too, then."

The little monk does his best to give strict instructions to the students. "While I am gone, you must practice good habits. You must wake up early, at 4:30, and practice meditation for at least an hour every day. Clean your sleeping areas thoroughly so that you can rest easy and be happy. Smile when you clean the bathrooms and the kitchen. Remember, when you clean more thoroughly than someone else, or you sit straighter than the other monks as you meditate, do not let it affect your ego. Say these two words, as many times as you need: "No ego. NO ego."

Pretend you can hear my footsteps and get ready for my inspection," he says to the crowd of students gathered together near the Bodhi tree to listen to their beloved teacher's instructions before he leaves for America.

When you want to sleep late or leave a mess or argue with one another, or when you want to disrespect Bhante Dhammawasa or another one of your teachers, remember the Buddha said there is no separation, we are all the same and each action influences the whole. Do your best to keep the Subodharama temple a beautiful place to practice the teachings of the great Siddhartha."

The little monk reminds the monk community of the 10 precepts that they promised to honor, and he speaks again about the idea that we are not separate from one another—leaving a mess or ignoring a precept for any person is leaving a mess and bad kamma for all.

"My friends, please remember this. Every time you offer service, you are training yourself to be a great leader who can spread our wonderful message of loving kindness. If you keep your areas clean, practice meditation and chanting, eat and walk mindfully, listen carefully, and cheerfully help with any task, even cleaning the bathroom, you will be welcome everywhere. If you help people, people are more likely to help you.

"Earn your merits, learn your karmic lessons and be happy! I know you will miss me, but I am not the reason for your happiness. The way you feel when you are with me is the part you might miss and that is the part that you can create in your mind. Practice your meditation diligently, chant mindfully, and cultivate mindfulness. I love you, and I will think of you in America, but I will not miss you. I know about impermanence and detachment. I will be happy. Pay respect to my great teacher Bhante Dhammawasa always and be good monks and happy people. Smile as much as you can. Goodbye."

Laughter and tears mix with murmured promises as the student monks wait in a line to say goodbye to their grateful teacher, Bhante Sujatha. At the embassy in Sri Lanka, the little monk tells the officer that he would like a one-week visa. "I will not be in America long. My students here need me."

The officer explains that he is sorry, but three weeks is the minimum visa he can issue.

Bhante Sujatha smiles at me as we sit in the back of a yoga meditation workshop he is leading, waiting for the yoga teacher to introduce him.

"Oh, my friend, when I think about that day, I was afraid, you know? I didn't have any idea how long I would be in America."

He shrugs his shoulders. Laughing. "I am thinking maybe 5, 10 days at most. That was in 1998, of course"

We smile at each other. The little monk has been in America for more than fifteen years.

Chapter Thirty-Two

Coming to America

As the plane circles over Detroit in February, Bhante Sujatha panics privately. His eyes are enormous in his reflection in the plane window as he views the landscape of Detroit when the plane is closer to the ground, getting ready to land. He breathes steadily, determined not to scare the other passengers. He wonders what they would do if he told them there was obviously a terrible fire.

All of the trees are bare and seem dry enough to crumble. The ground is bare of grass and greenery, clearly scorched by the fire. There are little patches of white snow here and there, and the little monk wonders if there was a drought. Surely plenty of snow would have put out the fire. He is a little confused when he sees pine trees, completely green and healthy looking.

He is thinking in his practiced language of Pali now, and he does not know English so he cannot ask anyone what happened. He wonders if he should try and warn the people, but he decides that the pilot must know and either the people know already that their town has burned or the pilot will tell them as they leave so they are prepared.

The cold weather sneaks in through the walls of the temporary walkway as Bhante Sujatha walks mindfully, carrying his small backpack, hoping he can find his way to the pick up place where Bhante Muditha is waiting for him in a car.

The people who were on the plane walk in the same general direction, and the little monk follows them, carrying his meditation cushion under his arm and listening to the slap of his sandals on the cold tile. He stops in a restroom, taking a moment and comparing the picture on the door to the one in the American guidebook for foreigners he brought along for the trip. Taking a breath for courage, he pushes open the door, relieved to see two men walking out.

There are so many signs on the walls that the little monk wonders how Americans can think straight. He pays attention to the sound of his sandals slapping against the floor and breathes, walking in the same direction as other people who have gotten off their planes. Unable to read any of the signs about exits or directions, Bhante Sujatha pays attention to his wounded mind, which is filled with doubts and fears about arriving in America. Because he practices meditation, he can let his disempowering thoughts go, and feel confident that he will find his way to his old teacher.

Stepping onto the people mover in O'Hare, the little monk holds the handrail and smiles, thinking to himself that this is the real America, the one he imagined as a young boy wanting to carry his wish to the west.

Bhante Sujatha is so calm that he is able to follow the crowd down to the baggage claim area and out the doors to the street, where the cold hits him like an icy beach towel, covering the whole front of him with a frozen heavy feeling.

"Oh!" he gasps, as the wet cold hits his bare toes.

He grits his teeth in pain and runs as best he can in his sandals to his beloved teacher, Bhante Muditha, waiting by his car. The older monk is wearing boots, a heavy coat over his robes, a turtleneck, and a thick green hat. He smiles broadly as he hands his student a coat and a hat, donated by temple members at the Grand Buddhist Vihara in Michigan.

Bhante Sujatha leans over in the passenger seat, hugging himself for warmth. Finally, he can speak with someone in his native language.

"It is freezing here! How can you stand this? And when was the terrible fire? Are you okay?"

Bhante Muditha keeps his eyes on the road as he talks. "Yes, it gets quite cold here. Today is actually not so bad. You'll get used to this. They make warm clothes in America. We'll get you some."

"Oh, no, no. This coat and hat should be enough. I am not staying long enough to need different clothes. I'll just spend most of my time inside."

Bhante Muditha is silent, allowing himself and his student to be mindful. After a few minutes, the little monk speaks again. "Well, I mean I guess I might stay longer, but I don't think I can live in this weather for long. So tell me about the fire! I want to know what happened!" The little monk sees more damage as they drive, boarded up buildings, bare trees and scorched earth. He marvels at the intact undamaged houses and buildings in Detroit, wondering how so many remained untouched.

Bhante Muditha frowns, wrinkling his forehead as he expresses concern. "Fire? Was there a fire?" Bhante Sujatha huffs in frustration. "Well, obviously! Look at the trees!"

Breaking out into helpless laughter, the older monk smiles as he shakes his head. "There is no fire, my friend! This is winter! All of the trees lose their leaves and the grass disappears. Usually there is white snow covering everything so it is beautiful, but most of the snow melted last week when there was an unexpected warm day! Oh," he says, slapping his thigh, "that was so funny! A fire!"

The little monk laughs too, smiling at his inexperience with winter in America. The sangha in the temple welcomes Bhante Sujatha, and he is very happy to be there helping the people, training monks from Sri Lanka and enjoying the practice with his beloved teacher.

Bhante Dhammawansa, the wonderful Sunday school teacher from the Subodharama temple is also there, supporting his brother monks

259

in their quest to spread loving kindness throughout the West.

It's not until I am almost done with the book that I understand; Bhante Dhammawasa was Bhante Sujatha's teacher in Sri Lanka, and Bhante Dhamawansa (note the n instead of the double s) was his Sunday school teacher, who now lived in Florida. It is a challenge to get these names right.

Bhante Sujatha is driving with a young monk from the Michigan Temple to visit a Christian church for a meditation service. The little monk clears his throat.

"My friend, may I ask you a question?"

"Sure," the younger monk replies.

"You have been in America a few years?"

"Yes, yes, I have," says the younger monk, eager to be helpful to this wise monk.

"Well, do people here die younger? I don't see old people anywhere. Do you know where they are?"

The younger monk frowns as he drives. "My friend, here in America, they do not always keep older people with their families. The older people live in special communities filled with other older people. Sometimes they even send them to a place they call a nursing home. Here in America older people are not seen as wiser."

"Special communities? Are these places only for old people?"

"Yes, yes, in fact, many of them do not allow anyone under a certain age to live there."

Laughing gently, Bhante Sujatha shakes his head.

"These Americans. They are so interesting, aren't they?"

260

Chapter Thirty-Three

Sponsorship

In Sri Lanka, Bhante Sumana is frustrated. His brother and his friends are joining the army in Sri Lanka to help with the battle against encroaching terrorism. One day, Bhante Sumana decides quietly to disrobe. He just has to help his brother and his people with fighting these terrorists!

Ten thousand miles away, Bhante Sujatha, Bhante Chan and Bhante San are living in a small condominium in Crystal Lake, Illinois, leading meditation services to larger and larger groups of practitioners. They are teaching in Woodstock, Las Vegas, California, and other places around the world. The monks need help. One morning during meditation, Bhante Sujatha remembers Bhante Sumana. The little monk remembers that Sumana wanted to come to America.

Bhante San is talking to me in the basement of the Blue Lotus Temple. "You know, Mary, when Bhante Sujatha came back to Sri Lanka, I really needed his support. It's really strange, but he always showed up right when I needed him. I would be just on the verge of breaking down, or disrobing, or giving up altogether, and he would be there. He has an uncanny ability to be there for people right when they need him."

After meditation, Bhante Sujatha calls Bhante Sumana.

"Would you like to come to America? Bhante Sumana is stunned. How did Sujatha know? "Yes, yes, I want to come!"

Bhante Sumana is excited. He does not answer mindfully. He is a treasured teacher in his village, and he doesn't take the time to think about the experience of leaving his sangha. As a young monk, he was impulsive when he said yes to the casual invitation to be ordained. Buddhists believe that we must practice every day. Being mindful takes diligence, and patience. And it does not last.

In the Buddhist philosophy, all experiences in life are impermanent, learning experiences. Meditation allows us time with our thoughts and our natures. If we are impulsive, we will be restless during meditation. If a seemingly good idea pops into our minds, we will want to do something about it. It will be a struggle to sit there quietly and focus on our breath. This practice, of sitting still when we want to act, allows us to resist other impulses as we go about our day. Mindfulness lessens our need to react quickly. We can take our time, and think about the best choice.

But there will always be an opportunity to lose our mindfulness, and we have to use our practice to calm our minds and react in a more considered manner. All of life, in the Buddhist philosophy, is an opportunity for practice, which does get deeper over time, but never reaches a stopping point. Even enlightenment, seeing the perfection that is life and us, is not an endpoint for a Bodhisattva who chooses to stay in this physical realm and continue to practice

America is seen around the world as the land of opportunity, and the monks at the Subodharama temple in Sri Lanka see our country as a chance to experience miraculous abundance and freedom. Those of us who are born here often become blind to the miracle of our freedom. We are like a fish, who would have a hard time describing water.

I feel the same way about Bhante Sujatha and his message of loving kindness.

In Sri Lanka , Michael Fronczak bows low before Lalitha, gently grasping her feet affectionately. I am moved to tears watching him. In Arizona, my friend bows to the ground in gratitude and respect before Ann Van Slyck, a noble friend of Bhante's. Writing this book is taking me all over the world. I wish I could bow low to every single person I encounter. The respect and love engendered by this simple action is hard to match. A handshake seems cold to me now. I appreciate Bhante Sujatha's unconditional respect and acceptance of our culture.

Bhante Sujatha tells Bhante Sumana that he will send a sponsor letter for him, allowing him to obtain a religious visa. Bhante Sujatha immediately writes and sends the letter when he hangs up the phone. For the little monk integrity is natural, built into his character through hard work and discipline. Within days, he notifies Bhante Sumana that he will need to go to the embassy for his visa, and then he can tell people that he is going to America. "You will need to study America and the facts about this country. Make sure you study hard."

In Sri Lanka, Bhante Sumana's days are filled with work at the temple, giving dhamma talks and leading meditation, chanting blessings for people in their homes and doing humanitarian work and temple services in his poor village. The people in the village have chosen their beloved monk to be the abbot of their small temple. Bhante Sumana does not look forward to telling them he is leaving.

When the young monk gets to the embassy for his visa, he is glad that he memorized the facts. He knows there are fifty states and five great lakes.

The embassy official asks the monk in English if he wants a translator. Bhante Sumana has never heard the word translator, and he doesn't like the sound of it. Translator sounds like alligator to the young monk. He shakes his head side to side, saying "No, no alligator!" His English is heavily accented, and the Embassy official thinks the young monk has rejected the idea of a translator.

263

"Okay, can you tell me the 8 fold path?

"Eight?" says Bhante Sumana, confused, "No," he says in faltering English, "there are five great lakes. Did you say lake?"

Confused, the official asks again. "Surely you know this. You are a monk! What are the ten precepts?"

"Ten? Hmmm.... Well, there are fifty states and five great lakes."

The compassionate official calls for a translator, and the three of them share a laugh over Bhante Sumana's misunderstandings.

A week later the young monk tells his family and the villagers that he is going to America. Practicing detachment is hard. The villagers were counting on Bhante Sumana to help them, and they truly love this funny, kind hearted, happy monk, but the young monk knows he must take this opportunity. He is certain it is the right path. People cry and tell him not to go, but Sumana, with years of training behind him, is able to breathe and practice compassion for himself and the people he is leaving.

"You know, so many of us go on silent retreats, and I think that is good, of course, but it's not reality. When you can focus on your breathing and be still in the middle of being angry or sad, that is when you are really using the practice. That is also when you can use your training and your cultivated mind to practice loving kindness. You see, that is the point of meditation here, to cultivate your mind so that you can practice more compassion and loving kindness. There is even a method of meditation with your eyes open. That is really good practice."

Meditation, as taught by Bhante Sujatha, is not about relaxation. It is about cultivating our minds so that we can be mindful as we live our lives.

Bhante Sumana turns aside as the villagers and his family members gather around him crying and wishing him well. He breathes in and out and remembers his mind. He finds his quiet inner self and stops himself from crying. Smiling, he says goodbye warmly, assuring the people that they are good practitioners and that they will be all right after he leaves.

"Just be happy! You can do it!" Bhante Sumana says, smiling, so simple and so deep at the same time. The next day, he leaves for America, going through the same humorous routine here, not knowing the language. Once he is here, he gratefully helps Bhante Sujatha, telling him that he is so happy for this chance.

"Is there anything you'd like me to be sure to include in this book about Bhante?" I ask Bhante Sumana. "Anything that you just feel like you want to say, 'Whatever you do, be sure to let people know this?'"

"Yes, yes there is, please, Mary. Let people know that for me, Bhante Sujatha is a great Bodhisattva, he is really a grateful guy. Really, I think he is on the path to enlightenment."

Most sponsorships to the US involve the exchange of serious money between the sponsoring temple and the temple in Sri Lanka. Most monks might sponsor one or two brother monks in a twenty-year service span. Bhante Sujatha has sponsored Bhante(s) Chan, Samita, Samantha ("Monk San"), Sumana, Sankicha, Mangla, Somananda, Rahula, Sathi, Rahula, Punna and Pamaratane at the time of this writing. He has never charged a cent for any of his services in this regard.

Chapter Thirty-Four

Noble Friends

Not associating with fools,
Associating with the wise,
Honoring those worthy of honor;
This is the greatest blessing
(Mangala Sutta [Sn 2.4] tr. John Kelly).

In an ancient Buddhist story, the Buddha's faithful attendant, Ananda, asked about the importance of having wholesome friends.

"Surely, great teacher, having noble friends must be an important half of a holy life."

The Buddha replied, "Do not say so, Ananda. Noble friends and companions are the whole of the holy life"

The Buddha said that there is no condition of life that more powerfully influences your development than cultivating wholesome friends and companions. Start with yourself, as you are today, and build on your strengths to become a better friend and companion to others. And use careful consideration when choosing your friends.

Michael Fronzcak was 19 years old, practicing meditation and studying martial arts in Detroit with a Chinese Sufi monk who generously introduced his students to many forms of Buddhist practice. He invited Bhante Sujatha and Bhante Dhammawansa to lead a meditation for his students.

The monks from Sri Lanka seemed to fill the small room as they entered in their flowing maroon robes, removing their sandals at the door. The robes and the sandals made an impression of otherworldliness in the chill of a Michigan winter. Sufi monks wear short jackets. This was the first time Michael had seen monks in their regal robes.

Settling in to meditate, Michael listened as the monks guided the participants in a long version of the metta sutra, the loving kindness meditation. The metta sutra is designed to encourage mindfulness and guide our thoughts to the pristine practice of loving kindness for ourselves and others. Smiling as he followed the instructions, Michael pictured his family members and wishes them happy, well, and peaceful. He feels peace flood through him as he pictures his father's face—and instead of thinking about what his father is doing, or feeling the usual guilt about not calling him more—he simply guides his mind to wish his father happy, well, and peaceful. The idea of wishing someone who is ill happy, well, and peaceful, rather than allowing worry to occupy our precious minds moves the young practitioner. When the meditation ends, Michael knows he wants more. He is moved by the simplicity and beauty of the practice of loving-kindness.

"It was really long. We were wishing all the beings in the universe happy, well and peaceful by the end of it, and I felt good about that. I especially liked Bhante Sujatha. There was something so easy about him."

The little monk and Michael stayed in touch, and Michael soon became a happy student of the middle path of Buddhism and a noble friend to Bhante Sujatha.

"He's taught me the true meaning of friendship. He is my first, Kalyana Mitta, my noble friend. The Buddha taught that you find great realizations and spiritual truths through noble friendships. The great truths live in the spaces with our noble friends. Without noble friends, you cannot attain enlightenment. So many people never understand this."

"The only thing Bhante Sujatha has ever asked me for is something that would improve my life. And he does it in the sweetest way, always asking my permission before he shares."

"He'll say something like, 'I need to ask you something, okay? You know, I want to see you practice a little more or are you considering this important person in your life?'"

Michael continues, "There's always been that acceptance, complete and utter openness, with no other interest except to help me. I've had lots of relationships but never one like this. It's this strong and gentle guidance with a complete absence of judgment. Just remarkable.

"And of course I have a special advantage in that I have known him a really long time, but I never see him treat other people any differently. Once, I questioned him about wanting to get married and have kids. I saw this as a missing in his life, and I wondered if he ever wished he could do that. I asked him if he misses having a home of his own, a family that welcomes him."

The little monk's answer moved Michael.

"If I were a husband and a father, I would take care of my family, of course. I know how to work, and I have energy. This could be wonderful. I would be a father to 2 or 3 children and a husband to a beautiful wife. The way I see it, though, is that I have all that and more. I am a son, a father, a brother, and an uncle to the whole world. In a way, I am married to my work, teaching people how to be happy through the practice of loving kindness meditation. I think I am helping to create a world where babies will be safe and happy. When I do baby blessings I remember this, that I am creating a home for all these families. A home where loving kindness is practiced everywhere they go. My home is the world. My wife is my work. My children are all the babies I get to bless. I am a son of the Buddha's teachings and an uncle to all the children in the world. My brothers are all the beings in this universe. I am father to my sanghas. After my travels in Australia, I saw this about myself.

Wherever I am, that's my home. Whoever I am with, they are my family. However it is; that is my world. This is the way I see my responsibility and my love for you. You are my brother or my child. I love you that much the moment I meet you. I give you my heart just like I would a family member. My renunciation of my parents and my family meant that I must love everyone as much as them. I must love more and judge less. From this view, I feel completely satisfied and motivated to make a difference, you know?"

"Mary, he is cultivating this universal form of friendship."

Michael and I are both quiet for a moment.

I cough gently, clearing my throat, feeling tears of inspiration. A world filled with loving-kindness is a big mission, and Bhante Sujatha views the world as his home. Yay for earthlings!

Bhante Sujatha has many close friends. Michael Fronzcak comments on this. Bhante Diviner, a teacher in Sri Lanka for fifty years, and a good friend of Bhante Sujatha's, tells Michael his thoughts on friendship.

"You know, my friend, the heart of the practice is this: You meet people, you give them your full attention, you give them your heart, then you let them go."

"There's so much dhamma (learning) in that, you know? I mean, how many times do we give our heart to someone—once or twice? These monks, Bhante Sujatha and Bhante Davindra, they give their hearts to each person they meet, over and over. I have seen Bhante Sujatha give unconditional love and friendship to everyone he meets, time after time. It's inspiring and seems impossible to me. I mean, how much emotional capacity do I have to give? How many friends can I handle? Bhante Sujatha doesn't ask himself these questions. He just gives over and over. It seems to fill him up, not drain him."

Chapter Thirty-Five

From Mexico to Woodstock

The little monk is talented, charismatic and hard working. He feels he has been gifted with gentle and strong teachers.

"I must have good kamma. I was so lucky to have my gentle mother and my tough father, and then to have that same gentleness in Bhante Dhammawasa and the tough way of training offered by Bhante Muditha. So, you know, I have both, and I can be gentle yet I am tough. I feel very grateful for this."

In two years, with unwavering support from his teachers, the little monk raises funds with the sangha and acquires a large home to use for a Michigan Temple. The practice in Australia, where Bhante Sujatha took part in raising funds with the sangha and creating a beautiful temple space, helped him in Michigan. As he goes about his daily activities he can hear the disciplined teachings of his father and Bhante Muditha whispering loudly in his ear, "Do it now! And do it right!"

When the sangha needs encouragement, the little monk can hear his wise and gentle teacher, Bhante Dhammawasa, telling him it's time to climb down from the mango tree and have some tea and conversation. Lalitha is never far from the little monk's mind as he calms himself with his breath, remembering her wonderful example of unconditional love and support. Bhante Sujatha combines strict discipline, unconditional love, his wish for a world filled with loving kindness, and his natural charisma to create a recipe for success.

The downside of this way of life, where Bhante Sujatha asks and receives quickly it seems, is that his mind is often in a restless state.

He must temper the celebration of success with a commitment to move on and make a difference for more people. It is important to remember that the goal of a Buddhist monk is to be humble and let go of attachments. Earning merits through the practice of loving kindness towards themselves and other beings is the goal; Nirvana is the destiny; the Buddhist teachings are the guardrails for the mountain road to this kind of achievement.

Material and personal success is difficult to handle. When Bhante Sujatha was notified that he would be celebrated as an Ambassador of Buddhism to the United States, he had to let go of his attachment NOT to accept a reward like this. He asked himself whether accepting this reward would benefit his practice, his wish, and his sangha. In the end, he saw that acceptance would benefit all. He would earn merits through the practice of humility and generosity in the face of success. Here in America, we encourage a drive towards a person's dreams, but there is very little information about how to handle the inevitable attachments and problems brought on by success.

Success is just as toxic as failure to our attempts at humility. Satisfaction is fleeting unless we can feel it fully with nothing more than our breath awareness. We can veer between arrogance and disowning the better parts of ourselves, refusing to accept responsibility for our talents and gifts. Mindfulness, reflected when Bhante Sujatha says "No ego," is the path to the middle, where our awareness of our gifts is balanced by our humility and our desire to serve.

During a silent moment in a dhamma talk at the Michigan Temple, the little monk sees that his work in that community is complete. Bhante Sujatha stares out at all the Sri Lankan faces and realizes that it is time to execute his mission, his wish, his heartfelt desire to teach Westerners to be happy through the practice of loving kindness and meditation.

"These people are born into Buddhism," he thinks. "They are wonderful, but they already know about the Buddha's teachings.

They know the benefits of meditation. I want to teach them, and I like the way they respect me. But I want to reach the typical American."

John Bardi, a philosophy professor at Penn State, is telling me what he thinks is so special about Bhante Sujatha. "You know, Mary, so much of the stuff I thought was deep about Buddhism, or amazing about Zen, was actually Japanese. I found that out when I lived in Japan. When you live in other countries you realize that so much of the stuff we think is this religion or that philosophy is actually the culture. Bhante Sujatha, raised in a serious Buddhist culture, is schooled beyond anyone I know in the deepest parts of Buddhist philosophy. I mean, it's almost as if he was in a Buddhist boot camp for more than 20 years. He knows Sanskrit, Pali and Singhal. He can cite almost any sutta, and I have had the pleasure of engaging in intellectual discourse with him. I'm a professor of philosophy. Of course I enjoy a good smart argument, but Bhante has somehow transmitted the idea of a global Buddhism with everyone he meets, without any of the cultural or intellectual barriers in the way. He is able to check his ego at the door and just love people."

I think about that for a few minutes and ask him to expand .

"America is the least prejudiced country in the world, you know? I mean we have our problems of course, but we are a real melting pot. In Japan or Tibet when I was there, I was a foreigner, and no matter how smart I was or how much I knew about their practices or even how long I would be there, I would not be Japanese or Tibetan. Bhante recognized this about America, this way that people come together from all the nations on the earth and call themselves Americans. He loves that. He can't get enough of that."

Bhante Sujatha smiles to himself as he thinks about reaching real Westerners, Americans, and teaching them about loving kindness meditation.

With that thought, the little monk begins to focus on the cool air as he inhales through his nose and the warm air blowing over his upper lip as he exhales, present to each mindful, loving breath. Before the dhamma talk is over, he knows that he must leave the temple in Michigan and go to a place where Buddhism is not practiced, a place where there are mostly western faces, western attitudes and Judeo Christian beliefs.

Bhante Sujatha can't help himself. He is a big thinker. Once a good idea is introduced in his mind, he feels compelled to follow through and make it happen. He knows that if he can inspire Americans with his message, if he can reach all the way down to the babies and even further to the unborn children, to the couples about to marry, he can see a generation of Americans practicing loving kindness meditation. That, he thinks, is the answer to the never-ending call to violence and self-seeking in this country. There is no judgment in this, only compassion.

"I am going in all the way," the little monk announces to his noble friend, Bhante Rishi, who encourages Bhante Sujatha to go.

Rishi, a noble friend, helped Bhante Sujatha see that moving to the middle of white religious America was a good path for his practice. Bhante Rishi was a psychologist named Richard Wright when he met Bhante Sujatha at a retreat center in Mexico. Moved by Bhante Sujatha's simple message of loving kindness and the practice of meditation, Mr. Wright was compelled to go deeper with his own practice. Eventually, he traveled with Bhante Sujatha to Sri Lanka, where he was ordained as a Buddhist Monk at the Subodharama Temple. The little monk gave him the Buddhist name Rishi, which means yogi, one who practices yoga. In Sanskrit, yoga means union, usually interpreted as union of the body, mind and spirit.

Bhante Sujatha and I are sitting in his condominium on a speakerphone with his noble friend now called Reverend Rishi.

"You can't learn universal truths if you stay in your own world. After about a month in Sri Lanka with me, Bhante Sujatha left, and I took on the teachings and practices of being ordained as a Buddhist Monk. It was tough. Even if I had known the language, the culture

was so different that I could not have expressed myself in any meaningful way. I couldn't buy my way out either. Trust me. Many times I would think of all the four star hotels in Sri Lanka, on the beach, and I would have thoughts about just leaving. But I didn't have my credit card. I had to learn to live without any of the comforts from home. And I came to see something important; this feeling that I called comfort was actually attachment. In Sri Lanka, I had nothing but the dhamma. This experience was invaluable for my practice.

So, when Bhante talked to me about his next step, I encouraged him. I went with him to Woodstock. We visited the junior college there so he could register for English as a second language. It was strange being with Bhante Sujatha and this counselor, who saw him as just another foreign student. A few times I wanted to help her understand who he was, but then I realized that was not the best way. I hope I returned the gift that he gave me. I think he and I agree that it's a good idea to let go of attachments whenever you can."

We are silent for a moment and Bhante Sujatha laughs. "My friend, now you are an Anglican Priest. You have let go of some attachments!"

Reverend Rishi kept his Buddhist name when he disrobed as a Buddhist Monk after five years, hearing the call to go back to his Christian roots. He eventually was ordained as an Anglican Priest and now serves at a parish in Canada. I ask him how Buddhism enhanced his Christian faith.

"Well, if you look at the life of Jesus Christ, it was really about suffering and the way out of suffering. There are many teachings in his life that parallel Buddhist philosophy. My church community has benefitted greatly from these insights, I think."

Bhante Sujatha smiles. "You know, Mary, maybe this is a good story too. The priest and the Buddhist Monk."

I smile. "Yes, it is."

At this point, there are so many good stories swirling around that I am afraid I might drown. I need to humble myself after being with these two holy men. I go home and pick up my yard littered by my dog all winter. Humbled. I am grateful for my noble friend who knows that it's important to temper celebration with hard work. I am starting to ask myself different questions. Rather than asking how I can make more money, or if something will bring me pleasure or even if it is the right thing to do, I am asking myself about which choice will lead to more wisdom, keep me humble, and support my practice efforts.

Bhante Rishi helps Bhante Sujatha compose an email requesting space to teach meditation classes and a place to stay. The emails are signed with the little monk's childhood name, Neil Bandara. They send the email to 60 Unitarian Churches. Unitarians are knows for being liberal and open to different spiritual practices.

Weeks later, two of them respond. After careful consideration between Atlanta, Georgia and Woodstock, Illinois, Bhante Sujatha chooses Woodstock. He wants to stay close to the Michigan Temple.

The day after making the choice, Bhante Sujatha sits with Bhante Sankicha for tea. He tells his brother monk that he is leaving Michigan, and that he needs him to take over the temple leadership. Bhante Dhamawansa has moved to a Florida temple, and Bhante Muditha is now an ambassador of Buddhism to Canada.

Bhante Sankicha takes a bite of his cookie and smiles as he eats mindfully, silent.

Bhante Sujatha talks. "I love this place and I am so grateful to Bhante Muditha for bringing me here. But my work is done. We have created a beautiful temple, and you will do well here. The people love you, and I know they love me, but they don't need me, my friend. They are already practicing Buddhists. I have outgrown this. I want my message to make a difference in America. I believe I can bring the Buddhist message of loving kindness and mindfulness to American people without the added pressures of our cultures. I feel I am meant to do this, that is my destiny. It is my wish."

The younger monk, mindful of his ego doing cartwheels, calms himself with a long drink of tea.

"Woodstock?"

"Yes. It is a Unitarian church in a suburb of Chicago."

"I have heard that Unitarian churches might be open to a different message."

The two friends sit together in companionable silence, thoughtful about the future. Bhante Sujatha is not complicated. He makes a choice and then moves. There is not much debate in his life, and little hesitation. There is thoughtfulness about the goodness of this or that and the impact on kamma. Actions are measured against the support or detraction from practice, not fear or doubt or the possibility of failure or success.

He has been raised in the idea of impermanence and no ego. The effort that might be required when making a life choice like changing the state in which you live, and leaving a long term project or employment situation, is removed by the simple act of letting go of permanence and ego. Nothing lasts, so even paralyzing fear will pass and the results of your endeavors are passing thoughts and nothing more. Ego, known in many circles as Edging God Out, is the great oppressor of so many good ideas, stopping us in our tracks as we hear the whistle of the oncoming train filled with people and their opinions. Most of us jump off the track or curl up as we hide in between the rails, afraid to get hit.

Bhante Sujatha stays on that track, letting the train be a ghost created by his thoughts, knowing it will pass through him like air even when it seems big enough to crush him.

Once again, the little monk is leaving a place where people love him. They are sad as he announces he is leaving, and he feels compassion for their thoughts of being abandoned or left without support. He tells them that they will be fine and that he is gifting them with a reminder about their responsibility for their happiness and their practice.

Well-meaning people do their best to talk the little monk out of traveling alone to this small midwestern town without cultivated English skills or knowledge of the area.

"You will be disrespected. You will be lonely," they say. All of their words are from places of compassion, of course, but after awhile the little monk hears all of their concerns jumbled together as the same tired refrain about why he shouldn't even try to change America, why he should insist that everyone follow the same rules and respect his robes and bow and pay homage to this and that. Finally, alone in the Michigan temple kitchen one morning, Bhante Sujatha faces himself and his reactions to these thoughts, as if they were a marauding gang. He raises his arm, remembering himself as a young boy, fighting off the angry cow, committed to protecting his mother no matter what, and he swings down hard, slamming his fist on the table, now committed to protecting his mission.

"I am going!" he says out loud to no one in his small sleeping quarters. He sighs after he yells, feeling a warm satisfaction spread through his body, wrapping him in reassurance that he is on the right path, finally on the way to spreading loving kindness and meditation practice to the West.

Chapter Thirty-Six

Children

"Okay kids, come on up now." Bhante Sujatha is asking the "Buddha Kids" to come up and sit near him, to tell the Sangha about their lessons for the day.

A mother sitting near me sits up straighter, pushing her daughter off of her lap, patting her back and encouraging her to walk up to the front with her bottle filled with colored sand. The children all hold these small bottles filled with their own beautiful sand designs.

Seeing the Buddha Kids always gives me hope. I am so happy that American children are being taught mindfulness and loving-kindness.

The teacher, a young woman dressed in jeans and a sweater, asks the children to explain their lesson for the day to the sangha.

"Remember?" she says, " Remember the monks who spent days making the beautiful sand designs by the water, and then what did they do?"

A little boy, holding his bottle, looks down at the ground shyly as he says, "They just wash it away." Bhante Sujatha and the other monks sitting near him smile. I do, too.

"That's right, kids, that's exactly right. We learned about impermanence didn't we?"

"Wow," says the little monk, a smile lighting up his face.

278

"Wow," I say along with several sangha members. "Wow."

The teacher continues, unaware of her impact.

"And what is the word for impermanence? The Buddhist word?"
Three of the children raise their hands. The teacher calls on a girl
who seems to be about 5 years old.

"A nee kea."

The teacher smiles, gently correcting her pronunciation by asking
another child to answer.

"Aneecha"

There is a palpable gasp in the sangha. We are surprised at the
depth of this teaching.

"Yes," says the teacher, smiling, "Yes, that's exactly right. Annica.
Impermanence. And what does that mean about your sand
sculptures?"

One boy shyly raises his hand. "It means we can shake them or
even drop them!"

Bhante Sujatha and the sangha laugh. There is some scattered
applause that dies off.

The teacher's smile broadens even more. "Exactly! That is it
exactly! You can take your bottles and give them away or shake
them up or even just dump them out! You can enjoy them and let
them go!"

The sangha bursts into applause, unable to repress the
spontaneous joy at watching children easily grasp this difficult
concept.

We visit a school, high in the mountains of Sri Lanka, to bring badly

279

needed school supplies and teach for a day. None of the children have ever met an American. They bow to us as we approach, touching their heads to the ground to express their appreciation for our visit. All of them wear crisp white school uniforms, impossibly clean in the middle of this jungle. I teach computer science in my assigned classroom. There are four old computers for about thirty children, who cram around the screen to see as I type simple English questions for them to answer. Where do you live? What do your parents do? What are you favorite classes? What do you want to be when you grow up?

My dad is a farmer. My mother is dead. I live in an apartment. I like science. I want to be a scientist. My mom is a teacher. My dad is not working. I live on a farm. I want to be a singer.

They read their answers out loud to me, proud of their English skills. I am moved by their enthusiasm and joy. I realize that these children have been taught respect and gratitude, gifts that rival any technology. Visiting that school is one of the best days of my life. I feel for these children and their poverty at the same time I envy their lifetime in a country with a strong, mindful center.

The daughter of a sangha member is being bullied at school. A girl larger than her has pushed her up against her locker, threatening and taunting her. She is afraid but knows from her time with the monks that this is a big opportunity to improve her practice of loving kindness. Her parents share the experience with me.

"She just thought, 'Happy, peaceful, well, the angry person is the one suffering from their anger. I can wish her happy, peaceful, and well. That is what I can do, I can practice compassion.'"

This teenage girl does not fight back or even seek revenge. She has learned what Thich Naht Hahn means, when he reminds us that the rager is the person suffering from rage. People observing someone who is raging are suffering from their personal reactions, not from anything the rager says or does. We can react with loving kindness in any situation. This does not mean that we put up with abuse. On the contrary, we don't add to the abuse by practicing hateful thoughts. Just like the Buddha said to the cobra mistaken for a rope, we can stand up for ourselves while wishing us and them happy, well, and peaceful.

"What do you think about this concept of reincarnation?"

The little monk is leading a class at Penn State University where about sixty students have come to see him speak. He smiles at the student who seems interested in the concept of rebirth.

"Oh, I don't know. It doesn't matter much, you know?"

The student tilts his head, pursing his lips and looking skeptical. "I think it matters. Isn't that something the Buddha taught?"

The little monk keeps smiling, breathing gently before he answers.

"My friend, the reason you want to know about reincarnation is the same reason that people want to know about past lives. Fear. We are afraid of what will happen after we die. We are afraid of what might happen when we die, and we are afraid that we won't know when we will die. We are afraid to leave this world and all of our attachments. All of this reflects the idea of permanence.

When you understand this moment, when you see the miracle of your breath, you will not care so much about what's next, you know? There is just this moment now. You will start to understand impermanence, and you will be more ready to die when the time comes.

So, let's practice simple meditation and learn about this moment before we move all the way to when you die and even further to when you are born again, okay?"

The class laughs and the little monk smiles as he closes his eyes and listens to the wonderful sound of young people moving around, whispering to each other, getting ready to meditate. The soft clicks of cell phones turning off and the crinkle of winter coats being removed makes him so happy that he feels tears start.

This is his dream, his wish for his lifetime. He is reaching young Americans. He is becoming his wish, a refuge for those without shelter, a ship for those with an ocean to cross.

Young people in this country are born into a world filled with lies shoved at them from the day they are born. We allow advertising to infants in this country! By the time people get to college, their trust level is at 0 or even less. Bhante Sujatha works with this. He takes their cynical questions and their complicated ideas and just diffuses them with loving kindness—with the best parts of Buddhism. He listens so carefully that he can get to the heart of the matter in the few seconds he has before the student pulls his cell phone out to respond to a text. Bhante Sujatha allows the student, or whoever he is with, to dictate the cultural background

In Sri Lanka, people do not share their life stories like they do here. People are private. Somehow Bhante Sujatha has adapted to the way we share here. He tells stories from his life to illustrate the Buddhist teachings. He observes that Americans like to learn through personal story telling, and so he uses his life stories to teach here. He is committed to teaching the practice, not the culture."

I am silent after Professor Bardi shares this with me, thinking about a dhamma talk at the temple, where Bhante Sujatha shared his views about separating the culture from the teachings:

The teachings of Buddhism are like water. They can be learned anywhere. The cultures are like shapes, or containers, into which the water is poured. I don't even like the name Buddhism. It implies that Buddhism is about the Buddha. It's not really. It's about the teachings, the dhamma. The Buddha lived 2600 years ago and his teachings are more popular than ever. Universal truths are like that. They live a long time."

Chapter Thirty-Seven

The Beginning of the Blue Lotus

The first few weeks at the Unitarian church were difficult. The little monk had almost no money and could only speak a smattering of English. The room the church provided for meditation was in the basement of the church, cold and a bit depressing.

People in the community, fearful of a threat to traditional religions, protested outside the church, carrying signs that said PAGAN. Although Bhante Sujatha smiled and did his best to practice loving kindness, he struggled with this lack of acceptance. He knew the solution was to practice loving kindness meditation.

As he cried himself to sleep one night, lonely and cold, he was reminded of his experience in the jungle as a young boy, sleeping without his mother nearby, waking up and crying in the middle of the night. He heard the gentle voice of Bhante Dhammawasa and feels the loving embrace of Lalitha as he breathes in and remembers, "Just wait. Just wait."

He practices patience as the group of three people meeting in the damp church basement to practice meditation with the Buddhist monk slowly grows into a group too big to fit downstairs.

"I said to myself, 'I will teach them meditation, I do not know English well, but I can share loving kindness with anyone.'

"So in the beginning, with just a little English, I am able to guide the people. And I smile frequently. That works too. I smile and people smile. They are happy when I smile. Smiling is one way to practice loving-kindness. If you are somewhere, and you don't even know the language, you can smile to practice loving kindness."

He laughs. "But, oh my, my dhamma talks! They were short, that's for sure. I just do the best I can. I think I do a bad job the first time, but I tell myself, if one person comes back, I will keep practicing meditation with Americans here. I was so surprised when one more person came back the next week, and then the group started to grow."

Quickly, the little monk realizes that he needs help. He calls on his good friend Bhante Chan to help him. He met Bhante Chan in Singapore and then spent time with him in Sri Lanka. Bhante Chan came to Michigan shortly after the little monk arrived there and worked tirelessly alongside his good friend, Bhante Sujatha.

Soon Bhante Chan and Bhante Sujatha are staying in houses with generous community members, attending the local college to learn English as a second language and leading meditation classes at the Unitarian church and other locations. Even with all of this, the two friends struggle with being in the Midwest community.

It is hot in July in Illinois, and so the Buddhist monks wear their robes and sandals, just as they did in the Sri Lankan community in Michigan. Neither of them anticipated the comments, the second looks, or the outright stares from Americans unfamiliar with their simple way of dressing.

In the grocery store one day a little girl pulls her mother's hand towards the friendly looking monks, begging her mother to come see the funny men with her.

"Mommy, mommy look! It's not Halloween; it's summer! Why are those men dressed for Halloween? Let's go meet them! Please!"

The mother gives up on ignoring her daughter and sighs as she puts down the fruit she was considering.

"Okay, okay, already! We're going to say hi!"

Bhante Sujatha and Bhante Chan hardly know English, but they do know how to smile, and they are experienced loving kindness practitioners. As the little girl runs over to them, both of the monks smile broadly, happy to see a child attracted to the Buddha's teachings. Of course, the little girl knows nothing about Buddhism and the training it takes to wear the robes representing the great Siddhartha.

The little girl is fascinated by these clever Halloween costumes. She grabs Bhante Chan's robe and feels it, asking him where he got it and why he and his friend are dressed for Halloween in the summer. She is a talkative little person, excited by life, telling the monks that her mom just read her the story called *Christmas in July*.

"Have you read it? Have you?? Well, I have! And you know, I say if we can have Christmas in July then, well, we can have Halloween in July! Can't we mommy? Can't I? I want to get a costume like them, mommy, can I? Where did you get your costume??"

The mother, out of breath from rushing after her daughter, grabs her daughter's hand and pulls her away from Bhante Chan.

"Darling! Please! These men are, they are, well, they are Dalai Lama Men! Please, they are not dressed for Halloween!" The mother smiles sheepishly at the monks. "Oh, I am so sorry! She is just so excited!"

Bhante Sujatha and Bhante Chan don't understand much English, but they know the words Halloween and Dalai Lama. Bhante Sujatha laughs and says hello to the little girl. His smile, as usual, instantly lightens the mood. Bhante Chan admires his friend and teacher as Bhante Sujatha, with almost no English, charms the mother and the daughter with his big smile and simple words.

285

"We are not dressed for Halloween and we are not Dalai Lamas!" Bhante Sujatha laughs, putting everyone even more at ease. "We are Buddhist monks, my friend, from Sri Lanka."

"Well, I'll be!" says the mother. The two monks do their best to tell the mother and her daughter about their meditation practices, hoping to teach a Westerner about the practice of loving kindness and help her to be happy.

Once again, the best loving kindness meditation salesman in the world has shown Westerners what happiness attained through loving kindness practice looks like. His smile is truly infectious, and people are attracted to him. They want what he has and they become willing to sit in silence with him, practicing meditation for the first time with this reassuring loving man.

Bhante Sujatha attended the local community college, learning English quickly, forcing himself to watch English-speaking television shows and converse only in English. The little monk is not entertained by television. He is using it to learn about our culture and to practice our language. As his English gets better, his dharma talks grow longer and more profound. Soon, the damp room in the temple basement is crowded with Westerners, eager to hear this little Buddhist monk from Sri Lanka with a smile as wide as the moon and a heart as big as the earth. The people meditating with the little monk start to notice changes in their lives, attracting other community members to the now twice weekly meditation practice in the basement.

Although it would never be allowed in Sri Lanka, Bhante Sujatha gets a job. He works in a center for mentally challenged people. The work is hard, and Bhante Sujatha is often tired. He practices meditation and goes to his almost full-time job where he enjoys a reputation as a compassionate, understanding worker with a rare talent for seeing what is possible in a patient's life and helping them along the path to recovery and functionality. I smile when I think of the people he worked with, having no idea that they were working with the future sanganayaka of North America.

286

"I always tell my friends and my parents that the people here are so nice, you know? Everyone is so helpful and trying to practice loving-kindness. But in my country and in other places, your country, well, it is doing some things that are not so nice. I feel bad, because I know the people here are so good, but well the bombings, killing children in Afghanistan and destroying Iraq, those are not seen as good actions in our country. Many of my people in Sri Lanka are afraid of your country. People that have been bombed have mixed feelings about America. And now these drones are causing more suffering. But I can tell you, if you visit Sri Lanka, the people will be so kind to you. We all know it is not the people causing the wars and suffering, it is the politics, you know? The politics."

Bhante Sujatha and I are in the car together, talking about the timeline for the book and the anticipated celebration and trip to Sri Lanka this summer. I am dismayed over the way my country must seem to a Buddhist nation who does not believe in war.

"Bhante, how can that be?" I ask, "How can the people in Sri Lanka feel kindness towards us when they see we have done so much damage?"

"Well, my friend, we are a Buddhist country. We see all the good in America. We are followers of the Buddha. We really think that loving kindness is always the answer, that practicing more loving kindness is the way to change the world."

Bhante Sujatha has proven himself as a Theravada Buddhist monk who is capable to building a sturdy bridge between the east and the west. He starts to sponsor and invite monks from Sri Lanka to walk across this bridge built over a previously impassable river of doubt, language problems, and cultural barriers.

287

Chapter Thirty-Eight

The Condo

Eventually, Bhante Sujatha needs his own place to stay. He asked Dan and Patricia, the people he was staying with, to show him some property. Dan becomes a little frustrated after showing the little monk several possibilities. None of them are satisfactory to Bhante Sujatha. They are all too large and luxurious. Smiling graciously, the little monk explains that he is a Buddhist monk, perfectly fine with sleeping on the floor.

"Really, I only need a place to cook, sleep and meditate. " At a small condominium in a town near the temple, Bhante Sujatha says no again and Dan breaks down.

"Bhante, you have to live somewhere! This is just about as simple as it gets! I'm sorry but people around here live in big places!"

They stare at each other a moment before they smile and start to laugh at the little monk's insistence on austerity.

"I mean, you'll just have to get used to it I guess! We're Americans! Rich! Big! Spoiled! Whatever! If you want to live here, you'll just have to put up with a little luxury!"

One morning in Sri Lanka, we all jump out of the van and snap pictures of monitor lizards by the side of the road. These alligator size creatures were crawling out of the muddy river in the middle of town. In the afternoon we enjoy a swim in the fancy hotel pool, looking forward to our safari that evening at the Yala National Park. We ride to the safari in our jeep like royalty, sitting on high seats in the back. As we passed by the river, now crowded with people and their children, bathing, I thought about those monitor lizards. I wanted to get out of the jeep and walk.

Soon, Bhante Chan comes to stay with Bhante Sujatha. Bhante Samita and Bhante San eventually come to stay as well. The little monk feels more comfortable with his brother monks in the condominium. Early one morning, Bhante Sujatha lies on his twin bed and smiles at the sounds of the other monks snoring, breathing and coughing as they sleep. He clasps his hands behind his head, raising his elbows and pointing his toes in a satisfactory stretch as he sighs, happy to hear the sleeping sounds of monks, the familiar beautiful sounds of his life.

Bhante San and Bhante Sumana sit with me at Starbucks and share their experience with me.

"We come to the Blue Lotus Temple, thinking it will be like Michigan. It isn't. It's a two-bedroom apartment. We don't have different areas. We have to share a closet and put all our socks and stuff in one box. Our books and study materials go in a kitchen cupboard. The living room is kept clear except for the statue of the Buddha and some meditation cushions. That's the temple."

They smile. "Sometimes we mix up our robes."

"I am taller," says Bhante Sumana, "So I usually end up with the right robe, but Bhante San and Samita are mixing up their robes all the time."

They share a laugh.

"At night, the temple becomes the sleeping area for San and me. We slept on the floor with a blanket. In the Subodharama temple, we had a wood bed with a thin mattress and a small blanket, so the floor of the condo was comfortable for us. There were funny times for sure. Visiting monks would stay with us, and sometimes we were sleeping next to each other in that living room, very close together. We would kick each other, and then laugh when we woke up and realized that each of us thought the other was the one

289

kicking. Poor San, he worked nights, so it was really hard on him. He never got enough sleep."

They both remembered wonderful discussions about the dhamma and lots of laughter as the monks talked into the night. Bhante Sujatha was a generous host, never asking for money, only that they do the best they can and work so that they can buy their own food. Bhante Sumana remembers being hungry frequently when the little monk encouraged his brother monks to wait for San, so that they could eat their meal together.

Bhante Sumana and I sit in a coffee shop in Woodstock, drinking lattes.

"You have to remember, in Sri Lanka, we use whatever people offer. My temple had one hundred monks. Everyone can't have a separate bed. Two or three monks always share a room. There were ten bathrooms total. So for us, one bathroom for four monks was just fine.

"In Sri Lanka, we didn't have indoor showers. We never heard of a shower in the bathroom like you always have here. We go outside with our brother monks, in our under robes, a short robe designed to wear when we bathe. Oh, that was so much fun, bathing! We are always splashing each other and joking. Monks throw water at us while they shower. We laugh so much. Just imagine a bunch of little kids outside, teasing each other. And the water was cold! Only the first people got water that was a little bit warm!

All the monks have three robes. Our regular robe, a double robe and a bathing robe. We use the double robe during the rainy season. We never wear jackets or a hat. We just put on two robes. We get wet when it rains.

In Sri Lanka, it's good because we have so many limits. I remember when I was a young monk and all the kids would be getting on the school bus, laughing and joking and wearing nice clothes. I would feel so bad! But then, I would remember to just rub my head. When

I feel it is bald, that is a way to remind myself that I am a Buddhist Monk. That was hard with those kids. Sometimes, you know, they would make fun of us."

Bhante Sumana looks down at his coffee, quiet for a moment. He smiles as he finishes his story. "But now I am so happy. My life is so good. And we had so much fun as little monks. So many friends and so much fun all the time!"

The image of the young monks splashing each other as they play by the showers stays with me a long time.

All of the monks staying with Bhante Sujatha are trained in loving kindness, cleanliness, and mindfulness. There is no mess and no crowding. For a monk trained at the Subodharama temple, there is no quest for individual space. They know that their only real home is inside of them, that self-reliance is the goal and the gift of their practice. They are easy to live with, each taking responsibility for themselves.

The monks work together to build a loving kindness practice in this small midwestern town.

At a workshop in Elkhart, Wisconsin, the little monk meets Judy Franklin, a practitioner who is searching for a spiritual home. She takes the precepts after a very short time, knowing they offered a serene way of life for her. Eventually she was ordained as a Buddhist Nun, first by Bhante Sujatha in Illinois and then formally in Sri Lanka.

She is given the name Bikkhuni Vimala, meaning pure of heart and mind. She joined the monastics as a part of the Blue Lotus Temple, completing a miraculous cast of characters.

Bhante Sujatha becomes known as a good teacher with a natural affinity for Westerners. People seek him out, asking him to speak at church events and lead meditation practices in various venues near Woodstock. Bhante Sujatha retains his vision as a leader always in service. He is willing to do anything to spread his message of the practice of loving kindness, meditation, and mindfulness as the way to happiness.

Chapter Thirty-Nine

Las Vegas

Monks in Las Vegas ask Bhante Sujatha to visit. They want to learn more about the processes that Bhante Sujatha uses to start temples and teach Westerners loving kindness meditation. The little monk is surprised to see a billboard in the middle of the strip.

"Your thoughts create your world. -the Buddha.

He smiles to himself, pleased to see words from the Buddha in the middle of Las Vegas. As he waits at a stoplight thinking about the billboard, he is jolted forward, locking his seatbelt and jarring his back. Car horns beep as they drive around the little monk and the car behind him, in a hurry to get to their destination.

Bhante Sujatha takes a deep breath as he experiences his first car accident. This is the fear of so many Buddhists, and the reason that monks do not drive in many Buddhist cultures and communities. Holy people should not be involved in a stress provoking legal entanglement like a car accident. Of course, Bhante Sujatha insisted on driving, and now he will insist on taking care of this accident, a logical consequence of driving.

As he unbuckles his seatbelt and opens his door, he is mindful, slowing himself down as he steps out of the car into the bright afternoon sunshine. A young woman, crying into her cell phone, occupies the car that hit him. She stops talking when she sees a Sri Lankan man, dressed in maroon robes, walking toward her car. She has hit a monk.

"I-I gotta go," she says into her phone, hanging up quickly and rolling down her window as Bhante Sujatha makes his way to her car. The little monk clasps his hands in the prayer position and smiles as he approaches her window.

"Hello miss, I am Bhante Sujatha. I have my insurance card. May I see yours and shall we call the police?"

"Oh, oh, no! I don't want the police!"

The little monk does not want this woman to suffer. He pauses, thoughtfully silent.

"Okay."

"Okay? You won't call the police?"

"No, but I do need to see your insurance."

"Okay, it's at my work."

The little monk smiles. "Okay, I will follow you there."

"Um, well, uh, okay."

Bhante Sujatha goes back to his car, silently wishing himself happy, peaceful, and well. He is relaxed as he gets into his car, practicing mindfulness as he drives behind her, wearing sunglasses and smiling as he drives. Although he was just involved in a car accident, he is able to smile. He knows that this is just a circumstance that will pass and he remembers the words on the billboard, "Your thoughts create your world."

The woman driving the car is filled with stress. She is struggling financially, and she is worried that she might have hurt a monk. She is suffering with the idea that she has hurt someone, and she does not know how to practice compassion for herself. The little monk knows that you cannot effectively practice compassion without first practicing compassion toward yourself.

294

After driving a few miles, the woman stops in front of a nightclub on the strip. Bhante Sujatha parks his car behind her and breathes mindfully, shrugging his shoulders and calming himself before he enters the dark club. He stops for a few minutes inside the door, waiting for his eyes to adjust. He immediately realizes that he is in the wrong place. There in front of him, is an almost naked woman writhing around a pole, dancing for men who are sitting at the bar with drinks and cigars in their hands.

The little monk notices his own judgment and dismisses it quickly, feeling compassion for these men and that woman. He wonders what drives people to this and then notices the judgment even in that seemingly compassionate thought. As he stands in the smoky gloom, he silently wishes the men and the woman happy, peaceful, and well. He is reminded of the power of meditation and a way of life bound by wholesome rules.

Buddhist people have easier lives in many ways, even though many of them are impoverished or oppressed in third world countries. They are born into a culture that values mindfulness, that honors the idea that we are always thinking and so that is the place to concentrate our efforts for a good life. The Buddha taught that if we can adjust our thinking, we can change our words, and if we can change our words, then we can change our life. Our thoughts really do create our world.

The woman is nervous when she comes out of a back room, accompanied by two beefy security guards.

"I am sorry!" she says, looking down at the ground as she sits across from the little monk in a booth.

"That's okay," says the little monk, smiling. "You can start again, you know? You can just start again." He laughs softly. "In fact, we can start our whole relationship again, can't we?"

Bhante Dhammaloka, a close friend of Bhante Sujatha's, is giving the dhamma talk at the temple. Bhante Sujatha is obviously happy to have him at the temple, shifting with excitement on his cushion, as he introduces him.

"We have a guest speaker, a good friend, Bhante Dhammaloka. He will give the talk."

The little monk smiles as his brother monk begins with a classic Buddhist story.

"There was a man who committed the worst crimes in the history of humanity. He killed 999 people, all by himself. He cut their fingers off and wore them like a garland. His goal was to have 1000 fingers on his garland.

"One day, his mother, horrified to hear of her son's actions, travels to the woods surrounded by village, emptied by these crimes. People would flee as he approached, never to return to their homes. The Buddha hears of this. He practices so diligently that he is in touch with people's kamma, and he knew that this man was capable of good. The Buddha even knew this terrible man was capable of following the path to become a monastic. He also knew that in his current state, this man would kill even his own mother, to complete his finger bone garland. To protect the man from suffering through the worst karmic hell for killing his mother, the Buddha steps between the criminal and his mother, letting the first good thought enter the marauder's mind.

"I will let my mother live. I will kill this monk instead." Of course, harming a monk brings terrible karmic retribution, but letting his mother live was a step in the right direction.

With great mindfulness, the Buddha walks ahead of the criminal, who no matter how fast he runs, cannot catch up to the great teacher. 'Why, this monk must be special! I can run as fast as a band of elephants! I am blessed with great strength. Whole villages have been destroyed because of the fear of my strength and yet I cannot catch up to him!'

With this thought, the man starts to experience faithfulness in the dhamma, seeing clearly the miracle of the Buddha's teaching. He cries out in desperation, out of breath and exhausted, 'Stop Monk! Stop!'

The Buddha smiles, still walking, 'I have stopped. You must stop now.'

The man, leaning over with his hands on his knees, panting, says, 'what are you talking about? I am stopped! Can't you see? I stopped already! You are still moving! You stop!'

Here, the man is experiencing despair about his own terrible actions, finally coming to the place of not understanding the great one, forgetting himself momentarily.

The Buddha speaks slowly. 'I have forsworn violence against all living beings. I have stopped all harm to any living being. I have stopped. Now you must stop.'

The man falls to his knees, hearing the dhamma for the first time "Finally, a wise monk even I must revere, has come to save me from myself! I will renounce all evil after hearing this dhamma!"

The man throws away his weapons, taking refuge in the Buddha's understanding and acceptance. The Buddha accepts him as a monastic in training. 'Come, Bikkhu, come.'

With these words, the man went on to become a faithful disciple of the Buddha, collecting alms, even while he was still scorned and feared by many who followed the teachings of the Buddha."

Bhante Dhammaloka, now addressing a mesmerized sangha, goes on.

My friends, you must understand, every moment we are reborn. Every moment your sight, smell, eyes, ears, and thoughts change. Each moment is new. You might be concerned about aging but

297

consider this. You are changing. Every cell in your body is changing, all the time. Aging is actually being reborn, you understand? You are new each moment. Every breath, you are new again."

That night, I read the angulimala (anguli –finger, mala-necklace) suttta again, learning that a teacher who became jealous of his student who was becoming a wiser sage than he poisoned the man's mind. He put the idea of collecting the fingers in his head by telling him that he must collect one thousand to complete his service to his teacher, who thought that surely the man would die in the attempt. The teacher does not know that the man was a great and terrible presence in his past life. The terrible instructions reawaken that root of crime in the man, who is unable to resist his own powerful kamma without the benevolence of the Buddha.

The Buddha and the man give us so many lessons. As I read and reread the story, I am moved. I am learning how much wisdom is contained in every story. The man's name changed when he became the evil one, and instead of choosing a Buddhist name or going back to his original name, he kept his bad man moniker as a warning to himself. This seems like such a good idea, to keep some token from our past as a warning to ourselves. People here do this in different ways. They keep fat clothes in their closet or they hang a photo of a lung cancer victim near their favorite place to smoke.

But so many times, we repress our past or hide in shame from our wrongdoings. What if we could wear our wrongdoings as warnings to ourselves, without judgment from others?

Later in the story, villagers who remember his terrible past deeds stone the man. He cries out to the Buddha for help as the villagers hurl rocks at him. Buddha does not interfere with the villagers, knowing they are helping his attendant improve his kamma.

"Surely brother, this is better than 10, 000 years of karmic retribution! Take it now! Stand up and take it!"

298

Take it now. Walk into the fire and face it. Aging is changing. All is impermanent. We are reborn every second. These teachings are touching my soul. I can feel myself change.

Before the little monk leaves the nightclub, the woman, the insurance agent and the club manager are asking about meditation and where and how they can practice it. People are almost always interested in how the little monk stays so happy and calm. In some ways, Bhante Sujatha is a natural born salesman who happens to be selling loving kindness. He is victorious when someone comes back to the temple to meditate or requests some one-on-one time with him. He donates almost all of the money he gets since his needs are very simple. He leaves a trail of happy, moved people almost everywhere he goes. These people are his loving kindness forces, changing the world through the simple practices of loving kindness and meditation.

Chapter Forty

Arizona

Bhante Sujatha describes the beautiful Arizona residence of his noble friends, Tom and Ann Van Slyck, as heaven. I visited Ann to help with a noble charity project. When I walk out into a glorious backyard in the foothills of the camel back mountains, I realize the distance Bhante has traveled to get here from his one room mud house in the jungle.

Ann worked with Bhante and Project Cure to fund the delivery of over one million dollars in hospital supplies to remote hospitals in the jungles of Sri Lanka. The trucks, filled with life saving equipment will be thundering up the jungle roads to these impossible to reach places this summer. It is a dream come true for the professionals who work tirelessly in these in these facilities to provide the very best care for their impoverished patients.

When I asked her why she chose to do this project, she told me a story.

"Mary, when I arrived at one of the hospitals, a nurse presented me with a bouquet of beautiful jungle flowers. Her shoes and her uniform were muddy, because she had run out into the jungle to pick these flowers for me that morning."

In the maternity ward at one hospital, experienced mothers are paired with first timers in a shared bed with their babies, a remarkable solution to the problem of inadequate staffing and cramped space. The EKG machine in one hospital was duct taped together and most of the facilities did not have even one of these valuable instruments. Ann is a retired nurse who has dedicated her career to improving patient care. She saw the need and responded in much the same way that she developed a revolutionary software company with her husband. The software greatly improved the ability of nurses to assess a patient's needs at their bedside.

The foothills near her home surround the Piestawa Peak, named for Lori Piestewa, the first Native American woman to die in combat and the first female American soldier who gave her life in the Iraq war.

Ann remembers a poignant moment, sitting in her back yard with Bhante Sujatha, asking him about capital punishment and whether it was practiced in Sri Lanka. Bhante was silent for a while before he answered. "We have capital punishment, but we don't use it."

In that moment, they both felt as if they were one with the mountain and all the people and the animals that had been there before them. Like the mountain, they chose to be still, just sitting while their thoughts swirled around them. Neither of them said another word about the conversation. Noble friends like Bhante and Ann hear great wisdom in the spaces left by their silence.

Chapter Forty-One

Charity

"People, there is a blow back! A wonderful blowback! Giving and Getting are exactly the same, you understand? You give, then you get! Right away! Lose yourself! Lose yourself! Stop looking for what you can get and look for what you can give! They are the same. Generosity is the way for us."

Bikkhuni Pannavati is giving a talk on Sunday night. This African American Buddhist nun sits on the cushion in the front of the temple and moves her shoulders in an exaggerated way, using her hands with outstretched fingers to pantomime a slow walk.

"We must be like the rhinoceros, you see, just slowly walking down the path, unafraid, walking right through anything in our way, strong and mighty."

I think of Bhante Sujatha's idea of a loving kindness force, and I am pretty sure I am witnessing a top soldier in that army of peace and compassion.

The nun tells us about her mission work, joking that every time she wanted to sit on her cushion, more work called her.

"When you wake up, you start to see. I woke up and looked and there they were. All over my community, homeless people. I saw them everywhere, and I decided to help them. We housed kids in our temple. Some of them were 25, but they were lost when they were much younger. They were still children. When I took them in,

302

my sangha wasn't very happy.

"How long will they stay here?" my Sangha asked.

Bikkhuni Pannavati smiles, patting her heart with her right hand.

'Well, as long as they need to, I guess,' I said. Then of course we had to educate these kids, so we started a school. Once they were educated, they needed places to stay and ways to support themselves. Eventually we bought some housing and a gluten-free bakery, where the kids could work."

I am just about to sit down, now that our kids are housed and working, when I get a call from India. We work with the untouchables there, 3500 people crammed into the end of a village. These people learn that even their shadow on someone from an upper caste is harmful. They are murdered and raped and no one cares. We do our best to teach them about loving kindness and meditation. These practices, they help with confidence. Oh, I have seen so much.

I get back from there, and sigh as I sit down on my cushion to meditate. But then Thailand calls. They need a nun to help ordain nuns there, to keep women safe and teach them the middle path. They have this problem with human trafficking and sex slavery. Of course, I go, because I remember, there is that blowback!" She smiles and looks around the room.

See, we have it mixed up. We forget that giving and receiving are the same act. The same. When you give, you get, right away. Stop trying to get anything and just give! Lose yourself and you will see that the blow back is better than you can imagine!"

After her talk, I ask her a few questions about Bhante Sujatha.

"You know, Mary, Bhante Sujatha helped me so much. He came to my temple and smiled. I needed to see that so badly. I needed to see that monks and nuns could be happy. And he protected me.

303

He helped me see that I could practice my way. He encouraged the best parts of me."

Bhante Sujatha's reach is so much further than I imagined. Every time he sponsors a monk or ordains a nun, more and more loving kindness and generosity are practiced around the world.

I remember listening to the monks tell me about collecting alms and not needing to say thank you. The giver and the receiver are equal, both important in the karmic path to enlightenment. Now I realize it's deeper. It is always deeper. Giving and receiving are the same. The act of giving does cause a blowback, right away. Real, unselfish generosity is one of the most beautiful qualities the Buddha taught. Of course. How can someone be happy, or enlightened without generosity? It's impossible, because you can't get anything without it. You can't give without getting. And you can't really get without giving. Wow."

Shortly after the little monk sponsors Bhante Sumana, and provides a beautiful temple and a home for the monks, Bhante Sumana's father falls ill.

"What's wrong?" Bhante Sujatha asks one morning, surprised to see plain toast and coffee for breakfast. Bhante Sumana loves to cook and usually prepares a more substantial meal.

"My father is ill in Sri Lanka. He has cancer," says Bhante Sumana.

The little monk does not hesitate. "Oh, well you must go to him!"

"But Bhante, you are ill, too!" Bhante Sumana knows that his teacher has just recovered from a rough time with his chronic pain.

Bhante Sumana tells me about his gratitude for Bhante Sujatha's help.

"Sometimes, Mary, I just go in the bathroom and cry, but Bhante San and Bhante Sujatha help me so much. Bhante Sujatha is so

patient and he waits, knowing I am crying. He doesn't embarrass me. He just helps me meet the people and shows me that they are so nice. He is such a grateful guy. Bhante San, oh my, he is so helpful, he tells me I must practice every day, at least five words from the dictionary, and I must watch American TV at least 6 hours every day while I practice writing and speaking English. It is so hard, but he and Bhante Sujatha never stop helping me. I am so lucky. I am so happy."

Bhante Sujatha insists on helping Bhante Sumana visit his sick father.

"No, no, thank you but don't think about me. You must go to your father. Be ready to leave in two days."

"Mary, I can't believe it. He helps me so much! Right away, he arranges a trip I know costs at least 5 thousand dollars. He gives me money and makes all the reservations."

To Bhante Sumana, Bhante Sujatha exemplifies the Buddhist teaching of generosity. This is the first training that the Buddha offered to his followers. Giving is seen as a path to end the suffering of attachment. In the little monk, his generosity is so highly developed that he feels pain or discomfort when he is NOT giving, rather than the common feeling of discomfort in giving away something to which we are attached.

"Mary, you know my dad is sick and while I am in Sri Lanka, I lose my green card! It is so hard to replace, and I just lose it! And you know, Bhante Sujatha never says a word! He just helps me get a new one. 'No problem,' he says, 'Don't worry.'"

"Accept and let go. Accept and let go. You do this over and over when you live a mindful life. You are comfortable receiving and giving, accepting and letting go. You are happy." Bhante Sujatha tells me this as he relates the details of his baby incubator project in

Sri Lanka. He tells me about a single family who received money for a suitable home, and then were able to care for their child born early with a baby incubator obtained through the good graces of Bhante Sujatha, Mike Fronzcak and their charitable project, Sanatha Suwaya.

"Mary, you know, we changed this family's whole life. It's just wonderful to be a part of this," Mike says to me on the phone.

The next summer in Sri Lanka, I am honored to walk next to the man who received this house in Bhante's parade. It is a dream come true for me.

While in Sri Lanka, the little monk almost always gives away his money, his time and whatever he can from the west. Instead of thinking about saving money or getting this or that as he makes choices, he is always thinking about what he can give and who he can help. In Buddhism, this is a mark of a Bodhisattva, someone who is enlightened.

The little monk started his scholarship fund by collecting cans from sodas and bringing them to the recycle center for cash. Once he received one hundred dollars, he started sending the money to Sri Lanka in the care of a good friend whom he instructed to find a deserving child. Over time the scholarship fund grew, and as of this writing, he has sent one hundred Sri Lankan children to high school and college. When the little monk collects money from his meditation workshops or retreats, he uses all of it except the amount he needs for basic necessities, for charity.

Any money he collects at the temple goes towards running the temple. Unless a patron specifically designates the money for Bhante Sujatha, he donates 100% of the monies collected to the costs of running this refuge of peace and love for the people of the Midwest.

Chapter Forty-Two

Choices

Bhante Sujatha is committed to freedom for himself and others. He purposefully kept his job at the pioneer center while he was creating the sangha in Woodstock, preferring to pay for his own expenses. In the dhamma talk at the temple, the little monk tells us that he is always confronted by too many choices.

"Americans say they want freedom, meaning they want choices. Real freedom comes when we limit our choices, when we live according the precepts of Buddhism or the Ten Commandments. These guidelines allow us freedom to live our lives in a satisfying way, and more importantly, they offer a path to mindfulness. When we are mindful, we can stop after making a choice and breathe for a few minutes, letting the certainty of our path sink into our minds. Regardless of how the choice turns out, we can live life with the quiet confidence of a mindful person."

I am listening carefully, having struggled with many choices in my life.

The little monk prefers simple and calm to big and busy. No matter how western he seems, how funny and friendly and accustomed to our ways, in his heart he is and always will be a follower of the Buddha, eschewing a life filled with too many choices.

Mike learns this when he comes to Crystal Lake to take Bhante shoe shopping, after the little monk compliments Mike's new sneakers.

Mike is happy about this.

"I will come to your house and take you shoe shopping! Let's go next week when I visit"

By now, Mike is assisting the little monk with his charitable work, traveling to Sri Lanka and living near the temple in Michigan.

Bhante Sujatha agrees, looking forward to seeing his friend. Mike chooses a store with plenty of choices, thinking that the little monk will be able to find the exact right pair for himself.

Bhante Sujatha sits down in a chair in a small shoe store while Mike picks out some comfortable looking shoes for his good friend. As he places one pair after another on the little monk's feet, he asks him the same questions.

"How do these feel? Do you like them? Are they comfortable? Do you like the way they look?"

The little monk gives the same answer to every question. "Yes, that is fine. Sure, I like that. Yes it fits. Yes sure, okay, yes."

After ten minutes of this, Mike becomes frustrated. "Bhante, you have to choose! There must be one pair you like more than another. They can't all feel exactly the same. Which pair do you like best?"

Bhante Sujatha backs up a little in his chair.

"Hey, friend, don't get angry with me. I've never done this before! I never shopped for shoes, you know?"

Mike clears his throat as he tells me this story, choking back tears. In that moment, he saw the hundred pairs of shoes on the wall and felt the overwhelm undoubtedly experienced by his noble friend, who had been raised in a family where he got new sandals once a year.

"You know, I saw it. I realized that I was getting angry that he

wouldn't make a choice, an easy choice I thought. This idea we have, that everyone enjoys and benefits from choices; it just isn't true! I mean, think about it. He has a shaved head; he wears one color; he lives simply. He's free. None of his brain power is used making meaningless choices."

Mike ends up buying his same brand of shoes in Bhante Sujatha's size.

Six years later, the little monk returns to Sri Lanka to work on his charitable institutions, including baby incubator projects, housing assistance, a scholarship fund and homes for older monks who can no longer live comfortably in the austere life of the temple.

As usual he greets Mike with armloads of presents from the West, for any children or families that might need it. Among those presents is a shoebox.

"Let's give this to some really good kid, okay? This is really nice."

Mike opens the box.

He laughs as he tells me about the contents.

"Mary, seriously, I never saw something like that. They were a different color. They were so old that the insignias were crumbling, literally dissolving! Oh my, we had a good laugh over my impatience and his acceptance. He let me buy him those shoes because I felt better doing it, not because he needed them or wanted them. I don't think he wore them twice!"

We both laugh.

Bhante Sujatha is continually surprised at the number of choices here, considering this a harder, not an easier way of life.

In Sri Lanka, a country renowned for Ceylon tea, surely far more popular than coffee in that country, tea is still just tea. There are not the varieties we have invented here. Bhante Sujatha tells the temple members about shopping for tea.

"I see there is tea for sleeping, tea for waking, tea for calming down, tea for digesting, tea for laughing,"

The Sangha bursts into laughter, as Bhante Sujatha continues.

I am pretty sure there was a tea for every single thing you could ever think of! You know, I come from the land of tea, and we don't have all of this there!

You see, too many choices makes life harder, not easier. Keep your life simple. Don't acquire too much. Leave yourself without too many choices. These kinds of choices, they are not worth your time. If you can practice mindfulness while you are shopping, you will be happier. I always think of who I can help with my money and my time. Who can you help? Be mindful with your time and your money. Don't look at so many choices if you can avoid it.

I decided to just get green tea. Then I had to choose between 15 kinds of that! If you can, make your life as simple as possible. This way you have time for meditation and loving kindness."

Chapter Forty-Three

Illness

Bhante Sujatha becomes so ill in Sri Lanka that his noble friend Mike contacts David, a sangha member in Illinois. Mike asks for help in getting Bhante Sujatha back to America where there are doctors familiar with his condition.

David, a noble friend in the Blue Lotus community, contacts the airport, holding on for an hour before he can speak with someone.

"Listen," says David earnestly. "This man is a Buddhist monk. He will not ask for help. Please, it is VERY important that he have a wheelchair and someone to assist him the moment he steps off that plane. Just walking from the plane to the gate may be too much. Will you be sure that someone meets him, please?"

David follows up carefully, wishing he could meet his teacher at the gate. Security precautions in America make this impossible.

On the day of their beloved teacher's homecoming, David and Lydia sit in their car and wait for the monk to be wheeled out the door. Lydia drives so that David can jump out quickly and help the little monk out of the wheel chair and into the car the moment they see him. They gasp when they see Bhante Sujatha, bent over in pain and sweating. He drags his heavy suitcase behind him, shuffling in his worn sandals to the waiting car. His maroon robes blow haphazardly around his bare legs, making the freezing weather even less bearable. David jumps out of the car and rushes up to his friend, grabbing his suitcase and taking his arm, letting the little monk lean on him for support.

"Oh my gosh, Bhante! Wasn't there a wheelchair there? What

happened??"

The little monk smiles at him, sweat beads popping out on his forehead.

"It is alright friend. It is alright. I am okay. I am happy.

The ride back to the condominium is quiet with Lydia and David lost in worry and respect while Bhante Sujatha breathes quietly, regaining his composure after his harrowing trip.

As David and Lydia leave their weakened friend at his house, he reminds David that he needs a ride to the Unitarian Church in the morning to speak about world peace. Then he would appreciate a ride to the doctor, so that he can get more medication or a better treatment.

"Bhante, shouldn't you rest? Mike told me he had to help you into the car you were so sick!"

The little monk smiles at his concerned friend. "I am all right. World Peace is really important. I can wait a little longer."

David knows better than to argue.

"Doesn't that bother you," I ask. "When he lets himself get so sick? Why didn't he insist on a wheelchair or take the next day off?

David smiles at me. "Yes, of course. But it doesn't bother Bhante. He is humble and quiet. If he doesn't absolutely need help, he will not ask. He is not stoic, really. He is accepting of more than you and I could ever imagine. It's his training. He doesn't suffer through something and then blame someone or hold a grudge or anything. He wasn't mad at the airport. He was just at peace with how it was. I noticed my ego, in that I wanted to be sure he knew that I requested a wheelchair, but I let that go after awhile."

The next morning, Bhante Sujatha gives an inspirational speech at the Unitarian church.

"I have some bad news for you. You are all too small to do anything about world peace. So am I. I am just a small person, working on himself, just like you are small people, working on yourselves. Well, actually, I am a little smaller maybe."

The community laughs a little, comparing their sizes to the eighty - five pound monk in front of them.

And now for the good news. You are just the right size to practice peace within yourselves, to love yourself, then your family. You can love your neighbors too. You can cultivate your wounded minds and learn to love even your most difficult people. We all know someone who is difficult. Some of us know many difficult people and they are right in our own families!"

More laughter and smiles spread throughout the audience, who is rapidly being attracted to the practice of loving kindness for themselves and their loved ones.

"If you want world peace, then you must find peace within yourself. Anger and peace can't exist at the same time. But until you can heal your wounded mind, you cannot begin to show the world how to practice peace. If you want to stop wars, first stop the wars within yourself and your family. Accept each other and practice loving kindness and mindful consideration with them before you ask people in the world who have good reasons to fight to stop fighting. If you cannot accept and practice compassion with a difficult person, how can you expect a country to make peace with its enemies?

It is only possible to achieve world peace one person at a time, starting with yourself. There is no other way."

The little monk smiles, without a trace of evidence of his great pain, and offers a final gift before he leaves.

Now, I would like to chant some blessings to you. If you would like,

313

close your eyes. Relax and receive these blessings, offered with loving kindness and compassion.

David is moved to tears as he watches his friend close his eyes and chant with a clear and beautiful voice, the same voice that moved the monks at the Subodharama temple so long ago.

"Mary it was just beautiful. He took his time and chanted so beautifully that I could see people moved to tears. I don't understand how he could do that when he was so sick, but he seemed at ease and joyful. When it was done, and we were outside, he started to collapse as I helped him to the car. I don't think he even slept, but he was determined not to miss the chance to spread his message of loving kindness."

Lying in a hospital bed surrounded by noble friends, the little monk smiles broadly at the doctor. Warily the doctor smiles back, confused by the happy look on his patients face.

"Do you feel better?"

"Oh, no," says the smiling little monk. "No, it is really bad."

"Okaaay, well, let's see, rate your pain on this scale." The doctor holds up a pain chart, showing the least pain near the number one all the way to agonizing pain at number 10. Number 9 is used to describe intense pain.

The little monk studies the chart for a moment.

"Number 9," he says, still smiling. "Yes, it is very bad pain but not the worst. Number 9, okay?"

The doctor looks up from his chart, over his glasses resting on the bridge of his nose. He raises his eyebrows, looking quizzically at the little monk.

"Are you sure it's a 9? That's really bad pain."

"Oh, yes, I am sure. You know I have been in pain many times with this. This time is one of the worst. That's why I call my friend to get me, you know?"

Everyone watching the little monk is moved. He is not tolerating the pain while smiling; he is actually happy, with the pain.

The hallway outside the hospital room is crowded with monks and concerned sangha members, who have grown to love Bhante Sujatha. He has brought the life-changing practice of meditation to so many people with his humble, simple ways of sharing the triple gem of the Buddha, the Dhamma and the Sangha.

The doctor frowns. "Then why are you smiling?"

"Oh, I am happy."

The little monk shrugs his shoulders and smiles even bigger, causing transformation from a sick bed, teaching profound dhamma, without uttering a word about Buddhism, without showing off with his massive and deep training and education in the practices of a Buddhist monk.

"I am a Buddhist monk, you know? I am happy."

The doctor's frown softens. "Oh, I see," he says quietly. "I see."

People who hear him are quiet, thinking about their lives and their complaints.

In chronic pain, in a small midwestern hospital room, surrounded by atheists and Christians and Buddhists and Jews, the little monk has succeeded again. He is the best salesman in the world it seems, for meditation, the middle path and loving kindness.

No one feels patronized or taught. There is no struggle with acceptance of the effectiveness of meditation or the depth of the dhamma. The evidence is in, the experiment is done, the results are clear. Meditation works. The middle path is a good idea. Loving-kindness transforms the world. Although the official designation has not been made, Bhante Sujatha is already an ambassador of Buddhism to the United States.

"Happy With. Happy Without. Empty Empty. Happy Happy. You see, I don't like my pain, but I don't dislike it either. It is still up to me to be happy, to be empty. I can let go of my thoughts and reactions to this pain, just like I can let go of any thought. I practice meditation. I cultivate my mind, so that I can accept great pain and great joy with equanimity.

"By equanimity, I mean that my mind is calm and steady, even under stress. I am calm no matter how bad the pain.

"I don't tolerate. That word is laced with anger. I Accept. I let go. Accept. Let go. Remember this. I know I say this all the time, but it is so simple and so difficult to practice loving-kindness. Accept. Let go. Practice meditation. Study the dhamma. You will stay busy and happy. You won't have time for drama. You will stop getting involved with unwholesome people and hurtful practices.

My pain helps me with my practice. I know people think, 'Well, if he is a Buddhist monk, why would he have so much pain? That meditation stuff really doesn't work, does it?' But my pain is here to serve me, you see?

My pain helps other people by reminding them that I am just a person like them. Also, Bhante Chan and the other monks have helped me so much and they get experience at running the temple and giving the dhamma talks when I am sick. If I am kind and I don't complain, people are inspired to deal better with their own problems. Doctors get to practice their medicine. So many people get to help me.

I think my pain is my kamma, and it is here to slow me down. My pain reminds me of my dependence and my reliance on my humble body. If I did not have this pain, I would be struggling more with ego

316

and restlessness, I think. I don't like my pain, but I think it is good for me. I can't change it. I have tried everything and it all works for a period of time, but then the side effects make some other part of me sick or the treatment of the moment wears off. So, I accept it and look at it as another Buddha for me. Pain can be a great teacher. If you experience pain, ask yourself what it is trying to teach you before you get a cure right away.

Pain is not always the enemy. Your untrained mind, which tells you that you can't be happy with pain, is the enemy. If your body is wounded, your mind is probably hurt more. Heal your mind first, then no matter what happens with your body, you can be happy. You can change your life. You can use pain as an opportunity for practice. I am mindful of complaining. If my mother calls me, I never complain to her. I want her to be happy. I listen to her and then I feel happier, knowing I am helping her, you see?"

I remember first meeting Bhante Sujatha, when he put me at ease by telling me he was not such a practiced Buddhist, that he trusted me to tell his story, that I would be just fine, he would be happy, that I should not worry.

Now that the book is almost complete, and I know the depth of Bhante Sujatha's experience and the expanse of his travels, I realize the kindness in this. I am overwhelmed by it. In a way, it is like his chanting, freely given with no expectations. It is grace.

Chapter Forty-Four

Moving People/Opening the Blue Lotus

Once again, the little monk finds himself surrounded by people's doubt and worry. He hears the compassion in the members of his meditation community as they share their concerns about buying the building owned by the Unitarian Church and turning it into the Blue Lotus Temple. In Buddhist teachings, the lotus flower is used as an example of the way that we must live in this world and practice loving-kindness.

Bhante Sujatha explains this to the temple during a dharma talk.

"My friends, the lotus flower is beautiful, so beautiful that my parents named my sister Manel after this flower. Manel means Blue Lotus and my sister is a wonderful example of loving kindness in action.

Yet the Lotus flower only grows in muddy water, usually clogged with seaweed and muck. Without the mud, the lotus flower cannot exist. Our lives as good practitioners are like this. We cannot practice without the world around us, you know? We need the mud too. We need the emotional messes and the financial pressure and the relationship problems so we can practice. We can be like the lotus flower, beautiful, yet dependent on our roots in the dirt. We can live in this society, while cultivating wholesome minds through the practice of meditation and loving kindness. If you do not have the mud of society, you cannot be so beautiful. Silent retreats are beautiful, for sure, but the practice comes when you are interacting with other people. Remember, my friends, you can be like the Lotus only if you remember that meditation is training for the practice of loving kindness. Meditation is not the practice; it is the training for the practice."

Eventually, with patience, kindness, relentless determination and big faith, the little monk succeeds in buying the Unitarian church. Many unexpected people and events come together to make this happen.

Bhante Sujatha was pleasantly surprised one day when he walked into the bank to make a car payment and found that a generous temple member had paid down the loan on his car. We could write a book about all the miracles that made the temple purchase possible. Bhante Sujatha will be forever grateful for the generosity and kindness of the congregation and the leaders of the Unitarian church

"I just knew what I wanted to do, you know? I wanted to build this temple and help Westerners with the practice of loving-kindness. I didn't know how. I knew who sometimes, but never how. I have a way that I can always see right away what is possible with people. But even that, I don't know sometimes. I just believe. The Buddha taught that our thoughts create our world so I think if I believe, I can do it. If I am willing to do all the work it will take, then it will happen. I am a monk. I am not attached. I am happy with, happy without. But I really see that I have this gift of vision. If I can see it, it can usually be done and I could see this temple right away."

Guy Spinelli, the president of the board of directors at the Blue Lotus Temple, tells me a wonderful story about a board meeting, where people were understandably objecting to the idea of the purchase and renovation of the Unitarian Church.

"They kept saying good reasons why it couldn't or shouldn't be done, you know? And I got up and just sat down next to Bhante Sujatha. I asked him what he wanted. 'What do YOU want, my friend?' He looked right at me and said, 'I want to build this temple. I want to keep those beautiful stained glass windows and make a beautiful refuge for the people.'

319

I said, 'Okay. Your mission is my mission.' And that's when I decided. That was that. My mission was his mission. At one point, he was traveling so much and someone told Bhante that he would have to be around more to accomplish all this, or he would have to give me the power of attorney to sign, and he just said 'Give me the form. I will sign. Now I am going to teach meditation.' He gave me his trust, and I was not about to let him or the community down.

Another time, everyone was panicking about the renovation, which was just an enormously expensive undertaking with an absolutely impossible deadline, and Bhante Sujatha raised his hands and said, 'Stop! Wait! Wait! We CAN get it done! We just have to think more positive thoughts! We don't know about the money or the time, but we can do it! Please, remember, we can do it!' His smile lit up the room.

I am that guy, you know? The one that stands in the background waiting for direction, willing to do whatever Bhante Sujatha wants.

I do my best to stay under the radar. I don't need any recognition.

He was traveling all the time and sometimes he was sick, and I knew what I was doing. I own three companies, and so I knew how to meet with banks and contractors and all that. I really wanted to help create this place, right here in Woodstock, Illinois. I want everyone to have the chance to feel like I've felt during the best times of my life, you know? I want to be a part of something that helps get rid of all the suffering out there. I wanted Bhante Sujatha's radiant smile to be broadcast into a warm beautiful space, where people could feel that love. I hope, really, that for centuries to come, this place is here for people, offering the middle path, not the extreme right or the extreme left, but the calm center of the middle path. I want that for my kids and their kids. You know, I came to Zen though Phil Jackson and basketball, and it changed my life. I want everyone to be able to change their life and practice that loving kindness."

Once the financing was in place and the building was transferred to

320

the Blue Lotus community in December, the biggest obstacle was time. Bhante Sujatha wanted the temple opening on Visakha Day, May 11th, that same year. He wanted to honor the Buddha and his community who had worked so tirelessly alongside him to make this refuge possible. Contractor after contractor said no.

"Absolutely not, no way, this will not be possible, if you want quality work, you have to give us more time. This is ridiculous!"

Bhante Sujatha, a natural born leader with a real talent for putting the right people in the right place at the right time, respectfully disagreed.

He would smile as he answered the doubters, nodding while they talked, listening patiently. 'No, I think we will do it by Visakha Day. We can express our gratitude for the teachings of the Buddha and give this community a place of peace.'"

Behind the little monks radiant smile is a steel resolve and a wealth of experience with team leadership. The little monk is a motivational speaker and a fearless leader in Saffron Robes. He may be small, but his influence is mighty. The exact right man was chosen for the job of completing the impossible task of creating a beautiful peaceful temple, fast.

As usual, Bhante Sujatha used his heart mindfully as a guide in this choice. No matter what people said, or how discouraged they acted, the little monk did not quit. He read "My Wish" to himself frequently, even though he knew it by heart. He wanted to see the words and remember the intensity of that first impression. It was a great reminder of his commitment to teach Westerners how to be happy, peaceful and well.

"You know, we always want to help the people. We want to help them practice loving kindness and meditation. I really mean it when I say 'My Wish.' If I say I want to be a refuge for those without shelter, well, then I had to create this refuge, you know? I wanted a place where you could come more than once a week, and I made

321

sure to keep it closed on Sundays, to honor the people who practice Christianity here. If I was in a mostly Jewish community, I might have closed on Saturdays. I want people to be able to practice their religion while they learn about the middle path of loving kindness and meditation. This is why I insist that we care for the stained glass windows, with the pictures of Jesus. I want people to know that we respect their individual and collective beliefs.

I know I say this over and over, but Buddhism is not a religion. Most of the religious feeling you get or the traditions that seem like a religion, well, those are cultural, not Buddhist. Buddhism, and I know something about this, Buddhism is simple really.

Heal your wounded mind, the one that tells you things like completing this refuge in 6 months is not possible, that people can't write a book or start a temple in the Midwest. With a cultivated mind, trained by practicing meditation, you really can do just about anything, can't you?"

Bhante Sujatha smiles at me, and I am quiet. Later I talk with Bhante Sumana about writing this book, feeling humbled by the capacity of my subject, and stunned by the impact of one man's life. Bhante Sumana smiles, as always, and says what he always says.

"You. Can. Do. It! You can! Look, how beautiful is your smile when you talk about the book! Just look at you! You can see it! This is your job, my friend. Yours."

People's concerns and doubts fly around the little monk like swarms of gnats. He uses the gentle pressure of determination fueled by wholesome desire to push the doubts, questions and fears out of his way.

"You know, it will be so beautiful to have this on Visakha day! Imagine the spring!" the little monk would say while a contractor said no and a board member said that it was too expensive and a temple member said it was impossible.

322

"Yes, well, let's see? Where do we start? What can I do?" Bhante Sujatha uses his profound training in being a humble leader. Whether a bathroom needs cleaning or a temple member needs encouragement, the little monk will roll up his sleeves and do the work. Absolutely nothing is beneath him. It is hard to say no to his request for help while he is doing the work. If he asks you to do the dishes, he's filling the sink while he talks. He picks up the broom and starts sweeping before he asks you to clean the floor.

"I just start doing the work, then I ask. When I came here to Illinois, I worked like crazy for two years before I asked Bhante Muditha for his blessing and support for the Blue Lotus Temple. I knew I had to show him some results first. I used my own money to support myself. I don't ask for help until I prove to myself the project can be done. Like I said, responsibility before rights. I also say, work before requests. Do it, then ask for help to do more."

Life in Peradiniya as a young boy and training at the temple as a monk made Bhante Sujatha particularly well suited to being the leader of an almost impossible project for a good cause. He called contractors and banks, prepared detailed accountings of his efforts, and kept his life rigorously clean and happy. He knows the most effective motivator is being an inspiration to people. He wakes up early and performs the rounds of encouragement, optimism and firm requests, closer and closer to the dream realized. He draws from his extensive schooling and experience in doing the impossible in Sri Lanka, Australia, Michigan, Peoria, Las Vegas, Pennsylvania and Arizona.

The Visakha Day opening of the blue Lotus Temple is beautiful, community members and monks together, dressed in white and saffron, marching behind colorful flags, celebrating the birth, life and death of the great teacher, Prince Siddhartha, the Buddha.

For the first time in public, the little monk breaks down, crying as he tells the tale, the whole story of the temple creation, including the ten years of almost constant struggle.

Heenbanda and Lalitha are there, along with Bhante Muditha and Bhante Dhammawasa. It is a day filled with joy and tears as the little monk proudly holds a statue of the Buddha in front of the marching crowd.

"So I hear that Bhante Sumana did a wonderful job in my absence."

The temple community claps, grateful for Bhante Sumana's leadership while Bhante Sujatha traveled around the world.

"You know I think I want to give Sumana a gift, and I cannot think of anything. I don't have anything. Then, I see, I am no longer at this temple I am already gone, traveling so much. So I gave Sumana the temple. He is now the abbot of the Blue Lotus Temple."

The little monk smiles at all of us, conveying deep love and appreciation, demonstrating the simplicity of detachment, of being willing to let it all go now and now and now.

When I was a little girl, I remember being at the very top of a slide at the beach. The slide is metal and very steep. To my nine-year-old eyes, it looks like it goes straight down. I hang on for dear life at the top while my mom stands in the water, demonstrating the patience of Job. "Let go," she shouts, "Let go!"

I hear her beautiful voice like a melody as I shiver with cold and feel the ache in my shoulders.

"Sweetie, you can do it! Let go! I am right here! I'll catch you! Let go!"

When I finally let go, the swoosh of my body down that slide feels like flying. I am free of doubt and fear and filled with happiness, knowing I am heading straight into the safety of my mother's arms.

This is the gift the little monk offers, too. Freedom from the constraints of our untrained minds. Freedom to let go of fear and make bold strides in self-expression. Learn about loving kindness and mindfulness meditation and make a strong determination to practice, at least five or ten minutes, every day. You can engage in a fitness regime for your mind, cultivating loving kindness and eschewing fearful doubt.

Let go. Let go. The loving kindness forces in McHenry County, Illinois and all around the world are waiting for you at the bottom of your slide into the practice of loving-kindness. Trust us. The freedom is worth the price of admission and then some!

The little monk and his team have created a refuge of love for all of us. His work is complete, and now he has moved on to spreading his message around the world. I can't wait to see what's next. I know it will be beautiful and I hope to be a part of this amazing man's journey for a lifetime.

Epilogue

In Sri Lanka last summer, I watched thousands of people line the streets just to get a glimpse of the monk I had come to know so well. I walked onto a stage in front of a crowd of thousands, and offered my translated book to the chief monks of Sri Lanka.

When I started the interview process, I did not know the depth of Bhante Sujatha's training or the meaning of his recognition as an ambassador of Buddhism to the United States.

When I confessed my doubts to John Bardi, he offered these words of wisdom: *"Oh, my dear, don't you know? Bhante Sujatha chose the right person! Of course you are an amateur! The root of that word is amore, love, love! You see, amateurs are in it for the love. This is exactly the innocence required to write this story. A professional or a cynic wouldn't stand a chance against Bhante's simple message. You allowed it to flow through you, you see? You are the channel! You are an amateur, a truly great achievement!"*

Walking behind Bhante on the crazy twisty staircase up the side of the mountain in Sigiriya, he reassured me, telling me not to worry, that he had good kamma that he would stay right by me. I'm certain now he was talking about more than our climb and my now diminished fear of heights. At the top of that mountain in Sigiriya, a man from Holland literally ran across the mountaintop with his family. He bowed low before Bhante, shouting that he was honored and asking me to take their picture.

Bhante Sujatha travels all over the world now, leading workshops and spreading his precious message about a simple path to peace and happiness. It would not be possible now for him to spend the time it takes with one person to tell the story of his amazing life. When I think about the chances of meeting the Chief Sanganayaka of North America in Woodstock, Illinois, and then add in the odds of being the one to write his story, it's still hard for me to believe that this actually happened.

Walking up the mountain to Nilambe, meeting Upul, sitting in the retreat center where Bhante sat with Godwin Samararatne, climbing to the top of the hill where the young monks played, walking up the steps to Bhante's family home and crossing the bridge over the Mahaweli River felt like being inside of a dream. Seeing the Subodharama temple and walking in Bhante's ceremonial parade next to a gaggle of little monks were some of the most precious moments of my life.

Several times during our trip, I realized that the monks had really brought me into their world. I had near constant déjà vu as I realized that I had never been here before, I just felt like I had. Sri Lanka was even more whimsical than I imagined. Monkeys were everywhere and the sounds of the jungle were so loud and constant that it felt like I was in a storybook.

Many times, I wanted to rewrite the whole book. I traveled to Bhante's home and met his family and friends in Sri Lanka. I feel far more qualified now, as a practicing meditator at the temple, but I can't ever again be the girl who walked into that first interview with Bhante Sujatha, unsure whether to bow or shake hands. I know too much now. I couldn't approach the subject of this book with the view of a novice, who felt like she had been transported into a fairytale world filled with loving kindness and peace. If you want to write your first biography, my advice is to choose an overwhelmingly kind Buddhist monk as your subject.

My experience of writing this book is a book in itself. I could title another book Driving with Bhante (if he didn't already have a CD by that name), as some of my most memorable moments were in the

327

car with Bhante Sujatha, listening to him share while he held a tape recorder on his lap. Once, we were stopped in traffic, on our way to a yoga retreat in Chicago. I looked over at him while he told me the story of his ordination. He was at the part where he watched his mom disappear down the hill and I saw tears in his eyes

"Bhante do you want to take a break? You know, you can tell me if this is too much, or you don't want to share something. It's ok."

He looked at me and smiled. "No, no, you know what? This has been really good for me. Telling my story. It feels so good."

As Socrates said, "an unexamined life is not worth living." I hope this book inspires you to see the miracle that is your life in a new way.

My goal is Bhante's goal, to fill you with joy. Bhante's noble friend, Ann Van Slyck, often asks me to feel the love she is sending as we end our calls.

I'd like to ask that of you, dear reader. Close your eyes, and feel the love and appreciation that Bhante Sujatha and I are sending your way, as you bear witness to the noble life of a great man.

May you be happy, may you be well, and may you be peaceful.

Metta,

Mary

Sponsors

This book has been completed and printed thanks to the support of these wonderful people.

Altruists

Tyler Lewke

Ann Van Slyck

Benefactors

Christine Gerulat

Mary Claire Moll

Patrons

Kellie Wilson, EVOLVE

Mary Jane McEwan

Noble Friends

Vimala Bhikkhuni	Rebecca Pajich
Susan & Erin Mathews	Kathy Gilbert
Arianne Lewis	Elizabeth Fitch
Charlie Poppell	Michelle L. Cerasani
Fred Gustafson	Nancy Schwab
Bob Krueger	Robbin Pierce
Kathryn Kresic	Greg & Michelle Kuhlman
Brent Steepe	Shawn Strach
Sai Sivakumar	Mary Garber
Allison Lewis	Christopher Trent

The Four Noble Truths of Buddhism

- There is suffering (Dukkha).
- There is the origin of suffering, which is   attachment to desire.
- There is the cessation of suffering.
- There is a way out of suffering, the Eightfold Path (Atthangika Magga).

The Eightfold Path

Wisdom (panna)

1. Right Understanding

2. Right Intention

Morality (sila)

3. Right Speech

4. Right Action

5. Right Livelihood

Concentration (Samadhi)

6. Right Effort

7. Right Mindfulness

8. Right concentration

The Ten Perfections

Generosity (Dana): Letting go. This alleviates the pain of attachment. The more you give, the wealthier you become.

Morality (Sila): Chastity, calmness, and quiet. These qualities help to diminish and eliminate the suffering caused by greed and selfishness.

Renunciation (Nekhamma): Giving up wordily attachments. Leading a holy life is seen a way to achieve freedom from the suffering engendered by lust, craving and desire.

Wisdom (Panna): Understanding based on the Four Noble Truths. This leads to the end of suffering based on ignorance.

Energy and Strength (Viriya): Sustained effort in overcoming unskillful ways. This does not refer to physical strength, although a well cared for body can be an important expression of self-love and an element of escape from suffering. The problem with physical strength is that our bodies are temporary shells, of no use in our next lifetimes. Viriya refers mainly to strength of character, and the development of energy for the engagement of persistent effort on behalf of the well being of others. In the absence of sustained effort, a meditator will lose focus and comes under the influence of the un-skillful ways that cause craving and desire.

Patience (Khanti): Patience with harsh circumstances and other upsetting experiences. Patience is offered as a gift, a way to grow closer to nirvana, rather than a way to "put up with" things. Patience alleviates the suffering caused by our attachment to "how it should be" or "where we would rather be."

Truthfulness (Saca): Familiarity with and adherence to the nature of reality, especially within the context of the four noble truths. A Buddha can only experience ultimate Saca. The practice of truthfulness alleviates the suffering caused by lying to ourselves about the nature of suffering and the path out of suffering.

Resolution/Determination (Aditthana): Aditthana translates as Highest or Best self (Adi) standing. (tthana). It refers to the Buddha's unceasing determination and resolve in discovering the nature of reality and the way out of suffering (the Four Noble Truths).

Loving-kindness (Metta): Love, without attachment. Loving kindness means that we love kindness for its own sake. Metta meditation is prescribed in Buddhism for sleeplessness, fractured relationships, and nightmares. People who practice Metta are thought to positively influence people and circumstances by their presence.

Equanimity (Uppekkha): Evenness of mind in the face of fluctuating life experiences. This is not cold detachment; it is the ability to practice loving kindness, mindfulness, calmness and compassion in the midst of challenging circumstances. It is being the eye of the storm, using our mind as a peaceful refuge instead of a chaotic fear producer.

Glossary

Bhante: This is a term, similar to "father" when referencing a priest. It is a warm and friendly way of addressing a monk. It is not Bhante Sujatha's first name. If he needs to sign a legal document, he uses his given Buddhist name and the name of his hometown, Sujatha Perediniya. He is never referred to by his family name.

Bikkhu: This term is used to describe a Buddhist monk. The word can be literally translated as beggar, referencing the idea that monks and nuns practice alms collection and rely on the sangha for support as a lesson in humility and wisdom, and as a way of giving the Sangha the opportunity to practice generosity.

Bhikkhuni: This is the female version of Bikkhu.

Dhamma: The teachings of the Buddha. This is the Pali way of saying Dharma, which is the Sanskrit translation. Theravada Buddhists use the Pali translations.

Kamma: This means intentional action, and refers to the universal law of cause and effect. It is the Pali version of the Sanskrit term, Karma

Sangha: The Buddhist community, including monks, nuns and lay people

The Triple Gem: The Buddha, the Dhamma and the Sangha

Dana Paramita: The idea that the giver and the receiver are the same. Both are equally important, as without receivers, we could not practice generosity, one of the most important qualities in all of Buddhism.

Theravada: A strain of Buddhist Practice, commonly referred to as the middle path

ABOUT THE AUTHOR

 Mary is relentlessly focused on bringing happiness and peace to this world. She uses inspirational storytelling to remind people of the joy that is their birthright.

She is a devoted meditator, a professional (and compulsive) writer, and a gifted speaker.

"No matter how tough the circumstances in which you were raised, you once saw the world through the magical eyes of a child. I want everyone to remember that joy. I want to show people that anything is possible with enough love."

You can connect with Mary on facebook, or at maryswriting.com.

If you have any questions or comments about this book, feel free to email Mary at mary@maryswriting.com

ABOUT THE MONK

Bhante Sujatha was born in Peradiniya, Sri Lanka
in 1967 and came to America in 1997. He is Chief
Sanganayaka of North America, which includes
the US, Mexico and Canada.   Also known as the Chief Sangha
Patron or an Ambassador of Buddhism.

He is the Abbott of the Blue Lotus Temple in Woodstock, Illinois, and
he practices loving kindness and continues to this day with his quest
to help Americans [and others] learn how to be happy, well and
peaceful.

Bhante Sujatha leads workshops and speaks all over the world. You
can find out more about him and his work at Bluelotustemple.org

You can also connect with Bhante on Facebook.

Visit the Blue Lotus Temple

On the web-

Bluelotustemple.org

In person-

Blue Lotus Temple 221 Dean Street, Woodstock, Illinois 60098

"Do not believe in anything simply because you have heard it. Do not believe anything simply because it is spoken and rumored by many. Do not believe anything simply because it is written in your religious books. Do not believe in anything merely on the authority of your teachers and elders. Do not believe in traditions because they have been handed down for many generations. But after observation and analysis, when you find that anything agrees with reason and is conducive to the good and benefit of one and all, then accept it and live up to it."

Buddha